flowers, foliage, and 12 months of interest make easy-care trees and shrubs the most valuable plants in the landscape. The following pages are filled with tips and techniques for choosing the best trees and shrubs for your yard.

table of contents

Better Homes and Gardens™

trees
& shrubs

NO LONGER PROPERTY OF ANYTHINK LIBRARIES RANGEVIEW LIBRARY DISTRICT

WILEY

John Wiley & Sons, Inc.

Better Homes and Gardens® Trees & Shrubs

Contributing Writer: Megan McConnell Hughes
Contributing Project Editor: Megan McConnell Hughes
Contributing Designers: Sundie Ruppert, Lori Gould, Cathy Brett
Editor, Garden Books: Denny Schrock
Editorial Assistant: Heather Knowles
Contributing Copy Editor: Fern Marshall Bradley
Contributing Proofreaders: Susan Lang, Barb Rothfus
Contributing Indexer: Ellen Sherron
Contributing Photographers: Dean Schoeppner, Denny Schrock
Contributing Photo Manager: Deb Wiley

Meredith® Books
Editorial Director: Gregory H. Kayko
Editor in Chief, Garden: Doug Jimerson
Art Director: Tim Alexander, Gene Rauch
Managing Editor: Doug Kouma
Business Director: Janice Croat
Imaging Center Operator: Tony Hunt

John Wiley & Sons, Inc.
Publisher: Natalie Chapman
Associate Publisher: Jessica Goodman
Executive Editor: Anne Ficklen
Assistant Editor: Heather Dabah
Production Director: Diana Cisek
Manufacturing Manager: Tom Hyland

This book is printed on acid-free paper.

Copyright © 2012 by Meredith Corporation, Des Moines, IA.
All rights reserved

Published by John Wiley & Sons, Inc., Hoboken, NJ
Published simultaneously in Canada

No part of this publication may be reproduced, stored in a retrieval
system, or transmitted in any form or by any means, electronic,
mechanical, photocopying, recording, scanning, or otherwise, except
as permitted under Section 107 or 108 of the 1976 United States
Copyright Act, without either the prior written permission of the Publisher,
or authorization through payment of the appropriate per-copy fee to
the Copyright Clearance Center, Inc., 222 Rosewood Drive, Danvers, MA
01923, (978) 750-8400, fax (978) 750-4470, or on the web at
www.copyright.com. Requests to the Publisher for permission should be
addressed to the Permissions Department, John Wiley & Sons, Inc.,
111 River Street, Hoboken, NJ 07030, (201) 748-6011, fax (201)
748-6008, or online at *www.wiley.com/go/permissions*.

Note to Reader: Due to differing conditions, tools, and individual skills,
Meredith Corporation assumes no responsibility for any damages, injuries
suffered, or losses incurred as a result of following the information
published in this book. Before beginning any project, review the
instructions carefully, and if any doubts or questions remain, consult local
experts or authorities. Because codes and regulations vary greatly, you
should always check with authorities to ensure that your project complies
with all applicable local codes and regulations. Always read and observe
all the safety precautions provided by manufacturers of any tools,
equipment, or supplies, and follow all accepted safety procedures.

Better Homes and Gardens Magazine
Editor in Chief: Gayle Goodson Butler

Meredith National Media Group
President: Tom Harty
Executive Vice President: Doug Olson

Meredith Corporation
Chairman of the Board: William T. Kerr
President and Chief Executive Officer: Stephen M. Lacy

In Memoriam: E. T. Meredith III (1933–2003)

Photo Credits
Photographers credited may retain copyright © to the listed photographs.
Agricultural Research Service/USDA (public domain photo): 148R,
    Derek Fell: 203R

Limit of Liability/Disclaimer of Warranty: While the publisher and
author have used their best efforts in preparing this book, they make
no representations or warranties with respect to the accuracy or
completeness of the contents of this book and specifically disclaim any
implied warranties of merchantability or fitness for a particular purpose.
No warranty may be created or extended by sales representatives or
written sales materials. The advice and strategies contained herein may
not be suitable for your situation. You should consult with a professional
where appropriate. Neither the publisher nor author shall be liable for any
loss of profit or any other commercial damages, including but not limited
to special, incidental, consequential, or other damages.

For general information on our other products and services or for
technical support, please contact our Customer Care Department within
the United States at (800) 762-2974, outside the United States at
(317) 572-3993 or fax (317) 572-4002.

Wiley also publishes its books in a variety of electronic formats. Some
content that appears in print may not be available in electronic books. For
more information about Wiley products, visit our web site at www.wiley.com.

Library of Congress Cataloging-in-Publication Data

Better homes and gardens flowering trees and shrubs.
     p. cm.
   Flowering trees and shrubs
   Includes index.
   ISBN 978-1-118-18237-6 (pbk.)
   1. Flowering trees. 2 Shrubs. 3. Landscape
gardening. I. Better homes and gardens. II. Title:
Flowering trees and shrubs.
   SB435.B485.2012
   635.9'7713--dc23
                                              2012031041
2010042156

Printed in the United States of America

10 9 8 7 6 5 4 3 2 1

landscaping with trees and shrubs

Call on trees and shrubs to create an inviting, artistic, and easy-care landscape. These versatile and long-lived plants are perfect for creating privacy in a backyard, sheltering a home from the sun, adding brilliant flowers to mixed borders, and providing treats for wildlife.

p.8
BENEFITS OF TREES AND SHRUBS
Trees and shrubs play an integral role in the landscape. Make an investment in these easy-to-grow plants today.

p.10
USING TREES AND SHRUBS
Trees and shrubs cast valuable shade, block unsightly views, add color and texture to the yard, and so much more.

p.20
PLANTING FOR WILDLIFE
See how easy it is to make your landscape a wildlife oasis with trees and shrubs. The birds will thank you!

The wonders of woody plants

Trees and shrubs are some of the most hardworking members of the landscape.

Standing tall year-round, woody plants perform the essential functions of blocking chilly winter winds and casting valuable shade on exposed homes, which lower summer cooling bills. While moderating temperatures in and around a home, trees and shrubs can also be employed to create a pretty living screen that blocks the views of a garage or neighboring property or prevents unwanted visitors from wandering into the yard.

These long-lived plants excel at many functional roles in the landscape, but don't let their task-oriented nature fool you. They do work hard, but add beauty to the landscape at the same time. Plant a favorite magnolia or a flower-packed butterfly bush in your yard, and you'll instantly add easy-care color and texture.

Lofty trees frame the front door of this quaint log home while tidy shrubs shelter the foundation. Well-maintained woody plants add value to every home.

Easy-care plants

Unlike annual flowers, trees and shrubs don't require annual planting. Woody plants thrive for at least 10 years to more than 100 years depending on the species. And unlike herbaceous perennials, many species of woody plants do not require frequent seasonal maintenance such as deadheading, pruning, or fertilizing.

Trees and shrubs do share some of the qualities of annuals and perennials, though: lovely flowers, intense fragrance, and intriguing foliage. Sweet-scented crabapples' pretty pink and white blooms perfume the yard in early spring. Perfect for small landscapes, Japanese tree lilac bears frothy white blooms that add valuable color, texture, and fragrance in early summer. And long-lived oaks, maples, and many other trees fire up the fall skies with red, orange, and yellow foliage.

When combined with annuals and perennials, trees and shrubs create a multilayer landscape that ensures you'll be surrounded by beauty all 12 months of the year. When freezing temperatures zap the annuals and perennials, evergreen trees and shrubs will continue to provide color and form. A diverse landscape also supplies valuable food and shelter for wildlife year-round.

Long-term investment

Because woody plants are longtime members of the landscape, sometimes gracing a garden for multiple generations, it's important to thoughtfully consider how they will contribute to the look and feel of your space before planting. The next several pages detail many uses for trees and shrubs. You'll find a wealth of tips and ideas for plant placement and plant selection to make the very best use of trees and shrubs around your home.

Place blooming shrubs, such as this handsome dogwood, near your home where you'll regularly enjoy their beauty.

Money tree Do trees, shrubs, and landscaping add value to your home? University studies indicate that they do indeed add value—a well-designed landscape that includes thriving, healthy plants increases your home value by as much as 12 percent.

The key to capitalizing on the value of landscaping is to landscape smart. Well-maintained trees and shrubs add far more to the bottom line than woody plants with broken limbs, crossing branches, and messy seedpods and fruit. Misplaced plants—those that are too close to a home or garage or those that encroach on walkways—are also detrimental. Easy-care plants will pay dividends and add charming curb appeal.

Create shade

A majestic oak or mighty maple is an intriguing

landscape element for its sheer size. Look beyond the size of the long-lived tree and you'll notice the oak's curvaceous branching structure provides valuable landscape interest year-round. And the maple likely lights up with hues of yellow, orange, and red in fall. Trees bring many aesthetic elements to your yard, and at the same time they are casting valuable shade.

When thoughtfully placed, a tree can cast a shadow to cool a once-sun-drenched patio. Or it can block sunlight from streaming in south-facing windows and raising the interior temperature of your home several degrees. Harness the power of shade that trees provide and you'll make your indoor and outdoor living spaces more inviting.

Deciduous trees, those that lose their leaves in fall, are the most common shade trees. Deciduous trees are especially useful for shading a dwelling because their foliage provides dense, light-blocking cover in summer when temperatures are high and the sun's warming effects are most potent. In winter the bare branches allow sunlight to blanket a home, warming it a few degrees.

Get the most shade impact for your investment in trees by planting them on the southwest, west, or east side of a home. The sun is most intense from these directions and well-placed trees will moderate it with ease.

Evergreen trees can also be employed as shade trees. They provide effective cooling in the summer, but because they retain their foliage year-round, they also prevent sun from filtering through in winter. Call on evergreens to shade the north or northwest side of a home where winter sunlight is less of a factor.

Evergreens are also an excellent choice for outdoor rooms, which are rarely used in winter.

The dense shade cast by Norway spruce or the graceful filtered shade of a white pine will create an inviting outdoor retreat.

A great shade tree

There isn't one particular species of tree that outranks others in creating shade. In fact, there are many great shade trees. Begin by considering the following qualities to determine what type of shade tree will complement your landscape. Once the specifications are in order, choosing a tree in the encyclopedias beginning on page 108 and 154 is easy.

Light shade or deep shade. A Norway maple casts dense, deep shade. The shade is so dense that grass has trouble growing under the canopy. This is a fine quality if the tree is near a patio or deck but can be frustrating if the tree is surrounded by lawn. A honeylocust tree, on the other hand, creates dappled shade. A few rays of sunlight can easily filter through the fine foliage.

Easy care. Trees that are notoriously messy, dropping fruit or countless branches, often don't make the best shade trees near a home. They'll quickly create more work than they are worth. Fall leaf drop is a given with deciduous trees. Autumn raking and minimal pruning should be all the care a mature shade tree requires.

Appropriate mature size. Trees are the longest-lived plants in a landscape. As they add years to their life, they add feet to their height and width. Too often people make the mistake of choosing a plant based on an inaccurate assumption about its mature size. A massive American sycamore grows up to 100 feet tall and nearly 40 feet wide at maturity. It's much too large for the average home landscape. Instead, aim for a tree that tops out at 40 to 60 feet tall and 30 to 40 feet wide.

Above left: **'Tricolor' beech is a large shade tree with lovely variegated foliage that turns yellow in fall.**

Above middle: **This low-growing deciduous tree is just right for this one-story home. A lofty maple or oak would complement a two-story structure.**

Above: **Redbud, a small tree with charming heart-shape leaves, is perfect for small gardens and urban landscapes.**

Opposite: **Pair large trees with understory plants that thrive in low-light conditions to create a lush, easy-care landscape that will bring to mind a hike through the forest.**

Plant for privacy

How about planting a living fence?
You could build a traditional wood stockade to shield views into adjoining yards, but a well-maintained living fence offers greater color and texture, plus it provides a valuable habitat for wildlife.

While a typical fence is drab brown in spring, a Koreanspice viburnum hedge, for example, is decorated with 2- to 3-inch-wide, clove-scented white flower clusters. Green fruit that turns red and then purple follows the flowers and is favored by birds. In fall viburnum's green leaves turn burgundy and then intensify to dark purple. A wood fence is hard pressed to compete with a viburnum's colorful show.

Deciduous trees and shrubs do an excellent job of creating privacy and muffling noise in the growing season, but their leafless branches provide little cover in winter. If year-round privacy is essential, choose an evergreen species. Evergreen rhododendrons and camellias offer beautiful blooms that rival those of popular deciduous shrubs while providing year-round privacy. Needled plants are always a good choice.

A living fence can mimic a traditional wood fence in style—a simple row of a single species of shrub, for example. Plants that tolerate pruning with ease can be trimmed to create a formal appearance. For an informal privacy hedge,

The flower-covered arching branches of Vanhoutte spirea are eye-catching for at least two weeks in spring. The pretty white flowers are delightfully fragrant.

look to nature for inspiration. Plant a living screen using a mix of deciduous and evergreen species in a variety of heights and shapes. As the plants grow, maintain a consistent outer edge by pruning overly exuberant branches so the hedge does not take on an overgrown appearance.

Plant spacing when creating a hedge will determine how quickly the plants grow together. The closer together shrubs are planted, the faster their branches will meet to create a solid visual barrier. Situating plants too close together, though, can promote weak and spindly growth. A rule of thumb is to space plants no closer than half the distance of their mature width. For example, if the mature width of a shrub is 10 feet, space plants 5 feet apart for rapid coverage.

A great privacy planting

Many trees and shrubs create excellent visual barriers. When choosing plants for your living screen, keep these concepts in mind.

Evergreen versus deciduous. Evergreen trees and shrubs provide privacy 12 months a year. They are especially useful for shielding views into swimming areas and limiting views of a busy street or property. Evergreens also do an excellent job of creating a sound barrier.

Deciduous trees and shrubs often offer more varied flowers, foliage, and fragrance than their evergreen counterparts. Deciduous plants are excellent for shielding views in summer and fall, but they offer sparse coverage in winter and spring. Employ them in areas where year-round cover is not essential.

Appropriate size. Hedges vary in size from knee-high to lofty 20-foot-tall barriers. Some species naturally top out at 5 to 10 feet tall; these are much easier to maintain at 5 feet tall than a species that grows 20 feet tall. Width is another important factor. How wide do you envision your hedge? Be mindful of property lines.

Color and texture. Spring flowers, brilliant fall foliage, and clusters of bird-attracting berries all introduce color and texture into the landscape. Would you like a hedge that not only creates a barrier but also offers visual treats?

Ease of care. Some hedges require frequent pruning to maintain their good looks. Other take on a lovely, tidy appearance with little pruning. How much pruning are you willing to do?

TEST GARDEN TIP

Green with envy

A tidy green hedge is a sight to behold. An excellent backdrop for a colorful perennial border or a nonobtrusive living screen, a hedge is a valuable landscaping tool. Here are a few favorite trees and shrubs for easy-care hedges.

Arborvitae
American holly
Boxwood
Forsythia
Hornbeam

Shade-friendly trees and shrubs

Many trees and shrubs thrive in the shade. These shade lovers are called understory plants because they typically grow under the canopy of larger trees. Understory trees and shrubs thrive in filtered light and compete well with large trees for soil moisture and nutrients. Use these plants to create a living screen in a shaded landscape.

UNDERSTORY SHRUBS

ARBORVITAE An evergreen shrub with soft foliage; will grow 20 feet tall but easy to maintain at lower height (pictured above).

BOXWOOD An evergreen with tiny, glossy leaves; tolerates frequent shearing.

FOTHERGILLA A native deciduous shrub with fragrant spring flowers and brilliantly colored fall foliage.

SMOKE TREE An easy-to-grow shrub with purple-leaf cultivars and airy seed flower in summer.

UNDERSTORY TREES

AMERICAN HOLLY An evergreen with bright red berries in winter; must plant male and female cultivars.

DOGWOOD A native tree with delightful spring flowers.

REDBUD A hardy plant whose vivid flowers cover leafless branches in early spring.

SERVICEBERRY A native tree with spring flowers, berries in summer, and colorful fall foliage (pictured above).

Screens and windbreaks

A row of trees or shrubs, often called a windbreak, is a good match for whipping winter wind that sends your hat airborne the moment you step outside. When oriented perpendicular to the prevailing wind, a row of trees with dense foliage significantly reduces the wind speed. Evergreens serve this purpose well.

A windbreak, also called a shelterbelt, can reduce winds speed by as much as 50 percent. This is particularly helpful when the windbreak is situated near a house, where it will greatly slow wind and reduce heating fuel consumption by as much as 25 percent.

The most effective windbreak consists of several rows of fast-growing, dense evergreen trees that reach a mature height of about one-and-a-half times the height of the house. Ideally the trees retain their stiff branches to ground level for maximum wind block.

Typically planted on the north and west sides of a home, a windbreak offers savings that increase as the portion of protected perimeter of a home increases. If a property doesn't have space for wind protection on multiple sides, add it where possible. Even a small windbreak will reduce heating costs.

Foundation plantings are also excellent at reducing wind speed and heat loss. Dense evergreen shrubs planted about 5 feet away from a house will create a trough of dead-air space. This dead-air space decreases heat loss from the house walls. Just like a traditional tree windbreak, a foundation-type windbreak is most effective on the north and west sides of a home, but the more foundation space covered, the greater the reduction in heat loss.

A great windbreak

A well-placed windbreak not only reduces winter heating costs, it also adds structure and form to the landscape. When choosing species for the windbreak planting, look for trees and shrubs that complement the style of your home and existing landscape elements. Here are a few more tips for creating a windbreak.

Opposite: **A long row of columnar arborvitae is a living wall around this patio. The trees block wind and create privacy.**

Location, location, location. The best windbreaks are planted in a line perpendicular to the prevailing winds. Windbreak plantings typically are installed on the north and west sides of a home. Wherever space permits, an extension of a windbreak will increase protection. Consider adding a row of trees to the east side of a home too.

The distance the trees are planted from a home is important. The maximum zone of wind protection exists at five to seven times the height of the windbreak. For example, if the mature height of a windbreak is 50 feet, the trees should be planted 250 to 350 feet away from the home to take advantage of maximum wind protection.

Mature size. A well-sited windbreak created using easy-care, long-lived trees can change from an asset to a headache if it outgrows its planting area and begins encroaching on your outdoor living space or the neighbor's property. Take time to consider the mature height and width of trees and shrubs when selecting species to create a windbreak.

Care requirements. The best windbreak plants require little annual care. Regular watering during the first growing season after planting and annual pruning when the plants are young is customary. A tree that has twig or branch drop requiring frequent cleanup is not a good choice. Choose plants that virtually take care of themselves. Limit maintenance around plants by blanketing the soil with a layer of organic mulch.

Best windbreak plants

Count on these species to provide excellent wind protection. Choose small or dwarf varieties for wind protection near a foundation. Large plants make excellent windbreaks along property lines.

NORTHEAST AND MIDWEST
Arborvitae (pictured above)
Eastern red cedar
Pine
Spruce
White fir

SOUTH AND SOUTHWEST
Crape myrtle
Eastern red cedar
Holly (pictured above)
Loblolly pine
Southern magnolia

NORTHWEST
Bristlecone pine
Colorado blue spruce (pictured above)
Eastern red cedar
Mugo pine
Rocky Mountain juniper

Year-round interest

A landscape with year-round interest

is ripe with color, texture, and beauty 365 days a year. A diverse palette of plants is essential to create a landscape that offers intrigue in spring, summer, fall, and winter. A thoughtful mix of trees and shrubs can easily ensure the view out a window in winter is just as lovely as the view in summer.

In most temperate climates the growing season kicks off in spring, when many species of trees and shrubs unfurl colorful, and often fragrant, blossoms. Species bloom at different times throughout the spring and summer. Flowering quince, for example, is prized for its early bloom time. Its fragrant miniature-roselike flowers decorate leafless stems as soon as the soil begins to warm. Old-fashioned lilacs begin flowering later in the season. Stage a multiweek bloom show by pairing early-season blooming plants with those that bloom later.

Foliage in shades of green, yellow, and purple adds color and texture to the garden in summer. A mix of leaf shapes will add energy to the landscape. Combine the simple oval leaves of magnolia with the petite foliage of European mountain ash. Another easy, energetic plant pair is a broadleaf plant with a needled plant—a maple with a white pine, for example.

The fall landscape lights up with shades of red, yellow, and orange and an occasional burst of purple or burgundy. A single magnificent tree displaying fall color can set an attractive seasonal scene. When choosing plants for fall color, don't overlook shrubs. Many shrubs have spectacular color on a small scale—an essential characteristic in small-space gardens.

Winter is a time of rest and renewal in the landscape, but shrubs with multicolored peeling bark, berries, and colorful twigs add a spark of energy to the quiet months in the garden. Gardeners in warm regions enjoy lovely camellia blossoms. Evergreen plants, such as pines and firs as well as rhododendrons, are a pleasing contrast to the bare branches of deciduous trees.

Year-round good looks

A patioside planting, entryway border, or backyard hedge that offers beauty every day of the year is a valuable asset. Keep these tips in mind as you plan for year-round good looks.

Multiseason interest. Plants that shine with interest in more than one season are always a good choice. Viburnums are a great example. Many varieties have striking spring blooms and their leaves take on shades of red and purple in fall. Multiseason interest is essential in small landscapes where planting space is limited.

Evergreen splendor. Offering color you can count on year-round, evergreen trees and shrubs are lovely backdrops for colorful deciduous plants in spring, summer, and fall. In winter their dense, oval and pyramidal forms reign supreme in the barren garden.

Early start. Get a jump on the spring bloom season by including trees and shrubs that wake up early. Witch hazel, camellia, daphne, and many viburnums begin blooming when there is still a smattering of snow on the ground.

Plant for wildlife. Enjoy the antics of birds, butterflies, and other critters in the landscape by including plants that offer food and shelter.

Opposite, top left: **Ring in spring with early-blooming trees and shrubs like this fragrant white crabapple.**

Opposite, top right: **Hydrangea blossoms change color over the course of a growing season. These blossoms debut lime green, turn magenta, and fade to tawny brown.**

Opposite, bottom left: **Japanese maples are known for their intense fall color. Choose your favorite variety from hundreds of cultivars.**

Opposite, bottom right: **Evergreen plants like the rhododendron and yew along this foundation offer color and texture year-round.**

Decorate for winter

Fuzzy buds, pretty peeling bark, and colorful twigs brighten up the winter landscape. Include a few of these easy-to-grow beauties to decorate the yard in winter.

CRABAPPLE Red, yellow, or green fruit persists into winter on some species of crabapple; small tree with spring flowers.

STAR MAGNOLIA Conical buds are tightly closed through winter, but the velvety covering is eye-catching; large shrub or small tree.

PAPERBARK MAPLE Bark peels and curls as tree ages to reveal trunks mottled with shades of brown and red; small tree with colorful foliage.

RED-TWIG DOGWOOD Young twigs turn brilliant red in winter; promote vibrant twig color by cutting this shrub to ground level every spring.

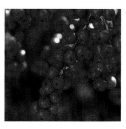

HOLLY Long-lasting red berries decorate plants for months in winter; must plant male and female plants for berry production.

Plant a room

Gain more living space by using trees and shrubs to plant lush outdoor rooms. No need to pour footings, extend the roofline, and build walls when you can plant trees and shrubs to create an inviting gathering space that offers close views of nature's delights.

Begin planning an outdoor room by defining the purpose of the space. Will your room be an outdoor kitchen with a grill and a dining table? Or maybe it will be a cozy spot for reclining with a good book. After defining the purpose, consider the materials you would like to use for the walls, ceiling, and floor of the space. The walls might be made of trees, shrubs, and the side of an existing building. Open sky, a leafy tree canopy, or a pergola might form the ceiling. The floor of a garden room can be as simple as a patch of grass or as intricate as a stone patio.

Wrapped with lush foliage and located just a few steps away from the door, this alfesco dining spot is an inviting retreat.

Open space around a patio or deck is a great place to begin planting an outdoor room. Think of trees and tall shrubs as the wall for an ideal outdoor space. Choose small columnar trees to create a narrow upright wall that doesn't infringe on the living space. Integrate flowering trees or shrubs into the scheme and enjoy a bit of nature's art as you kick back in your alfresco living room.

Trees and shrubs are excellent at transforming an open, grassy expanse into a series of intimate rooms. When thoughtfully divided, a small yard can feel more expansive when plants are used as living walls within the space. Trees and shrubs prevent the eye from taking in the entire landscape in one glance. Instead the plants mask views, creating a sense of mystery and encouraging visitors to explore the space.

Plant a great garden room

Planting a garden room begins with choosing the best trees and shrubs for the job. Look for plants that have a strong upright habit so they don't become excessively wide and extend into the room. Here are a few more essential tips to keep in mind as you select plants for your garden room.

Go simple. Many of the best garden rooms are defined by uniform hedge or tree plantings. A repetitive wall planting will create a neutral backdrop, allowing the purpose of the room to shine rather drawing attention to the border planting.

Frame with fragrance. Perfume a garden room with a fragrant hedge or tree border. Lilac, mockorange, crabapple, and several species of viburnum are prized for their pleasing fragrance. Their blooms are stellar too and will adorn the walls of a garden room with lovely color.

Pair trees and shrubs. If a garden room calls for walls any taller than 10 feet, use a combination of trees and shade-tolerant shrubs. While trees create a leafy canopy up high, shade-loving shrubs will define the room near ground level. A few great shrubs for shade include boxwood, red-twig dogwood, and summersweet clethra.

Low boxwood hedges encircle multiple outdoor rooms in this small backyard. A tall arborvitae hedge in the background creates a visual barrier.

Be mindful of size

An adorable little spruce at a garden center can become a lofty specimen in a few years. Underestimating the growth of trees and shrubs is a common mistake. But it is one that is easy to avoid by doing a little homework before making a purchase.

Not only do different species of plants mature at various heights and widths, assorted cultivars within the same genus or even species often grow to different sizes. For example, the mature size of crabapple varieties varies from 10 feet tall to nearly 30 feet tall.

Check the plant tag to be sure the mature size of a plant will complement the planting area you have in mind. The tag has hardiness information as well as the plant's expected mature height and width and other important growing notes. The plant's size can vary slightly depending on the growing conditions. To be safe, plan for the plant to slightly exceed the size listed on the plant tag.

Wildlife habitat

Habitat for all kinds of wildlife is disappearing at an alarming rate.

The continued growth of suburban areas reduces food sources, nesting sites, and water access for songbirds, squirrels, chipmunks, butterflies, and a host of other welcome backyard visitors.

The good news is that a few trees and shrubs can quickly transform a barren landscape into a rich oasis of food and shelter for hundreds of species. In short order the yard will come alive with cardinals winging in to munch on berries. Butterflies will flutter through shrub borders searching out nectar. And songbirds and hummingbirds will nest in dense, shrubby plants.

A wildlife-friendly landscape includes plants that provide food and shelter. Many woody plants produce fruit or nuts that offer food for both birds and animals. When selecting plants, put together a mix of species that will provide food throughout the year.

Provide shelter

Cover, or shelter, is a key ingredient in providing a rich home for wildlife. In winter, wildlife need shelter from the cold, wind, and precipitation. Evergreen trees and shrubs, especially those with branches close to the ground, make some of the best shelters.

Another great source of shelter is dead plant material. Fallen trees provide cover for salamanders and small mammals. Brush piles are ideal as cover, nesting sites, and dens for many wildlife species. Instead of quickly getting rid of

Crabapple trees are an important food source for blue jays and other wildlife during fall, winter, and early spring.

fallen branches, stack them in an out-of-the-way corner of the landscape. Wildlife will find them and set up house.

Look to nature when designing a landscape for wildlife. Plant trees and shrubs in groups, just as they grow in nature, instead of as isolated specimens. Pay attention to plant height when designing a planting. Plant tall trees, short trees, shrubs, and perennials together. Wildlife will find food and cover at varying heights.

Include water

Complete a great wildlife planting by providing a source of fresh water. This is as simple as placing a birdbath or shallow saucer near an outdoor faucet. The proximity to the faucet will make the birdbath a cinch to fill and clean. Here are a few more tips for creating a wildlife oasis.

Create a diverse plant collection. A mixed border that consists of several species of trees and shrubs will attract more songbirds, butterflies, and insects than a uniform hedge. Include plants that birds and animals favor for shelter as well as food sources in the mix.

Plant a year-round buffet. Feed wildlife 12 months a year, and they are likely to make the area a permanent home. Be sure to include plants that produce food that is available in late winter and early spring—the time of greatest food scarcity. Hawthorn, crabapple, holly, American cranberrybush viburnum, and staghorn sumac are early spring food sources.

Add nesting cavities. Trees and shrubs offer protection from the elements and ideal nesting sites for many species. Tree cavities in both living and dead trees provide nesting sites for a variety of species including woodpeckers, nuthatches, chickadees, and gray squirrels. These cavities are rare in new or young landscapes. Encourage wildlife to take up residence by providing birdhouses and nesting boxes.

Left: **Hummingbirds will nest near nectar sources. Create a nectar buffet by pairing flowering trees and shrubs with long-blooming annuals and perennials. Aim to have several plants in bloom throughout the entire growing season.**

Below: **Beautyberry is an easy-to-grow, 3- to 6-foot-tall shrub that produces amethyst berries in late summer. The berries disappear quickly, because birds devour them as soon as they ripen.**

Best trees and shrubs for wildlife

Put out the welcome mat for songbirds, squirrels, chipmunks, and a host of other backyard critters with trees and shrubs that offer them food and shelter. These easy-to-grow species are an especially welcome sight to creatures that are forced to travel farther and farther to find food in new subdivisions. Share the joy of landscaping for wildlife with your neighbors and create a neighborhood-wide habitat.

AMERICAN HOLLY Glossy evergreen leaves provide cover and nesting sites for a variety of wildlife. The large tree's fruit draws songbirds, ruffed grouse, and deer.

CANADIAN HEMLOCK Dense evergreen branches make this large tree an excellent shelter and nesting site. It also provides food for birds and small animals. It has graceful arching branches.

CRABAPPLE This spring-blooming small tree produces fruit relished by many songbirds and mammals. Butterflies and bees seek nectar from the plant's fragrant flowers.

GRAY DOGWOOD Fruit decorates this medium to large native shrub in fall, providing sustenance to birds during migration. It tolerates wet, dry, or poor soil.

HACKBERRY An easy-to-grow, adaptable tree, hackberry produces fruit that attracts many bird species, including cedar waxwings, flickers, cardinals, and robins.

HAWTHORN These thorny trees are good nesting sites for birds. Hawthorns produce fruit eaten by cedar waxwings, sparrows, small mammals, and deer throughout winter.

OAK The acorns of these tall trees offer an important food source for both birds and mammals. Oaks also provide valuable nesting sites.

RHODODENDRON Evergreen varieties of this shrub offer year-round cover. Spring flowers provide nectar for bees and butterflies. Rhododendrons thrive in shade.

SERVICEBERRY A small tree or large shrub, serviceberry produces fruit in early summer and attracts robins, cedar waxwings, rose-breasted grosbeaks, and other birds.

STAGHORN SUMAC A great shrub for tough growing sites, staghorn sumac has fruit that persists through winter and is an important emergency food for a variety of birds in early spring.

VIBURNUM Many varieties of these medium to large shrubs are attractive landscaping plants and provide fruit and cover for wildlife, particularly during late summer and fall migration.

WINTERBERRY A small shrub with pretty red berries, winterberry provides a valuable winter food source for birds. The fruit of this deciduous holly is eye-catching in winter.

beauty from trees and shrubs

From sweet-scented flowers in spring to bold red twigs in fall, trees and shrubs add brilliant beauty to the landscape year-round. Explore the many attributes of woody plants and choose a few favorite species to enjoy in your yard.

p.26
FANTASTIC FOLIAGE
Green is only one part of the leaf color spectrum. Embrace the many hues of leaves as you choose plants for your landscape.

p.30
FLOWERS AND FRUIT
Jewels of the garden, flowers and fruit decorate trees and shrubs for weeks at a time. Add many of these beauties to your garden.

p.34
BARK AND TWIGS
Often overlooked, the woody parts of trees and shrubs boast many unique colors and textures.

Beautiful leaves
and needles

Leaves and needles are the powerhouses of trees and shrubs.

They capture the sunlight that powers the important process of photosynthesis. While they house the biological machinery that turns carbon dioxide into life-giving sugars, leaves and needles also play an important aesthetic role in the landscape. Tree and shrub foliage enriches the landscape with hefty doses of color and texture. Its influence on the landscape is especially striking when a leafless winter scene is compared to the same scene in summer. The lush feel of the summer scene is thanks in large part to copious amounts of foliage.

From palm-shape maple leaves to intricately cut pin oak foliage, leaf shapes, and the textures they create, vary greatly. Finely textured ornamental trees, such as Japanese maples, and shrubs are excellent focal points in shrub borders or foundation plantings. Highlight the intricacies of their foliage by pairing them with plants with simple large leaves. The contrast will create interest and draw the eye to the finely textured plantings.

Needled plants also offer diversity. The soft thin needles of white pine vary greatly from the long, stiff needles of Austrian pine. Plants with flattened scalelike foliage, such as arborvitae, juniper, and bald cypress are beloved for their ability to block wind and protect wildlife from the elements.

Celebrate color

Color, like shape, varies among woody plant species. Leaf and needle color is generally green, yellow, gray, or blue-green. Red, maroon, orange, and purples are common in fall. Choose plants with bright green, red, or yellow foliage to add excitement and energy to a space. Create a calm atmosphere by integrating trees and shrubs with gray and blue-green foliage.

Leaf color of many species varies by cultivar. Spirea is a good example. Old-fashioned bridal wreath spirea has medium green foliage while closely related Magic Carpet Japanese spirea has chartreuse leaves. See the encyclopedias, beginning on page 108, to learn more about the popular leaf and needle colors within each species.

Opposite: **Finely cut foliage of a Japanese maple takes center stage near this patio while creating a brilliant privacy screen.**

ASK THE GARDEN DOCTOR

My variegated maple has a couple of branches with all-green leaves this year. Is something wrong with it?

ANSWER: Variegated plants occasionally revert back to their all-green form. There is nothing wrong with your tree; its coloring is just a little off. Preserve the variegated nature of your tree by pruning off the branches that have all-green leaves.

A hint of blue

Aside from the hue of a cloud-free sky, blue is rarely found in the landscape. Scan the perennial garden for cerulean, cobalt, indigo, and sapphire blossoms and you're likely to strike out. Woody plants, on the other hand, offer several hints of blue year-round.

BLUE SPRUCE
The most best-known blue-tinged beauty is Colorado blue spruce. Growing 30 to 60 feet tall, this spruce has an especially distinct blue color on new growth.

BLUE JUNIPER
Several cultivars and species of juniper sport icy blue foliage. Blue coloring on junipers often intensifies in winter.

BLUE CYPRESS
Some cypresses are known for their blue-green coloring. 'Blue Ice' Arizona cypress grows about 15 feet tall and is a great choice for foundation plantings.

Fabulous fall color

A glowing sugar maple, ablaze with shades of orange and yellow and backlit by the setting sun is a magnificent way to celebrate the changing seasons. While many large trees light up with brilliant color in fall—maples, oaks, birches, and honeylocust are just a few—hundreds of other woody plants also display color-rich leaves for several weeks in autumn. If planting space is limited, just one or two species prized for their autumn finery will easily create a lovely scene.

Temperature, moisture, day length, and soil conditions all influence how fall leaf color develops. Here callery pear and sumac sport vibrant orange and red end-of-season color.

Color on a small scale

Shrubs and small ornamental trees offer a host of opportunities for adding color to petite suburban lots and courtyard gardens where a massive oak isn't an option. The leaves of gray dogwood turn a velvety, rich shade of deep red as the days get shorter. Oakleaf hydrangea sports Technicolor foliage in hues of red, orange, and yellow.

Shrubs and small ornamental trees are perfect for adding striking fall color to entryways, patioside plantings, and other popular outdoor areas calling for plants that maintain a small stature. Amplify the deciduous plants' autumn coloring by pairing them with evergreen shrubs. A dark green backdrop of yew or arborvitae is the perfect foil for a blazing red crape myrtle.

Varying color

Decreasing day length and cooling temperatures trigger woody plants to prepare for winter. The plants' major visible preparation is changing leaf color. The leaf shedding, or senescence, process is complex and closely connected to the local ecology. Prior to the leaves dropping from the branches, the plants absorb many of the sugars and amino acids from the leaves. These nutrients are used by the plant during winter and fuel production of new leaves in spring.

As sugars and amino acids are removed, some other biochemical reactions break down components of the leaves and the remaining components, which are responsible for fall coloration, become visible.

The hue and intensity of leaf color is influenced by growing conditions. A sweet gum tree might produce a bright red display one year and follow up with a dull red-brown cloak the following autumn. Soil moisture content is a common factor in fall color production. Ample moisture often allows biochemical reactions inside leaf cells to be quick and efficient, and then few of the colorful compounds are revealed. A dry growing season tends to produce the opposite effect.

ASK THE GARDEN DOCTOR

This fall my white pine dropped a lot of needles. They turned brown-orange before falling off the tree. Is something wrong?

ANSWER: There is no need to worry. Your tree is simply going through seasonal needle drop. It is a natural process. Contrary to their name, evergreens have needles that do not stay green forever. Triggered by the weather and the season, evergreen trees cast off some of their needles. Some trees shed many needles every year—white pines are some of the most dramatic—and others have a big needle drop every couple of years.

A rainbow of color
Add your favorite hues to the landscape with this roundup of colorful foliage. Some cultivars within a species produce more intense color than others. Be sure to read the plant tag to get a good idea of fall color potential.

YELLOW
Birch
Ginkgo (near right)
Honeylocust
Hornbeam
Katsura tree

ORANGE
Staghorn sumac
Sugar maple

RED
Black gum
Burning bush
Callery pear
Japanese maple (far right)
Red maple (middle right)
Scarlet oak

PURPLE
Blackhaw viburnum
Smoke tree
Wayfaringtree viburnum

Flowers for every season

The perfect contrast to woody twigs and branches,

flowers do an excellent job of softening the rugged texture of trees and shrubs. From dime-size witch hazel blossoms to massive magnolia flowers, woody plants offer a range of unique blooms that rival many perennial plants.

Many flowering shrubs will bloom for weeks at a time, surpassing their herbaceous perennial counterparts. Combine long-blooming shrubs and perennials for a colorful foundation planting or brilliant easy-care mixed border that is rife with flowers, fragrance, and wildlife interest year-round.

Spring is the spectacular flowering season of most trees and many shrubs. Heralders of

Shade-loving, spring-flowering rhododendrons and azaleas are excellent shrubs for the north and east sides of a home.

spring—flowering cherry, crabapple, forsythia, and rhododendrons—add bold swaths of color to the still-drab landscape in early and mid-spring. Be sure to include a few of these beauties within sight of windows so they can be enjoyed from inside the home as well as outside.

Continue the bloom show in summer with pagoda dogwood, Washington hawthorn, and Japanese tree lilac. These small to medium trees top out at less than 30 feet tall. Plant a cluster of three or five trees near a property line and enjoy the benefits of a blooming privacy screen. Add summer-flowering shrubs, such as hydrangea, smoke tree, and summersweet clethra, and the flower show will extend from ground level up.

Unlike annual flowering plants and many perennials, blooming trees will not rebloom if their faded flowers are removed. Trees generally bloom once a year.

Some shrubs, on the other hand, will rebloom if their spent blooms are removed. Butterfly bush, hydrangea, and weigela are just a few examples of shrubs with repeat-bloom potential. Snip spent flowers off these shrubs in spring and summer to promote a second flush of blooms in late summer or early fall.

Fall and winter splendor

Flowering woody plants are few in the fall landscape, but many summer-flowering species hold their blossoms well into fall. Tawny, cone-shape hydrangea flowers are nearly as pretty dried on the shrub in fall as they are when they first debut in summer. Smoke tree offers similar airy floral delights.

What trees and shrubs lack in fall flowering, they make up for with color-drenched foliage. Count on many species of viburnum, fothergilla, and spicebush to bloom in spring or summer and then light up with shades of red, orange, or yellow in fall. These hardworking plants with multiple seasons of interest are always valuable members of the landscape.

Camellia, also called winter rose, is the queen of the winter bloom show in warm climates. Hundreds of colorful and sometimes fragrant cultivars are available. Be sure to choose a variety that blooms in winter; some camellias bloom in fall or spring. Gardeners in northern climates will enjoy sweet-scented winter blossoms of witch hazel and daphne. These tough shrubs often bloom when a few inches of snow still covers the ground.

TEST GARDEN TIP

Bloom partners

Tulips, daffodils, hyacinths, and crocuses are great planting partners for spring-flowering shrubs. The bulbs emerge in early spring, suppressing weeds around the base of the flowering shrubs. After the bulb blooms fade, allow the foliage to remain and slowly turn yellow to ensure the bulb has plenty of energy for blooming next spring.

Early season splendor

A sure sign that spring is on the way, the first flowers of spring are a welcome sight. Add easy-care early color to the landscape with these top spring performers.

FLOWERING QUINCE New double-flowering cultivars give this old favorite even more flower power. Zones 4–8.

FORSYTHIA Sulfur-yellow blossoms make this twiggy shrub a beacon of color in early spring. Zones 5–8.

LEMON BOTTLEBRUSH Blooming nearly year-round, this hummingbird favorite has a citrus aroma. Zones 8–11.

REDBUD Tiny pink to purple flowers decorate the leafless branches of this tough tree in early spring. Zones 4–9.

RED MAPLE Tiny, delicate maple flowers are some of the earliest flowers to open in spring. Zones 4–9.

SPICEBUSH A native plant, spicebush (*Lindera benzoin*) perfumes the garden for weeks in mid-spring. Zones 4–9.

STAR MAGNOLIA Tissue-paper-like petals make star magnolia a favorite. Excellent large shrub. Zones 4–9.

WITCH HAZEL Often blooming in late winter when snow is still on the ground, witch hazel is delightfully fragrant. Zones 5–8.

Fruit, nuts, and treats for wildlife

At first glance the glistening red berries

decorating an American holly are a lovely seasonal adornment. Keep your eye on the plants during the chilly days of winter, and you'll quickly note that the berries are a popular source of calories for many songbirds, including mourning doves. Many trees and shrubs are essential sources of nutrients for wildlife. Include fruit- and nut-producing plants in the landscape to ensure a thriving ecosystem.

Diversity is essential when creating a wildlife buffet. Include plants that produce fruit, such as crabapple, hawthorn, and American cranberrybush, alongside nut-producing plants. Oak, hickory, and beech produce nuts that are popular with squirrels and chipmunks as well as birds. Some fruit and nuts are quickly consumed while others remain on the plant well into winter. Plant several long-lasting food sources.

Thriving in full sun or part shade, American cranberrybush viburnum produces clusters of glossy red fruit. Birds devour the fruit in winter.

Planting different types of woody plants is just as important as the types of fruit and nuts they produce. A diverse planting that includes low-growing St. Johnswort and some holly cultivars, small ornamental trees such as dogwood and crabapple, and lofty oaks will attract far more wildlife than a planting made up entirely of trees or only shrubs. Wildlife feed at different levels. A mix of shrubs, small trees, and tall trees offers many options.

Plant with care

Fruit- and nut-producing trees and shrubs occasionally litter sidewalks and patios with their bounty. Birds and wildlife may further contribute to the messy situation as they flock to the buffet and leave droppings behind. Maintain a clean patio and a debris-free walkway by planting fruit- and nut-producing plants 10 to 15 feet away from outdoor living areas.

A property line is a great place for a mixed border of trees and shrubs that bear fruit or nuts. The planting will make a lively living screen. Call on shrubs and small ornamental trees to create a similar front yard border and share the beauty of a planting for wildlife with passersby.

Right: **A source of food for birds, raccoons, opossums, and others, beautyberry is an easy-to-grow native shrub.**

TEST GARDEN TIP
Choose natives

Native plants are always a good choice, especially when it comes to planting for wildlife. Native plants are accustomed to the soil and climate conditions of a site and often require less maintenance than nonnatives. Native trees and shrubs provide the best food and shelter resources for local wildlife because the animals are adapted to the species. Not sure which plants are native to your area? Contact your local extension service or state department of natural resources.

Year-round smorgasbord

A landscape with an ongoing food supply will encourage wildlife to make it a permanent home. The best landscape includes plants that offer fruit and nuts in every season. Here are some of the best food sources by season.

SPRING
Elm
Hawthorn
Holly

FALL
Eastern red cedar
Flowering dogwood
Hackberry

SUMMER
Serviceberry
Viburnum

WINTER
American beech
Black chokeberry
Black gum
Crabapple
Holly

Unique bark and twigs

Finely cut leaves, pretty berries, and fragrant flowers

often overshadow the subtle, yet intriguing, bark and twigs of trees and shrubs during the growing season. As soon as fall turns to winter, peeling bark, zigzagging twigs, and a host of other lovely characteristics add style and glamour to the winter scene.

A leafless winter landscape calls attention to the lines and forms of trees and shrubs. Trees with pendulous branches, often called weeping, make a striking silhouette. The angular branching pattern of honeylocust makes a bold statement against a pale blue winter sky. Leafless lilacs are a twiggy mass while barren hydrangeas have a more open, upright habit.

When choosing trees and shrubs, take note of the lines and forms their leafless branches present in the landscape. In many regions deciduous trees and shrubs are without leaves for at least six months a year—a surefire reason to consider their winter appearance.

Beauty of bark

The diverse character of bark is a surprise to many. Some trees and shrubs are cloaked with a smooth brown or gray protective coat; other plants have rough-textured bark that has many crevices. Play up the variation in texture by pairing opposing bark textures in a planting area.

Fast-growing gum tree has colorful, smooth bark. Thriving in warm regions, gum trees make good privacy screens.

Some of the most dramatic bark variations include colored bark. Many species of crape myrtle have warm cinnamon-color bark that brighten the winter landscape. Red-twig dogwood is beloved for its bright cherry red twigs that are especially prominent against a snowy backdrop.

Peeling, or exfoliating, bark adds another layer of interest to the landscape. A few popular trees with peeling bark include river birch, shagbark hickory, paperbark maple, and crape myrtle. Peeling bark tends to develop with age. A newly planted river birch, for example, will have little peeling bark, but by the time the trunk reaches 4 to 5 inches in diameter, it will be covered with curling paperlike strips of bark.

Some of the loveliest trees with peeling bark exhibit multiple hues when their outer layer of bark sloughs off. Lacebark pine does just that, revealing a patchwork of colors ranging from brown to gray to russet and green.

TEST GARDEN TIP

Go red!

Red-twig dogwood develops its most intense coloring on one-year-old stems. Ensure your plant has fire-engine red coloration by cutting the shrub back to 6 inches above ground level in early spring. New stems will quickly develop and they will display flashy red hues in winter.

Tree and shrub forms

Winter reveals the form of deciduous trees and shrubs. Knowledge of their forms is especially helpful when combining trees and shrubs in borders, such as foundation plantings, and in the overall landscape. For an energetic mix, pair plants with angular and rounded forms. For a calm, restful feel, combine similar plant forms. Here's a rundown of common tree and shrub forms.

SHRUBS

ROUNDED A perfect contrast to columnar plants, rounded shrubs are useful throughout the landscape.

COLUMNAR Like an arrow shooting toward the sky, a columnar shrub is a dramatic focal point.

PYRAMIDAL When seen from a distance, these shrubs tend to lift the eye upward. Plant them to contrast with a round or spreading tree.

SPREADING When paired with upright plants, spreading plants add interest at ground level while surpressing many weeds.

TREES

ROUNDED, OVAL Trees with this lovely shape often achieve their most perfect form when planted alone in an open yard. Or plant a group of three or five and enjoy their billowing mass.

SPREADING Useful for creating a canopy over a patio or continuing the horizontal line of a house, spreading trees will also frame a view.

PENDULOUS Ideal focal points, pendulous or weeping trees are lovely living sculptures.

VASE-SHAPE OR MULTISTEM Trees with vase shapes or multiple stems have a striking natural look. Plant several multistemmed trees together to achieve the look of a forest.

planting
plans

Create easy-care mixed borders, living privacy fences, and much more with plant-by-number plans. Use the woody plants listed in the following plans or create a custom design by replacing the designated trees and shrubs with plants of similar size and color.

p.**38**
SMALL-SPACE SOLUTIONS
Many shrubs and small trees thrive in containers, creating a year-round garden on a porch or patio.

p.**40**
EASY-CARE GARDENS
Keep landscape chores to a minimum by making woody plants an intregral part of a new garden.

p.**50**
CREATIVE SCREENS
From decorating a luckluster foundation to screening a view into a neighbor's yard, trees and shrubs stand up to the challenge.

TEST GARDEN TIP

Shrubs for containers

From dwarf pines to floriferous hydrangeas, shrubs are great container plants. Unlike annuals and perennials, they add interest year-round, making them good choices for entryways and other high-traffic areas. When grown in containers, most shrubs mature at less than their normal size.

PLANT LIST	
A.	**1 Purple beautyberry** (*Callicarpa dichotoma* 'Issai')
B.	**4 Pink chrysanthemum**
C.	**4 Ornamental cabbage**
D.	**4 Creeping wire vine** (*Muehlenbeckia axillaris*)

Seasonal showcase
A salvaged cornice filled with lush, quick-growing beautyberry creates a high-impact entryway. Shrubs make excellent container plants. Here beautyberry holds court among ornamental cabbages and chyrsanthemums in fall. In winter its berried branches will attract birds. Change out the annuals at the base of the beautyberry with the seasons to add a new punch of color. Pansies are perfect for spring, and trailing calibrachoa or bacopa and purple African daisies make a statement in summer.

Cornices, along with a host of other architectural elements, make great planting vessels. Too precious for the junk pile, the elegant pieces take on new life when filled with potting soil. Visit salvage businesses and flea markets to find bits of antique architecture worth preserving, then convert them into planters using a little resourcefulness, a few screws, some wire, and high quality potting soil.

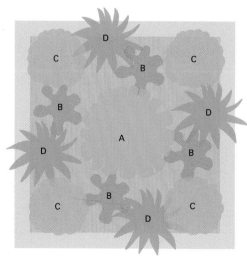

TEST
GARDEN
TIP

Slow-release fertilizer

Container-grown trees and shrubs don't have the ability to mine deep into the soil to acquire nutrients. Confined to their containers, the plants can become nutrient-deficient. Fertilize plants annually with a slow-release, general-purpose fertilizer. A slow-release formulation will make nutrients available over a long period and prevent a flush of tender growth that is susceptible to insects and diseases.

PLANT LIST

A.	**1 Crape myrtle** (*Lagerstroemia* cultivars)
B.	**2 'Inky Toes' coleus** (*Solenostemon scutellarioides*)
C.	**1 Variegated shell ginger** (*Alpinia zerumbet* 'Variegata')
D.	**1 Asparagus fern** (*Asparagus densiflorus*)

Color on high

Perfect for anchoring the corner of a deck or patio, crape myrtle adds color for weeks in summer. Situate this lush container in full sun for the best bloom show. A multistemmed tree was used here but a single-stem specimen would work equally well. Be sure to choose a small to medium crape myrtle cultivar. A plant that grows 10 to 15 feet tall is optimal. If crape myrtle is not hardy in your area, use serviceberry or flowering dogwood instead.

High quality potting soil is essential to a healthy tree or shrub container planting. Use a bagged product specially formulated for container gardening. A product that contains slow-release fertilizer is a good choice.

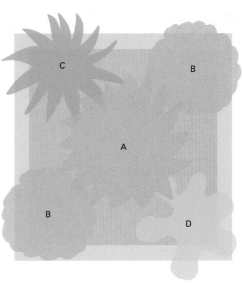

Blooming foundation

Adaptable to full sun or part shade, the plants in this simple foundation plan thrive in moist, well-drained soil. The bloom show begins in April with fragrant Indian hawthorn blossoms.

Light up a lackluster foundation with flowers.

Low-maintenance shrub roses and easy-to-grow Indian hawthorn provide months of blossoms. When the shrubs are paired with long-blooming daylilies and perennial salvia, the flower show extends from mid-spring to fall. A blooming foundation like this one creates a welcoming transition from the house to the landscape beyond.

Easy-care plants are essential for this front-and-center garden. The shrubs require only annual pruning. Caring for the perennials is as easy as removing spent flowers and foliage in fall. When the growing season ends, evergreen Indian hawthorn continues to add structure to the garden bed, and the leafless shrub roses will play a part too. The winter appearance of high traffic foundation plantings is important. Include evergreen and deciduous plants in foundation plantings to ensure interest in the off-season.

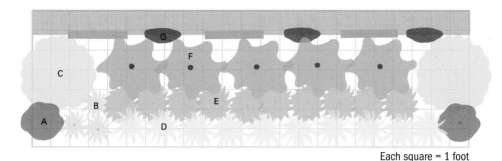

Each square = 1 foot

PLANT LIST

A. **2 Miniature roses**

B. **3 Dwarf Asiatic lilies** (*Lilium* hybrids)

C. **2 Indian hawthorns** (*Raphiolepis indica*)*

D. **10 Miniature daylilies** (*Hemerocallis* hybrids)

E. **10 Perennial sage** (*Salvia* × *sylvestris* May Night)

F. **5 Shrub roses** such as 'Betty Prior'

G. **3 Large-flowered clematises**
(*Clematis* hybrids) such as 'Jackmanii' and 'Henryi'

*In cold regions substitute Meyer lilac
(*Syringa meyeri*) or rhododendron.

ASK THE GARDEN DOCTOR

Japanese beetles decimated my shrub roses last year. What can I do to keep them away?

ANSWER: Japanese beetle is a frustrating pest that is tough to control. Begin by treating your lawn for grubs and you'll reduce the number of Japanese beetles (unless your neighbor doesn't control grubs, in which case beetles will invade your garden). Don't use adult beetle traps as they'll likely lure more beetles than you have in your yard. Your best line of defense is planting trees and shrubs that beetles don't like to feed on. Lilac, holly, and rhododendron are good substitutions for shrub roses.

TEST GARDEN TIP

A roundup of shrub roses

There are hundreds of shrub roses on the market. These no-fuss plants are more like shrubs than exhibition-worthy roses. Here are a few popular, reliable groups of shrub roses.

Buck Prized for their exceptional winter hardiness, roses bred by Griffith Buck at Iowa State University are medium-size—to 5 feet tall—with a wide range of bloom forms and colors. 'Carefree Beauty' and 'Polonaise' are both fine Buck roses.

David Austin Combining the bloom forms and fragrance of Old Garden Roses with the repeat-blooming habit and extended color palette of modern roses, David Austin English roses have vintage charm. Plant habits range from small shrubs to climbers.

Knock Out A medium shrub with single or double blooms available in a range of colors, Knock Out has become the best-selling rose in the world. It is adaptable to most soil conditions and has good disease resistance.

Morden Bred at the Agriculture Canada Research Station in Morden, Manitoba, the many varieties in this series all include the word "Morden" in their names. The plants are low to medium in height and extremely winter-hardy.

Color under a canopy

Long-blooming annuals hold court under a river birch. The birch and annuals benefit from regular watering.

Plant a shade garden under the cool canopy of a tree.

The perfect planting spot for shade-loving annuals, perennials, and shrubs, an open swath of soil under a deciduous or evergreen tree is especially useful for adding color and interest to small-space gardens. The shade garden can easily expand as the tree canopy enlarges.

Boxwood anchors the edges of this planting. Long-blooming annuals including red wax begonias, purple lobelia, and blue ageratum add a tapestry of texture and color under the leafy boughs from early summer until fall. Change up the design and color scheme with a host of other shade-tolerant annuals. For a more permanent planting, substitute perennials for the annuals. Reblooming fringed bleeding heart (*Dicentra eximia*), perennial geraniums (*Geranium*), deadnettle (*Lamium*) and hostas will provide months of easy-care color.

TEST GARDEN TIP

Planting around trees

Add interest to the base of a tree with a lush, colorful garden. Follow these pointers for blooming success.

Assess shade. Trees with high, open canopies, such as honeylocust and Kentucky coffee tree, create little shade and are good choices for gardening around. Dense, light-blocking shade hinders even the most valiant garden efforts. As a rule of thumb, if grass does not grow well under the tree, other plants will likely struggle.

Consider soil moisture. One of the greatest obstacles to gardening around trees is limited soil moisture. Mature trees quickly absorb available water, leaving nearby plants high and dry. Combat dry soil by growing drought-tolerant plants.

Don't add soil. Tempting as it may be to build a raised bed around a tree, burying roots with only a few inches of soil can kill a sensitive tree.

Dig with caution. It's okay to slice through a few small roots with a trowel, but avoid cutting roots that are thicker than an inch in diameter to avoid damaging the tree.

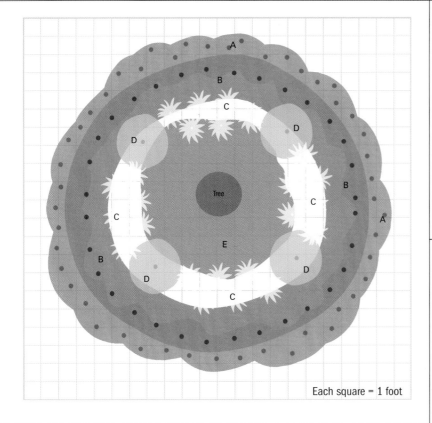

Each square = 1 foot

PLANT LIST		
A.	**48 Lobelias** (*Lobelia erinus*)	
B.	**32 Ageratums** (*Ageratum houstonianum*)	
C.	**24 Dusty millers** (*Senecio cineraria*)	
D.	**4 Boxwoods** (*Buxus* spp.)	
E.	**28 Red wax begonias** (*Begonia × semperflorens*)	
F.	**1 River birch** (*Betula nigra*)	

ASK THE GARDEN DOCTOR

Can I fertilize the plants growing under a tree?

ANSWER: Yes. Fertilizer will not harm the tree. Use a slow-release fertilizer and follow the label directions for application.

Entry garden charmer

Barberry and juniper shrubs mingle with sweetly fragrant roses to create a fragrant garden entrance.

Create a gracious garden entry with shrubs.

Burgundy Japanese barberries, seafoam green creeping junipers, and sweet pink and white roses mingle together in a cottage garden composition that is fitting for the crisp white picket fence they flank. Foliage and flowers are equal partners in this easy-care garden. The tiny, semievergreen leaves of Japanese barberry are a lovely foil for the pink blossoms of 'The Fairy' roses. At ground level, the tufts of green juniper foliage ramble along the slate steps, framing the path.

Creeping or low-growing shrubs, such as creeping juniper, are great weed barriers. Their dense foliage prevents light from reaching the soil, thereby preventing seeds from sprouting. Unlike wood mulch or other mulch products that need to be refreshed every year, creeping shrubs require minimal annual care. If they grow out of bounds, simply prune them back.

There are many excellent creeping shrubs. In addition to low-growing junipers, several species of cotoneaster and wintercreeper euonymus grow 1 to 3 feet tall and spread several feet wide. Fragrant sumac and Japanese holly are also excellent groundcovers.

PLANT LIST

A. **2 Creeping junipers**
(*Juniperus horizontalis* 'Bar Harbor'):
Zones 5–9

B. **4 Japanese barberries**
(*Berberis thunbergii* 'Atropurpurea'):
Zones 5–8

C. **4 'The Fairy' roses**
(*Rosa* 'The Fairy'): Zones 5–9

D. **2 'New Dawn' climbing roses**
(*Rosa* 'New Dawn'): Zones 5–9

E. **1 'Constance Spry' shrub rose**
(*Rosa* 'Constance Spry'): Zones 5–9

F. **2 Jackman clematises**
(*Clematis* 'Jackmanii'): Zones 4–8

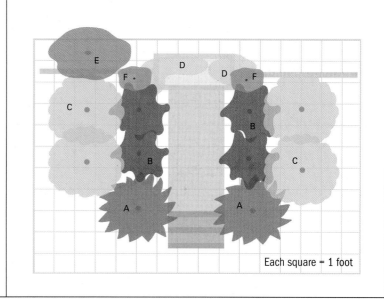

Each square = 1 foot

TEST GARDEN TIP

Shrub rose know-how

Use shrub roses to add weeks of carefree color to foundation plantings, perennial borders, and nearly any other landscape situation. Grow great shrub roses with these tips.

Seek sun. Shrub roses bloom best when they receive at least eight hours of direct sunlight a day. They tolerate four to six hours of direct sun well, but they will not bloom as vigorously.

Know your zone. Be sure the shrub roses you select are hardy to your area. Frigid winter temperatures can freeze some shrub roses to ground level. The roses will often regrow from their roots, but their size and shape will be compromised. Shrub roses in the Buck and Morden groups are particularly cold-hardy. See page 41 for more about cold-hardy roses.

Space smart. Keep fungal problems at bay by encouraging air circulation among plants. When planting, allow for adequate space around plants by following the plant spacing recommendations on the rose's plant tag.

Prune annually. Take 10 minutes in early spring to give shrub roses a quick trim. Prune away dead or damaged canes and canes that are crossing or rubbing on one another. Prune any wayward canes to create a plant with a pleasing shape.

Creative living sculpture

Slow-growing boxwood is a popular knot garden plant. Here it is used to outline the garden and create gentle curves inside the square.

Calming blues, silvers, and greens make for a

sophisticated and very serene knot garden. A not-so-formal knot garden is a great focal point in the landscape. When viewed from several feet above—such as from a deck or second-story window—the graceful lines and sharp corners are prominent. From ground level the tapestry of textures and vertical elements take center stage.

Easy care green boxwood outlines this design. More boxwood is used to create gentle curves around upright evergreens. The pyramid-shape yews in each corner serve as punctuation marks to add vertical interest. The evergreen nature of boxwood and yews ensures that the knot garden offers interest year-round.

At first glance you might assume that the carefully sculpted boxwood in this garden requires frequent pruning. That's not the case. Boxwood is very slow growing. It looks neat and tidy with just one or two shearings a season. If you prefer a finely manicured look, trim it once in late spring and again in late summer.

The planting spaces between the evergreen plants are filled with short rows of mealycup sage, heliotrope, and dusty miller. For a more permanent planting, substitute perennials for the annuals. Perennial sage (*Salvia officinalis*), perennial geranium (*Geranium*), and lady's mantle (*Alchemilla mollis*) are long-lasting, easy-to-grow perennials.

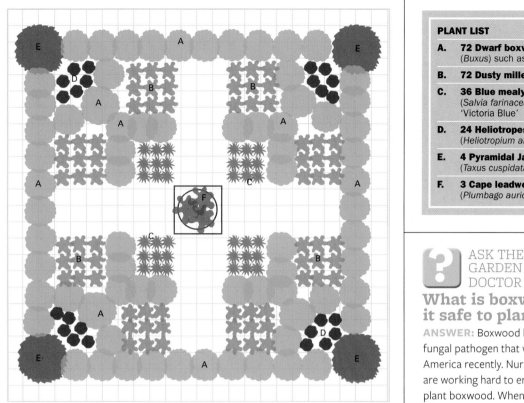

Each square = 1 foot

PLANT LIST

A.	**72 Dwarf boxwoods** (*Buxus*) such as 'Green Gem'
B.	**72 Dusty millers** (*Senecio cineraria*)
C.	**36 Blue mealycup sages** (*Salvia farinacea*) such as 'Victoria Blue'
D.	**24 Heliotropes** (*Heliotropium arborescens*)
E.	**4 Pyramidal Japanese yews** (*Taxus cuspidata*)
F.	**3 Cape leadworts** (*Plumbago auriculata*)

ASK THE GARDEN DOCTOR

What is boxwood blight? Is it safe to plant boxwood?

ANSWER: Boxwood blight is a destructive fungal pathogen that was found in North America recently. Nurseries and scientists are working hard to eradicate it. It is safe to plant boxwood. When purchasing plants, choose healthy, vigorous plants from reputable nurseries.

TEST GARDEN TIP

Hedge worthy

Boxwood is an excellent edging material for formal gardens. However, some boxwoods can soar to well over 12 feet, so be sure to choose a dwarf variety for your knot garden. Also avoid boxwoods that have pyramidal shapes, such as 'Green Mountain', since they don't work well for trimming into a low hedge. The follow selections are great for edging.

Dwarf English boxwood (*Buxus sempervirens* 'Suffruticosa'), which grows just 2 to 4 feet tall.

Littleleaf boxwood (*Buxus microphylla*), which grows 3 to 4 feet tall.

Korean boxwood (*Buxus sinica insularis*), which grows 2 to 3 feet tall.

Hybrid boxwoods (*Buxus* cultivars) 'Green Velvet' grows 3 feet tall and is reliably cold-hardy to Zone 4. Antarctica and Chicagoland Green ('Glencoe') are also low growing and hardy to Zone 4.

Year-round foundation

Mixing evergreen and deciduous shrubs with a few perennials is a surefire way to ensure a foundation is lively and colorful year-round. Too often, foundation plantings become twiggy, leaf-filled borders for three to six months a year. Create an inviting entry in the depths of winter as well as high summer with the collection of easy-to-grow plants included in this foundation plan.

Many perennials and some shrubs will bloom for weeks if their spent blooms are removed.

This process is called deadheading, and it is as simple as pinching or pruning off the withered blooms. Count on the hibiscus to bloom from midsummer until fall if you regularly pinch off the faded flowers. Clip away tired bluebeard flowers, and the plant will likely debut new flowers a few weeks later. Spend 10 minutes a week deadheading, and the plants will reward you with weeks of fresh flowers.

TEST GARDEN TIP

Foundation renovation

An easy way to give a home a fresh look is to update the foundation plantings. Add color to a tired collection of junipers and yews, and you'll create an inviting entryway. Here are a few tips to get you started.

Work with what you have. As long as the existing plants are simply overgrown—too tall or extending out of the garden bed—keep a select few. By thoughtfully leaving healthy, mature plants, your new foundation planting will avoid the awkward immature stage as it slowly fills in.

Plant for every season. Ensure eye-catching colors and textures year-round by selecting plants with multiseason interest. Use perennials and bulbs to add a burst of color periodically throughout the season.

Shop the sales. Keep your foundation renovation budget in check by buying plants on sale at the end of the season. Plant at least six weeks before the first anticipated fall freeze to ensure that the plants have plenty of time to expand their root systems in the new locale.

The best foundation plantings boast color and texture from January through December. Hibiscus and bluebeard provide abundant color here in summer. Yew and juniper anchor the garden in winter.

PLANT LIST

A. **1 Yew** (*Taxus* × *media*)

B. **2 Hardy hibiscuses** (*Hibiscus moscheutos*)

C. **2 Bluebeards** (*Caryopteris clandonensis*)

D. **1 Summersweet clethra** (*Clethra alnifolia*)

E. **12 Ajugas** (*Ajuga reptans*)

F. **1 Smoke tree** (*Cotinus coggygria* Golden Spirit)

G. **1 Juniper** (*Juniperus squamata* 'Blue Star')

H. **1 Japanese barberry** (*Berberis thunbergii* 'Atropurpurea')

I. **1 Shasta daisy** (*Leucanthemum* × *superbum*)

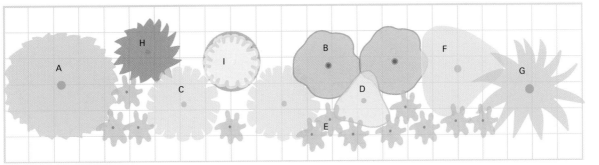

Each square = 1 foot

Bird-friendly border

Much more inviting than a simple wood fence, this diverse planting screens views while providing abundant resources for wildlife.

The surest way to attract winged visitors to your yard

is to provide them with a rich habitat. This diverse shrub and perennial border includes plants for forage, shelter, and nesting. Complement the plants with a simple water source, such as a birdbath, and get ready for a parade of songbirds flitting among the plants.

A smoky-hued Colorado blue spruce is the centerpiece of this easy-care planting. Growing 15 to 20 feet tall and 6 to 10 feet wide, 'Bakeri' Colorado blue spruce is well-suited for small residential lots. Its dense branch structure makes it an ideal shelter or nesting spot for birds. The tree's blue needles are a lovely complement to the blue-green juniper and warm green hebe. Employ this planting plan as a living screen and the evergreens will block unsightly views year-round.

Each square = 1 foot

PLANT LIST

A. **1 Variegated red-twig dogwood**
(*Cornus alba* 'Elegantissima')

B. **1 Juniper**
(*Juniperus chinensis* 'Blue Point')

C. **5 Cape fuchsias**
(*Phygelius × rectus* 'Devil's Tears')

D. **5 Asters** (*A. novi-belgii* 'Professor
Anton Kippenberg')

E. **1 Forget-me-knot**
(*Myosotis sylvatica*)

F. **1 Boxleaf hebe** (*Hebe odora*)

G. **1 Colorado blue spruce**
(*Picea pungens* 'Bakeri')

H. **2 New England asters**
(*A. novae-angliae*)

I. **1 American cranberrybush**
(*Viburnum trilobum*)

J. **1 Stinking iris** (*Iris foetidissima*)

K. **1 Golden hakone grass**
(*Hakonechloa macra* 'Aureola')

L. **1 Blue oatgrass**
(*Helictotrichon sempervirens*)

M. **2 Arborvitaes**
(*Thuja occidentalis*)

N. **1 Euphorbia**
(*Euphorbia characias wulfenii*)

TEST
GARDEN
TIP

Create a neighborhood oasis

Your landscape will quickly become a favorite respite for all types of wildlife when you follow the planting plan on this page. Here are a few more tips for welcoming birds, mammals, and insects of all sorts.

Let perennials stand through winter. Resist the urge to trim back perennials and deadhead flowering shrubs. The fruit and seeds produced by perennials and shrubs are a valuable food source for wildlife during winter. Trim perennials back to ground level in early spring. Prune shrubs as necessary in early spring to encourage dense new growth.

Limit herbicides and pesticides. The best weed and pest control in a wildlife-friendly environment is to employ mechanical controls—such as pulling weeds, tossing bad bugs in soapy water, or spraying plants with a strong stream from the garden hose to dislodge pests—when Nature is not able to keep pest numbers in check. Pesticides are particularly troublesome because they are likely to harm good insects while eradicating the pests.

Create a Certified Wildlife Habitat. Join thousands of other gardeners and create a Certified Wildlife Habitat through the National Wildlife Federation. A simple four-step program ensures that your garden provides the necessary food, shelter, water, and nesting sites for wildlife. By certifying your space you'll help get the word out that habitat restoration is easy and important!

Fantastic fall foliage

As soon as cool nights and short days prevail, deciduous trees begin to prepare for winter by revealing bold-color foliage like the reds and yellows of these maples.

Delight in the natural joys of fall with this color-rich

tree, shrub, and perennial planting. Set it along a property line and watch the large swaths of color intensify from late summer until early winter. The autumn hues of the two large maples in this plan are dependent on the planting area and seasonal conditions. One year might produce a Technicolor display like the one pictured here, while the next year the trees may take on more muted tones. An ever-changing planting like this is one of the many joys of gardening.

Several evergreens are included in this mixed planting. Evergreens are especially important because they provide color, texture, and structure for many months when other garden plants are without leaves. Increase the evergreen nature of this planting by including more arborvitae behind the maples.

TEST
GARDEN
TIP

Perennial partners

Pair trees and shrubs with perennials that shine in fall for a brilliant show of late-season color that beckons you outdoors to enjoy the splendor. Here are a few favorite, easy-to-grow perennials that keep their good looks late into fall.

Aster has daisy flowers in white or shades of pink or purple. This large mounding perennial grows 2 to 4 feet tall and wide. Full sun and well-drained soil. It tolerates drought well. Zones 4–10.

Blanket flower has cheerful daisylike blooms in warm yellow and red tones. It tolerates poor, infertile, and dry soil with ease. Blanket flower grows 1 to 2 feet tall and wide. Full sun and well-drained soil. Zones 3–8.

Chrysanthemum is a stalwart in the fall perennial garden. Its daisy flowers are available in a multitude of hues. A reliable bloomer, it is blanketed with flowers for weeks. Plants grow 1 to 3 feet tall and wide. Full sun and well-drained soil. Zones 5–10.

Goldenrod is a North American native perennial that is known for its yellow plumes in late summer and fall. It is deer-resistant and drought-tolerant. Plants grow 1 to 4 feet tall and wide. Full sun and well-drained soil. Zones 3–9.

Grasses are year-round garden plants, but they are particularly striking in fall when their feathery seed heads are present. Many excellent ornamental grasses are available. Full sun or part shade and well-drained soil. Zones 3–9.

Joe-pye weed has mauve blooms that open atop stately burgundy stems in late summer. The blossoms beckon butterflies, bees, and birds. Plants grow 4 to 6 feet tall and 4 feet wide. Full sun or part shade and moist to well-drained soil. Zones 3–9.

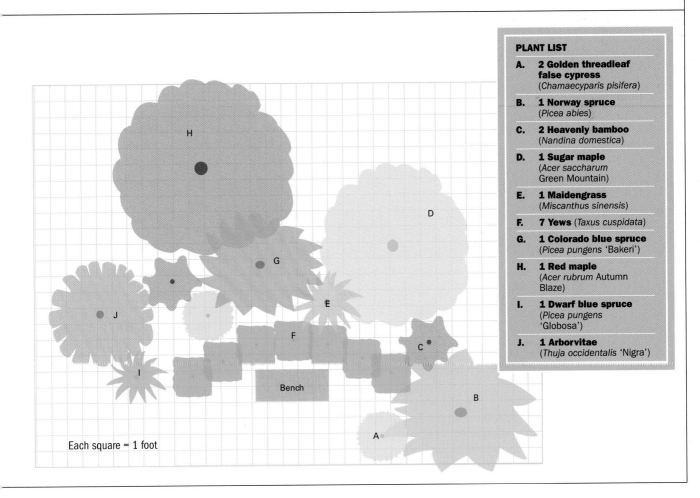

Each square = 1 foot

PLANT LIST

A.	**2 Golden threadleaf false cypress** (*Chamaecyparis pisifera*)
B.	**1 Norway spruce** (*Picea abies*)
C.	**2 Heavenly bamboo** (*Nandina domestica*)
D.	**1 Sugar maple** (*Acer saccharum* Green Mountain)
E.	**1 Maidengrass** (*Miscanthus sinensis*)
F.	**7 Yews** (*Taxus cuspidata*)
G.	**1 Colorado blue spruce** (*Picea pungens* 'Bakeri')
H.	**1 Red maple** (*Acer rubrum* Autumn Blaze)
I.	**1 Dwarf blue spruce** (*Picea pungens* 'Globosa')
J.	**1 Arborvitae** (*Thuja occidentalis* 'Nigra')

Bench

Easy-care hedge

Chartreuse 'Rheingold' arborvitae makes this simple border pop with color. The shrubs maintain their intense color year-round and contrast with 'Rose Glow' barberry.

A mixed shrub planting is almost always a great choice for screening an unwanted view, enclosing an outdoor room, or simply adding color and texture to your landscape. The plants included in this easy-care border are adaptable to a multitude of growing conditions. In soils from dry and quick-draining to clay, the evergreen arborvitae, red-hued barberry, and ornamental grasses will thrive, provided they receive at least eight hours of sunlight a day.

Plant this pleasing combo along a property line or use it as a living border near your patio to partially enclose the space. The planting plan illustrated here is about 24 feet long and 8 feet wide. Create a longer mixed hedge by simply repeating the planting scheme as needed to fill the space. Be sure to blanket the soil around the young plants with a 2-inch-thick layer of mulch to suppress weeds.

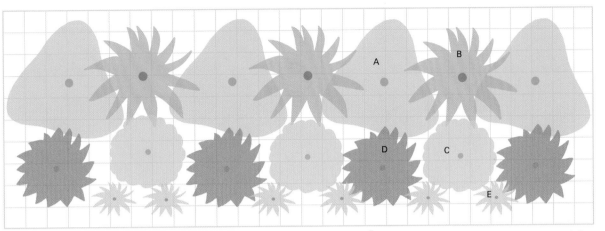

Each square = 1 foot

PLANT LIST

A. **4 Pyramidal arborvitae**
(*Thuja occidentalis* 'Emerald')

B. **3 Maidengrass**
(*Miscanthus sinensis* 'Gracillimus')

C. **3 Globe arborvitae**
(*Thuja occidentalis* 'Rheingold')

D. **4 Japanese barberry**
(*Berberis thunbergii* 'Rose Glow')

E. **6 Sedge** (*Carex albula*
'Frosty Curls')

ASK THE GARDEN DOCTOR

I can't plant barberry where I live. It is considered an invasive species. What is a good alternative to this tough shrub?

ANSWER: Japanese barberry self-seeds easily in some areas and quickly multiplies. It tolerates drought and is rarely browsed by deer, giving it a competitive advantage in woodlands and native areas where it displaces native plants. Japanese barberry is deemed an invasive species in 20 states.

If Japanese barberry is invasive in your area, plant inkberry, winterberry, arrowwood viburnum, or ninebark instead. Spirea is a another great substitution for barberry in this planting plan above.

TEST GARDEN TIP

Hedge care 101

Shrubs are some of the easiest-care plants in the landscape, which makes them excellent as candidates for a low-maintenance, informal hedge planting. Enjoy the benefits of a beautiful hedge for decades with these simple tips.

Analyze size. Carefully consider a shrub's mature size when purchasing it for a hedge planting. If the plant matures to a larger size than the allotted space in the landscape, it will require annual pruning.

Mulch, mulch, mulch. A thick layer of mulch will significantly cut down on weeds between plants in a newly planted shrub border. Prior to spreading the mulch, consider applying a granular preemergent weed product. The herbicide, combined with a 2- to 4-inch-thick layer of organic mulch, keeps weed growth to a minimum.

Prune annually. An annual two-hour investment in pruning in midsummer sets the course for a long-lived, healthy hedge. Selectively remove stems and foliage that are encroaching on nearby plants or growing too tall. If plants are allowed to grow out of bounds, severe pruning will be necessary and the hedge will lose its good looks for several months while it puts on new growth.

selecting trees and shrubs

Match the growing conditions in your yard with woody plants that suit the site, and you'll set the scene for a beautiful outdoor retreat full of flowers, foliage, and sweet shade.

p.58
CONSIDER HARDINESS
Zone ratings are a guide to knowing which plants will overwinter with ease in your area. Learn about woody plants and hardiness ratings.

p.60
SOIL, LIGHT, AND WATER
Match the soil, light, and moisture conditions of a site with a plant that thrives in those conditions, and the new plant will thrive.

p.64
SIZE MATTERS
Avoid the hassle of wrangling an overgrown shrub back in bounds by choosing a specimen whose mature size matches the available growing space.

p.66
PLANTS FOR DIFFICULT CONDITIONS
Need a shrub for dry soil? Or a tree that deer will not devour? Check out the summary of trees and shrubs for tough sites.

Know your Zone

A mimosa in Minnesota is a rare sight.

Woody plants are particular about temperature. While oaks and forsythia thrive in Minnesota's cold winter temperatures, mimosas, camellias, and other tender plants are accustomed to the moderate winter temperatures prevalent in warmer climates. A plant's tolerance of cold temperatures is summarized in its USDA Hardiness Zone rating.

North America is divided into 12 Zones based on the lowest expected winter temperature in each area. Trees, shrubs, and perennials are assigned a Hardiness Zone based on growing trials in many regions. A plant's Hardiness Zone rating represents the coldest Zone where the plant will thrive. For example, many hydrangea cultivars are hardy to Zone 4. Hydrangeas will grow in Zone 3, which is colder than Zone 4, but harsh winter weather is likely to damage or even kill them.

Find the growing Zone for your landscape on the Zone map on page 216. USDA Plant Hardiness Zone ratings are available in the encyclopedias beginning on page 108. Plant tags also contain zone information. Be sure to check a tree or shrub's zone rating before purchasing it.

Upper limit

Often a plant's rating is presented as a range of Zones. Littleleaf linden thrives in Zones 4 through 7, for example. Plant littleleaf linden in Zones 4, 5, 6, or 7 and it will thrive. Zones 3 and lower are too cold for overwintering, and Zones 8 and above are too warm year-round. Many woody plants require cool winter temperatures for strong growth. Be mindful of the upper as well as the lower zone limit, and plants will thrive.

Opposite: **'Summer Chocolate' mimosa, with lacy dusky purple foliage, thrives in Zones 6 to 9. Go to page 216 to find your gardening Zone.**

Microclimates

Pockets of warm and cool air are easy to find throughout the typical landscape. These are called microclimates. A planting bed next to a south-facing brick foundation is often several degrees warmer than a garden area in open lawn, thanks to the radiant heat from the brick. The same is true for a shrub border protected by dense evergreens. The evergreens shield the shrubs from cold, drying winter winds.

Microclimates are helpful when you would like to grow a plant that is tender in your Zone. Plant tender camellia near a south-facing wall where temperatures will likely not dip as low as they do in open areas. Microclimates can moderate temperature changes by a few degrees; however, they rarely make it possible to grow plants more than one Zone outside the plant's true Zone rating.

Winter protection

While not practical for tree trunks and roots, adding a layer of winter protection to a shrub's stems and roots is possible. A 3- to 4-inch layer of mulch, such as shredded bark, compost, or pine straw, around the base of a tender shrub will help protect its roots from extreme temperatures. Wrapping the branches with a couple of layers of burlap will offer protection for upper parts of the plant.

These tactics do not always prevent damage on marginally hardy species, but for a small investment of time and money, you might be able to overwinter a tender plant.

Go native

Native plants are adapted to local soil and climatic conditions. They provide valuable food and shelter for wildlife. Because native plants are adapted to local conditions, they usually require relatively low maintenance. Once a native tree or shrub is established, it needs little annual care.

Which plants are native? Scientists have been wrestling with this question for decades. While some people insist that native plants can only be species that are found in nature, and not cultivars, others suggest that native plants include any cultivars within a native species. Bottom line, landscaping with native species or native-derived cultivars is always a benefit.

Contact your local extension service or talk with a trusted professional at your local garden center to learn about great native plants for your area.

RED CHOKEBERRY

Soil considerations

Soil rich in organic matter drains well and provides ample nutrients for woody plants.

Most trees and shrubs grow best in soil that drains freely and provides ample nutrients for building strong roots, stems, and leaves. There are exceptions to this rule, of course—bald cypress and river birch thrive in constantly moist soil beside a pond or stream or in a moist depression in the landscape. Potentilla and juniper, on the other hand, are prized for their ability to survive and even thrive in dry soil that supplies limited nutrients. Hackberry and honeylocust can grow well in wet or dry soil.

Soil components

Four components determine a soil's ability to hold water and provide nutrients: clay, silt, sand, and organic matter. Knowing a few basic facts about how these soil components influence water and nutrient availability will go a long way toward helping you select the best trees and shrubs for the soil conditions in your yard.

Loam is the ideal soil for most plants. In a loamy soil, the four basic components are combined in the right proportions for plant growth. Many home landscapes, especially those around newly constructed homes, have less than ideal soil. It is too moist or dry or ranges to both extremes in different areas of the site.

Soil with a high clay content retains nutrients, but the tiny particles also trap water, creating a drainage issue. Prolonged rainfall creates waterlogged soil as water replaces oxygen around plant roots. Wilted leaves and drooping branches are a common aboveground sign of soggy soil and lack of oxygen below ground. Poorly drained clay soil is just fine for growing willow, hackberry, and swamp white oak trees, but it produces deadly results for magnolia and spruce. To tell whether your soil has a high clay content, grab a handful of moist soil and squeeze it. Clay soil feels sticky and forms a tight clump.

Smaller than grains of sand but larger than clay particles, silt particles form soil that drains freely and holds nutrients. Loam includes a large percentage of silt. Camellia, hydrangea, and weigela, along with many other trees and shrubs, grow well in soil high in silt. Silty soil feels powdery when dry, silky when wet.

Sandy soils drain very quickly and hold few nutrients. Plants that thrive in lean conditions, typically those that are native to arid regions or the Southwest, are excellent choices for sandy soil. Sandy soil crumbles when you try to form it into a ball. A few great shrubs for sandy soil include juniper, potentilla, Japanese barberry, spirea, and mockorange.

Working with your soil

Once you know the components of your soil, you can easily match your landscape's soil conditions with the best plants for those conditions. As you study individual plants in the encyclopedias, which begins on page 108, you'll discover clues about pairing plants with the appropriate soil. Each plant description includes "best site," which describes the conditions in which the tree or shrub grows best. For sandy soil, look for plants that require excellent drainage. For loam or sandy loam, look for trees and shrubs that need well-drained soil. If an entry notes that a plant tolerates infertile soil, it will likely grow in sand or clay, depending on its moisture requirements. If an entry mentions soils of average fertility, that refers to any reasonably fertile soil.

TEST GARDEN TIP

Soil for containers

Many shrubs and a few small trees thrive in pots year-round. Great soil is key to success. Fill the pot with a high-quality potting soil that includes a slow-release fertilizer. Specially formulated potting soil drains quickly, creating air spaces for oxygen to reach plant roots. Garden soil behaves differently in a container. In the restricted root zone, it tends to hold too much water and deprive roots of oxygen.

What about water? The most critical watering period for trees and shrubs is the first growing season after planting. For about six months after planting, trees and shrubs funnel a great amount of energy into creating a strong, healthy root system in the surrounding soil. Promote strong root growth by watering plants deeply just before the soil feels dry to the touch. Depending on the weather conditions, this might mean watering plants every few days, weekly, or every couple of weeks. Apply enough water so the soil is moist at least 6 inches below the surface.

After trees and shrubs establish a deep root system, they rarely need additional watering if they are adapted to the local weather conditions. Periods of extreme drought are an exception. Water deeply—moistening the soil to at least 6 inches below the soil surface—and infrequently until soil moisture is replenished by rain.

Sun and shade

Satisfy trees' and shrubs' needs for sunlight
and you're well on your way to creating a thriving landscape. Many woody plants require bright sunlight, but several grow and bloom in part shade or even full shade. Pairing a plant with its preferred light level begins with studying the sunlight that bathes your landscape.

Take inventory of sunlight
Start by assessing light patterns every couple of hours during the course of a day, noting where shadows fall, linger, and pass. Where you see sunlight trails during spring, bare-branched trees are creating the illusion of sunny spots beneath. What you think is a sunny area may be swallowed by shade after leaves emerge. Buildings and walls also cast shadows; don't overlook those structures as you plot the sun's path.

As you assess light patterns, consider plant growth. A 15-foot-tall maple will cast a much greater shadow in five years than it does now. Base sunlight estimates on mature plant size. Find out more about a plant's mature size in its entry in the encyclopedias beginning on page 108.

Once you have a general idea of how many hours of daily sunlight various areas throughout your yard receive, begin considering the best plants for those conditions. As you read about trees and shrubs, you'll encounter light requirements. Light needs are often expressed as full sun,

Shade patterns change over the course of the season. The perennials near this deciduous tree receive ample sunlight in early spring before the tree's leaves emerge.

part sun (partial sun), part shade (partial shade), or full shade. These terms refer to the sunlight a plant needs to yield top-notch performance. Deciphering these labels can be confusing. Here's a quick primer.

Full-sun plants require at least six hours of sun per day. The quality of the sunlight is important. A tree or shrub labeled as requiring full sun needs six hours of direct sunlight, not light filtered through a canopy.

Part-sun plants should receive three to six hours of direct sun per day, preferably in morning or evening, not during the hottest parts of the day.

Part-shade plants will thrive with three to six hours of sun per day, but definitely require shade during the afternoon, when the sun is hottest. These conditions describe small trees and shrubs growing underneath mature trees where the sun slants in during the morning. The east side of a building also offers part shade.

Full-shade plants need fewer than three hours of direct sun per day. Filtered sunlight or light shade is necessary for the rest of the day. This could describe plants on the north side of a structure or under a spreading tree where sunlight briefly penetrates the canopy at some point during the day and plants grow in light-filled shade the rest of the day.

Regional influences

A tree or shrub's light requirement shifts throughout the country. In the South and Southwest, shrubs that grow well in full sun in the North, such as many hydrangeas, need shade during the hottest part of the day. In the Pacific Northwest, cloud cover can prevent sun lovers from flourishing. Where cool, wet summers prevail, plants that prefer part shade can thrive in sunnier conditions.

ASK THE GARDEN DOCTOR

My butterfly bush grew very little this year and had only a couple of blooms. It is growing in a shade garden under some large pine trees. Is it getting enough light?

ANSWER: Limited growth and few flowers are signs that a plant is not receiving enough light, water, or nutrients to thrive. Butterfly bush requires at least eight hours a day of bright sunlight to thrive. It also grows best in moist, well-drained soil, but it will tolerate dry soil. The nutrient content of your soil is likely not a problem; butterfly bush doesn't require excessive nutrients. Most likely, your butterfly bush is not receiving enough sunlight. Lack of light, coupled with exceptionally dry soil, limited its growth and flowering. Move it to a full-sun location and water it regularly for a few weeks until it establishes a strong root system and can mine for its own water.

Flowering shrubs for shade
Count on these shrubs to bloom in part shade. Perfect for the north or east side of a home or a near shaded outdoor room, they will add color to the landscape for weeks.

BOTTLEBRUSH BUCKEYE White flowers are 8 to 12 inches long in earlysummer; spreading shrub grows 12 feet tall and wide. Zones 4–8.

CAMELLIA Flowers in shades of white, pink, or red bloom in fall, winter, and early spring; plants thrive in the shade of pines. Zones 7–11.

FOTHERGILLA Cream-color bottlebrush-like flowers in spring; bold yellow, orange, and red fall color. Zones 5–8.

MOUNTAIN LAUREL Showy white to deep pink flowers in late spring or early summer. Evergreen foliage is a valuable asset. Zones 4–9.

OAKLEAF HYDRANGEA Showy, large cone-shape flower clusters in summer; striking red, orange, and yellow fall color. Zones 5–9.

SPICEBUSH Green-yellow flowers in mid-spring; scarlet fruit ripens in late summer through October and attracts birds. Zones 4–9.

SUMMERSWEET CLETHRA Fragrant white, pink, or rose flowers in mid-summer; grows well in moist soil. Zones 4–9.

WITCH HAZEL Boldly fragrant yellow or red flowers bloom for several weeks in late winter or early spring. Zones 5–8.

Size matters

Hydrangea, dwarf
conifers, and a
magnificent weeping
spruce transform this
petite lot into a
spectacular garden.

Take the mature height and width of a tree or shrub into account

before adding it to the landscape. It is very easy to become enamored with a young, small plant at the garden center. Consider a blue spruce, for example. Petite and plump, the young tree might appear to be a great fit for planting near an entryway or in a patioside planting bed. In 5 to 10 years, that knee-high tree will rise two stories tall and span 15 feet or more wide. If planted in too-tight quarters it will have to be removed. Valuable growing time and money are lost. A little planning will ensure a plant will complement the landscape in a decade or two.

Mature size

Each entry in the encyclopedias, which begin on page 108, includes the mature size of the tree or shrub: the estimated height and width of the species or cultivar at maturity. Mature size is based on plant trials and is not absolute. Some plants remain shorter than their estimated mature size while others may exceed the listed value by several feet.

Sunlight has a great influence on plant growth. Plants in shade will often grow taller with a thinner crown as they stretch toward available light. A plant not competing for light might attain the same height, but it will likely be much broader. Moisture and soil conditions also influence growth. Bottom line, if a site's growing conditions match a plant's preferred conditions, it will likely reach its estimated mature size.

Growth rate

Some woody plants grow slowly while others sprout upward practically overnight. Rhododendrons are notoriously slow-growing plants. This is a welcome attribute in a shade garden, where they will maintain their form for years without encroaching on nearby plants. Slow growth rate can be detrimental if you would like the rhododendrons to quickly expand to screen a view. If a plant grows particularly slowly or quickly, that is highlighted in its encyclopedia description.

Pruning is an option for reigning in plants that outgrow their boundaries. When given the choice though, avoid planting a species that will require regular pruning to maintain a desired size. Instead, search out a smaller cultivar or consider a different species.

Keywords for small sites

Small lots call for small trees and shrubs. Not only is planting space limited, but the proportions of the house and lot call for small plantings for a cohesive look. Trees and shrubs described as dwarf are often good choices. Generally, the term "small," when used to describe trees, indicates that the tree will not exceed 25 feet or two stories tall.

TEST GARDEN TIP

Embrace diversity

Take a walk in a woodland and you'll see hundreds of plant species. Thanks to the diverse plant palette, many of animal and insect species also coexist in the woodland, creating a healthy ecosystem. Mimic nature's diversity in your own landscape by including a variety of trees and shrubs. A uniform hedge is pleasing to the human eye, but a mixed-species hedge is a greater benefit to the wildlife that shares your backyard. Be sure to include native plants in the mix.

Petite plants for small lots

In the right-size lots of one-quarter and one-third acre that are prevalent today, these small trees and shrubs will add easy-care interest to your landscape.

SPRING BLOOMERS
MEYER LILAC Small, fragrant lilac flowers in spring. Pleasing upright, rounded form. Shrub. Zones 3–7.

PAGODA DOGWOOD (pictured above) White flowers and striking horizontal branching. Tree or shrub. Zones 3–7.

RHODODENDRON Slow growing, evergreen. Flowers in many different hues. Select a small cultivar. Shrub. Zones 4–9.

STAR MAGNOLIA Graceful white or pink flowers in spring. Smooth green foliage. Tree or shrub. Zones 4–9.

SUMMER STARS
CRAPE MYRTLE White, pink, purple, or deep red flowers in summer. Tree or shrub. Zones 5–9.

JAPANESE TREE LILAC Frothy white flowers in early summer. Tree. Zones 3–7.

SMOOTH HYDRANGEA White flowers decorate plants for weeks in summer. Shrub. Zones 4–9.

SPIREA (pictured above) Selections with chartreuse, dark green, or burgundy foliage provide contrast in the summer border. Colorful flowers. Shrub. Zones 3–8.

FALL FAVORITES
FRAGRANT SUMAC Foliage turns orange to red to reddish purple in fall. Shrub. Zones 4–8.

NANNYBERRY VIBURNUM (pictured above) Small fruit attracts birds in fall and winter. Shrub. Zones 3–7.

OLEANDER Evergreen with long bloom season beginning in summer and extending into fall. Shrub. Zones 8–11.

SERVICEBERRY Red, orange, and yellow foliage. Spring flowers and summer fruit. Tree or shrub. Zones 3–9.

Trees for tough sites

Trees and shrubs are living problem solvers.

Select woody plants carefully and they will take on shaded sites, dry soil, wet soil, deer pressure, and many other challenges with grace. Changing with the seasons, trees and shrubs turn problem spots into beauty as they create shade, add a burst of color, feed and shelter wildlife, and soften the rigid lines of homes and buildings. Match your landscape challenge with the right plant and you'll set the foundation for a long partnership.

Is your dry backyard devoid of shade? Honeylocust and hackberry tolerate dry soil with ease and cast cooling shade. For an inviting outdoor room, complement the tough trees with shrubs that grow in part shade. Perhaps your landscape is plagued by too much shade, thwarting previous attempts to grow trees and shrubs. Adding foliage, flowers, and interest to a shaded landscape is simply a matter of choosing shade-loving plants. Dogwood, camellia, and rhododendron are all at home in shade and light up the landscape with a springtime flower show.

Bring new life to a boggy area, such as a low spot along a driveway where water collects briefly after a rain or an open swath of soil near a downspout. River birch and bald cypress trees thrive in wet soil. Red chokeberry is at home in wet soil and its red fruits add interest for weeks.

If an ever-growing deer population is wreaking havoc on your landscape, select from a host of deer-resistant plants. Unpalatable for a number of reasons including texture and fragrance, deer-resistant plants offer a planting solution for deer-dense areas. It's important to note that no plants are deer-proof. Hungry deer will devour thorny rose canes or almost any other plant in search of nutrition.

Use the listing of trees and shrubs adapted to various conditions on the following pages to draft solutions to your landscape problems.

WILLOW

HONEYLOCUST

WET SOILS

AMERICAN HORNBEAM Adaptable small tree for sun or shade. Native. Fall color is a pleasing shade of yellow to yellow-brown.

BALD CYPRESS Deciduous conifer native to swamps in the Southeast. Foliage is yellow-green in spring and russet in fall. Large tree.

BLACK GUM Native tree with lustrous dark green foliage that turns bright scarlet, yellow, orange, and purple in fall.

HACKBERRY No outstanding ornamental features, but it is a great large tree for wet soil.

RIVER BIRCH Has exfoliating bark and tolerates heat and wet soil. Often planted as a multistemmed clump. Yellow fall color.

SWEETBAY MAGNOLIA Small tree with fragrant flowers. Its evergreen to semievergreen leaves have silvery undersides.

WILLOW Graceful pendulous or upright branches. Yellow fall color and twigs. Drops many branches. Plant away from outdoor living areas.

DRY SOILS

AMERICAN LINDEN Fragrant flowers in summer and large green leaves. Susceptible to Japanese beetle. Pleasing round to pyramidal shape.

BUR OAK Long-lived native tree. Slow growing but worth the wait for its spreading, gnarled branches.

CRABAPPLE Small ornamental tree with fragrant red, pink, or white spring flowers. Choose disease-resistant cultivars.

GINKGO Striking fan-shaped leaves turn clear yellow in fall. Slow growing with few disease problems. Pick male cultivars to avoid odoriferous fruit.

HAWTHORN Rounded, low-branched tree with white blooms in spring and red fruits in fall. Choose a thornless cultivar, unless you want to create a barrier.

HONEYLOCUST Large, spreading tree with tiny leaflets. Casts filtered shade.

WHITE FIR Pleasing pyramidal shape when mature. Medium to large evergreen with bluish-green needles.

HEMLOCK

COLORADO BLUE SPRUCE

RIVER BIRCH

AMUR MAPLE

SHADE

AMERICAN HORNBEAM Dark green leaves change to yellow, orange, and reddish in fall. Best in moist sites. Rounded shape and low branching.

CANADIAN HEMLOCK Graceful, arching branches. Soft evergreen needles. Grows best in cool sites with moist soil. Large tree.

OHIO BUCKEYE Yellow fall color and prickly fruit that opens to reveal buckeyes, which are favored by wildlife. Medium size tree.

PAGODA DOGWOOD Fall color is reddish purple. Native. Broad spreading habit with horizontal branching pattern.

REDBUD Dark pinkish-purple or white flowers in early spring before leaves emerge. Heart-shape leaves. Small tree with an open habit.

SAUCER MAGNOLIA White or pink flowers in spring. Broad, spreading tree with rounded outline when mature.

SERVICEBERRY Orange, yellow, or red fall color. Spring bloom; summer fruits attract birds. Small tree or multistemmed shrub.

DEER PRESSURE

AMERICAN HOLLY Glossy dark green, evergreen foliage and pyramidal shape. Separate male and female plants needed for fruit set.

CHINESE FRINGE TREE Small tree with pendulous white flowers in late spring. Dull yellow fall color.

COLORADO BLUE SPRUCE Evergreen with blue-tinged foliage. Pyramidal outline. Choose a small cultivar for residential landscapes.

JAPANESE BLACK PINE Evergreen with long dark green needles and an irregular habit. Tolerates salt spray.

KATSURA TREE Pyramidal outline and dense foliage; yellow fall foliage. Prized for its foliage. Grows best in moist soil.

PAPER BIRCH Medium green leaves. Bark turns papery white with age. River birch is also deer-resistant.

SCOTCH PINE Evergreen with attractive reddish bark. Medium to large tree. Red pine is also deer-resistant.

COOL CLIMATES

CRABAPPLE Spectacular spring blooms and persistent fruits attract wildlife. 'Donald Wyman' and Red Jewel are good choices.

EASTERN RED CEDAR Blue-green evergreen foliage. Low maintenance. 'Skyrocket' has a pleasing columnar habit.

ELM A large shade-producing tree. Lovely umbrella-like shape. Select disease-resistant hybrids.

KENTUCKY COFFEE TREE Large, spreading tree with bluish-green foliage that turns yellow in fall. Brown seedpods. Adaptable to many soil types.

LITTLELEAF LINDEN Medium tree with small dark green leaves that are blue-green underneath. They turn yellow in fall. Fragrant flowers in early summer.

RIVER BIRCH Peeling bark on trunk reveals coppery-bronze bark underneath. Adaptable to many soil conditions.

SMALL SPACES

AMUR MAPLE A small to medium tree with scarlet and yellow fall color. 15 to 20 feet tall and wide.

CALLERY PEAR Fragrant white flowers in spring. Pyramidal outline. Red to purple fall color. 20 to 40 feet tall and 10 to 20 feet wide.

COLUMNAR ENGLISH OAK A narrow, tall oak. Slow growing and long-lived. 40 to 60 feet tall and 10 to 20 feet wide.

CRABAPPLE Hundreds of varieties available with narrow upright forms. Showy spring flower display. Most cultivars 15 to 25 feet tall and wide.

CRAPE MYRTLE Prolific summer flowers and heat- and drought-tolerant. Hundreds of cultivars available. Choose a small tree form. Many such cultivars are 20 feet tall and about 15 feet wide.

GOLDEN RAIN TREE Upright panicles of yellow flowers in summer. Good tree for dry sites. 20 to 40 feet tall and wide.

SERVICEBERRY Orange, yellow, or red fall color. Spring bloom; summer fruits attract birds. Small tree or multistemmed shrub.

Shrubs for tough sites

NINEBARK

FLOWERING QUINCE

WET SOILS

EUROPEAN CRANBERRYBUSH VIBURNUM Maplelike dark green foliage turns yellow-red and red-purple in fall. Red berries ripen in late summer and persist into winter.

MOUNTAIN LAUREL Broadleaf evergreen. Lovely flower clusters in late spring and early summer. Needs acidic soil.

NINEBARK Striking chartreuse, copper, or burgundy-to-purple summer foliage. Very easy to grow. Prune annually to keep vigorous plant in bounds.

RED CHOKEBERRY Bright red fruit in late summer and fall. Red and purple fall color.

SILKY DOGWOOD A Midwestern native with flat-top yellowish-white flowers and bluish fruit.

SUMMERSWEET CLETHRA Bees and butterflies love its white or pink flowers. Blooms in summer and has long-lasting flowers. Grows in sun or shade.

WINTERBERRY Deciduous holly with bright red fruit in fall. Plant male and female plants for fruit set.

DRY SOILS

CREEPING JUNIPER Cultivars with blue-green, green, or yellow-green foliage are common. Spreading plant; good for hillsides and as a groundcover.

FLOWERING QUINCE Flowers in winter or very early spring. Shrub has an informal rounded habit. Look for new double-flowered cultivars.

FRAGRANT SUMAC Brilliant fall color and aromatic leaves. 'Gro-Low' grows 2 to 3 feet tall and 6 to 8 feet wide. Good groundcover shrub.

JAPANESE BARBERRY Green, maroon, or yellow summer foliage changes to red, yelllow, or orange in fall. Showy red berries in fall.

POTENTILLA Covered with yellow, pink, red, or white flowers from summer to frost.

PRIVET Popular hedge plant. Medium green foliage. Adaptable and easy to grow.

SIBERIAN PEASHRUB Good hedge or screen plant. Exceptionally cold-hardy. Yellow blooms in late spring.

Dry, rocky crevices along this stream call for shrubs that can withstand extended dry conditions.

DAPHNE

BOXWOOD

VANHOUTTE SPIREA

BLUEBEARD

SHADE

ARROWWOOD VIBURNUM Creamy-white flowers in spring and blue-black fruit in fall. Medium to large native shrub.

BOXWOOD Evergreen broadleaf shrub that tolerates pruning well. Use as a hedge or edging plant in a mixed border. Slow growing.

DAPHNE Fragrant flowers in late winter or early spring. Plant near entryway to enjoy fragrance of the small flowers. Rounded shape.

RHODODENDRON Evergreen foliage and bright spring flowers. Plant several together for a showy display. Slow growing.

SMOOTH HYDRANGEA Creamy-white flowers in summer fade to tan in fall. Large flower clusters.

WITCH HAZEL Flowers in winter or early spring, depending on cultivar. Many cultivars have good fall color.

YEW Dark green foliage. Evergreen. Upright or spreading forms available. Deer favorite.

DEER PRESSURE

BOXWOOD Evergreen broadleaf shrub that tolerates pruning well. Use as a hedge or edging plant in a mixed border. Slow growing.

CREEPING JUNIPER Cultivars with blue-green, green, or yellow-green foliage are common. Spreading plant; good for hillsides and as a groundcover.

FORSYTHIA Sulfur-yellow flowers in early spring. Vigorous grower; often requires pruning after bloom.

JAPANESE BARBERRY Green or purple-maroon summer foliage changes to red or scarlet in fall. Showy red berries in fall.

LILAC Showy fragrant white, lavender, purple, or pink flowers in spring. Best in sun; tolerates many sites.

MUGO PINE Small to large evergreen shrub. Dwarf cultivars available. Adaptable to many soils.

VIBURNUM Native shrub with spring blooms and fall fruits for wildlife. Shade-tolerant.

COOL CLIMATES

'ANNABELLE' HYDRANGEA Flower clusters up to 12 inches in diameter. Grows well in shade.

'MISS KIM' LILAC A compact shrub with fragrant lavender flowers in late spring. Good for foundation planting or shrub border.

POTENTILLA Small shrub with several flushes of bloom throughout the year. Flowers are yellow, red, pink, or white.

RED-TWIG DOGWOOD Broad shrub that spreads by suckers. White flowers in spring followed by white berries in summer and red twigs in winter.

SIBERIAN PEASHRUB Upright shrub with yellow flowers in late spring. Good for windbreaks and informal hedges.

VANHOUTTE SPIREA Arching stems and fragrant white flowers in late spring. Plant is an old-fashioned favorite.

WINTERBERRY A holly that loses its leaves in winter; small red fruits persists well into winter. Plant male and female cultivars for fruit set.

SLOPES

BLACK CHOKEBERRY Has medium green foliage. Fruit and flowers attract birds. Tolerates most soils.

BLUEBEARD Blue-purple flowers for weeks in mid- to late summer. Attracts bees. Low, mounding habit. Tolerates dry soil and heat.

CREEPING JUNIPER Blue-green foliage turns purplish in winter. Spreading plant; excellent groundcover.

JAPANESE YEW Hardy needled evergreen that spreads.

RUSSIAN ARBORVITAE A low, spreading evergreen. Green foliage turns bronze to burgundy in winter.

SMOOTH SUMAC Native shrub that creates a colony as it spreads by suckers. Bright red fall color.

WINTERCREEPER EUONYMUS Fine-textured shrub with narrow leaves. Look for a low, spreading cultivar. Very hardy.

planting and care

The following pages are full of essential buying tips and planting advice. Take time when planting a new tree or shrub. Proper planting techniques go a long way toward establishing a healthy, thriving landscape.

p.**72**
BUYING TREES AND SHRUBS
Learn all about quality trees and shrubs so you know what to look for when you go to the garden center or nursery.

p.**74**
WHEN TO PLANT
Choose the best planting time for trees and shrubs for optimal growth and ease of maintenance during their establishment period.

p.**76**
HOW TO PLANT
Set the scene for good growth and minimal maintenance with easy-to-follow planting techniques.

p.**82**
CARING FOR TREES AND SHRUBS
Water and occasional pruning are the chief maintenance requirements of most trees and shrubs.

p.**86**
PEST PATROL
Combat pest problems by following the advice in the pest entries and the solutions from the Garden Doctor.

Choosing a healthy plant

Plants with strong root systems

and healthy leaves, stems, and trunks easily transition into their new planting place. Because trees and shrubs command a sizable investment, it pays to shop smart and examine plants before making a purchase.

Where to shop

Trees and shrubs are sold at garden centers and home centers and through mail-order and some online companies. Garden centers likely have the largest selection of plants and the greatest diversity of species for your area. Often staffed with knowledgeable salespeople, a garden center is a great place to ask questions about the best plants for your yard and seek planting advice appropriate for your Zone.

Try a home center or big-box retailer if you need a large number of uniform plants. The woody plant selection at a home center is slimmer than at a garden center, and plants may not be well-tended. The prices at a home center will often be less than those at a garden center. The best way to succeed with home center plants is to purchase them as soon as possible after they arrive at the store. Most home centers receive

Most garden centers stock many container-grown shrub and tree cultivars. Be sure to read plant tags carefully to ensure you purchase the plant you desire.

plants on certain days of the week; learn the delivery schedule and shop shortly thereafter.

What to look for

Search out quality rather than quantity when choosing a woody plant. A small tree with a sturdy, straight trunk and a few well-positioned branches is a better long-term investment than a large tree with many wayward branches and a blemished trunk. Foliage color and shape as well as branching structure should be appropriate for the plant. Learn more about plant characteristics in the encyclopedias beginning on page 108.

Nurseries grow trees and shrubs in many different ways. Plastic containers are a common method for raising woody plants. Some plants are grown and sold in fabric bags or containers. Field-grown trees and large shrubs are harvested and burlap is wrapped around the root balls and secured with nails, string, or wire. These plants are called balled-and-burlapped (B&B). Because their root balls contain field soil, as opposed to lightweight potting mix, they are heavier and harder to handle than container-grown plants. But because their roots are established in water-holding field soil, they will not dry out as quickly as plants growing in fast-draining potting soil.

Healthy roots

Be sure to inspect a plant's root system. A healthy root system helps trees and shrubs overcome transplanting stress and quickly establish in the landscape. Container-grown plants should be firmly rooted in the soil. Check the strength of the root system by pushing the tree trunk or shrub back and forth while holding the root ball still. The base of the tree or shrub should not move. Next, check for the location of the top layer of the plant's roots, which should be within an inch or two of the soil surface. Sometimes plants have been planted too deeply in the container. The raised soil level can hinder growth and even cause death. This is especially true for trees.

Balled-and-burlapped trees and shrubs should have a solid root ball. A loose or droopy ball indicates the plant does not have a strong root system and may not grow well in the landscape.

Be wary of large plants

Bigger is not always better when it comes to buying trees and shrubs. Container-grown plants with a large amount of aboveground growth should have a sizeable root mass as well. If a 4-foot-tall shrub is squeezed into a 1-gallon pot, its root system is likely compromised, and transplanting into the landscape will stress the plant and slow its growth. When given a choice, opt for a smaller plant relative to the size of the root ball. When the stems and leaves are somewhat proportional to the roots, the plant will establish rapidly in a new setting.

TEST GARDEN TIP

Avoid circling roots

Before purchasing a plant, slip it out of its growing container. Look at the outside of the root ball. You should see several small, fine roots and maybe a few larger roots on the edge of the soil ball. Avoid plants that have masses of thick roots circling the outside of the root ball. These plants have been in containers too long and are difficult to establish in the landscape.

Tree and shrub buying tips

HEALTHY ROOTS Check the roots close to the base of the trunk. Look for kinked or circling roots near the soil surface. These are signs of root problems. Don't buy the plant. Inspect the bottom of the container for escaping roots. The escaping roots should be no larger than the diameter of a pencil. Next, lay the plant on its side and slip it out of the container. The root ball should stay together and a few roots should be visible near the outer edge of soil. If many roots create a ring around the outside of the root ball, the plant is likely pot-bound. Choose a different plant.

STRONG TRUNK Strong trunks are thickest near the ground and taper as they rise. They do not need stakes for support. Test trunk strength by taking the tree into an open area and removing all stakes. If the tree is in leaf and it remains erect, it is probably strong enough. The trunk should be free of scrapes and dents. Trunk damage at a young age is challenging to overcome. It could compromise the health and strength of the tree as it ages.

APPROPRIATE BRANCHING Well-positioned branches are important on trees. Branches should be distributed along the trunk and not clumped toward the top. Look for a pleasing branch arrangement, inspecting all sides of the tree. Branching is also important on shrubs, but because shrubs have many branches and are typically shorter-lived than trees, branching is not as critical. Look for a plant that has a balanced appearance on all sides and strong, unblemished branches.

Spring and fall planting

Cool soil and regular moisture encourage newly planted trees and shrubs to put down deep roots. These root-friendly conditions are abundant in spring and fall, making the beginning and end of the growing season the best times to plant. While Nature's explosion of new growth in spring makes it appear to be the leading time to plant, the extended cool soil temperatures in fall offer several distinct advantages.

Plants quickly produce new roots in the moderate soil and air temperatures that prevail in fall.

Favor fall

After the heat of summer, soil in most climates cools slowly over a period of three or four months, typically beginning in September and reaching a low point in December or January. As soil cools to 45°F, plant roots expand. Couple the cool temperatures with sufficient moisture, and you have a great recipe for growth. Most container-grown and balled-and-burlapped deciduous trees and shrubs sold at garden centers are excellent candidates for fall planting. Conifers, such as pine and spruce, prefer slightly warmer soil for root growth and are best planted in late summer or spring.

Fall planting is especially beneficial when moving established trees from one place to another. In some cases, as much as 95 percent of a plant's roots are severed as it is dug out of the ground and moved to a new site. Rapid root regrowth is essential.

Years of research reveal that plants with shallow, fibrous root systems are easiest to establish in fall. Maple, buckeye, hackberry, honeylocust, hawthorn, crabapple, and linden all thrive when planted in fall.

Plants with taproots and those that are slow to expand their root systems include fir, birch, hornbeam, ginkgo, sweet gum, oak, willow, and bald cypress. Plant these species in spring, when they'll have many months to grow before cold weather hits.

Easy-going shrubs

Most deciduous shrubs (those that lose their leaves in fall) tolerate planting anytime during the growing season. Fall does offer advantages in that less care is required because plants are rarely stressed by scorching temperatures or weeks of dry soil. Of course, spring presents similar advantages, but for a shorter period of time.

Some shrubs are susceptible to drying winter winds. Broadleaf evergreens such as rhododendron, and evergreens conifers such as yew and arborvitae, quickly dry out in whipping winter winds. Plant broadleaf and needled evergreens in spring.

ASK THE GARDEN DOCTOR

Last year I had a large maple planted in my yard. It looks like it has hardly grown. What's going on?

ANSWER: Larger trees take longer to establish in the landscape. They will expand their branches as soon as a strong root system is in place. In the meantime it is important to water deeply and infrequently to encourage the plant to build a deep, extensive root system. A small tree—one with a 1- or 2-inch-diameter trunk—often establishes much more quickly because not as much of its root system was severed in the transplanting process. Small trees like this will likely reach the same size as a 3-inch-diameter tree in 5 to 10 years.

The best trees for your dollar

When purchasing trees for your landscape, it's important to know that some trees are more valuable than others. A strong, long-lived oak, for example, adds greater value to the landscape than a weak-wooded cottonwood or a messy willow. Cottonwood and willow have their place in the landscape, but when making a significant investment in trees, look for plants with reputations for strong, sturdy growth and longevity, such as live oak.

The following species will give you the most value for your dollar.

BALD CYPRESS	**MAPLE**
BIRCH	**OAK**
CRABAPPLE	**PINE**
GINKGO	**SPRUCE**
LACEBARK ELM	**SERVICEBERRY**
LINDEN	

Preparing
the site

Site preparation is dependent on the size of a planting project.

A single tree requires just a few minutes of prep time, but a mixed shrub border can easily encompass a day's worth of work. Whether your site demands five minutes or five hours of preparation for planting, don't skip this important step. An investment of time now will reward you with trees and shrubs that have years of strong, healthy growth.

Tree tips

If the soil and light conditions in a planting site are a good match for the new tree, very little site preparation is required. Take time to thoroughly remove sod from the planting area with a sharp spade. Rogue grass will quickly regrow around the young tree's trunk. Grass close to the tree trunk increases the chance of trunk injury during mowing. Also remove any construction debris from the planting site. Pieces of lumber, chunks of concrete, shingles, and other debris have the potential to impede growth.

Prepare a shrub bed

Large planting beds are excellent sites for shrubs as well as trees. Mimicking how plants grow in nature, planting beds create a mass of color and texture that blends well with the existing landscape. Large beds are a benefit from a maintenance standpoint too. Instead of many small trees and shrubs to mow around, a planting bed creates one contiguous shape that makes for fast and easy mowing. A thick blanket of mulch between young plants suppresses weeds. The plants will quickly grow together, shading the soil and preventing weeds.

Removing existing vegetation and eliminating compaction are the main goals when preparing a planting bed. Use a sharp spade or rent a sod cutter to skim away sod. Soil around newly built homes and high-traffic areas, such as near an entryway, is often compacted. Compacted soil has little space for oxygen to make its way to plant roots and is often poorly drained. Combat compaction by incorporating a 3-inch layer of well-decomposed compost in the topmost 8 to 12 inches of soil. Not only does compost make soil more porous, it also adds valuable nutrients. If you have the opportunity, always incorporate compost prior to planting.

Opposite: **A supple garden hose is an excellent tool for marking the edge of a new shrub bed. Arrange the hose until the bed outline pleases you.**

Make a planting bed

Time and effort preparing a planting bed for shrubs is always a good investment. A sharp spade and well-decomposed compost are all you need, but a sod cutter and rototiller will make quick work of the project. Prepare the planting bed when the existing soil is moist but not wet—a handful of soil should form a clump that breaks apart easily when squeezed.

1 REMOVE SOD

Begin by skimming off the sod. Use a sharp spade or rent a sod cutter from your local home improvement center. Be sure to cut deep enough to remove the sod's entire root zone. Cutting about 2 inches below the crown of the plant is usually sufficient. Add the sod to your compost pile, where it will decompose to form rich compost.

2 ADD COMPOST

Blanket the planting bed with a 3-inch-thick layer of compost. Well-decomposed compost is essential. The material should be black, soft, and sweet smelling. Compost that contains chunks of bark, leaves, and other brown debris is not fully decomposed and can limit nitrogen available to new plants.

3 MIX INTO SOIL

Incorporate the compost into the top 8 to 12 inches of soil. Using a sharp spade, turn and mix the compost and soil together. Use a rototiller to quickly incorporate compost in a large planting bed.

How to plant trees

Container-grown trees, like this lovely crabapple, are easier to plant than bulky balled-and-burlapped plants.

Proper planting depth is the most important part

of the tree planting process. If you plant a tree at the right depth, it will have the resources to overcome a host of landscape challenges. If it is planted too shallow or too deep, growth is compromised, water and nutrients are not readily available, and the plant is more susceptible to a variety of pests.

Thankfully, root flares make it easy to plant at the correct depth. At the base of every tree trunk, you'll find the root flare. This is the slightly swollen area at the trunk base where the uppermost roots emerge. In most cases the root flare should be level with the surrounding soil.

Often trees are planted too deep in the nursery and the root flare is covered with soil. At planting time, remove the excess soil across the top of the entire root ball to expose the root flare. When backfilling the tree, be sure to keep the area free of soil.

High and dry
If you are planting in poorly drained soil or clay, set the tree so that the root flare is about 2 inches above the surrounding grade. As roots emerge from the root ball, they will expand into soil near the surface, where water drains more freely and oxygen is more abundant.

How to plant a tree

There is an adage about the importance of a good planting hole. It goes something like this: It is better to put a 25-cent tree in a 2-dollar hole than put a 2-dollar tree in a 25-cent hole. The saying holds true today. Take time to carefully dig an adequate-size planting hole, and the tree will be well on its way to a long life.

1 DIG HOLE
Using a sharp spade, dig a planting hole. The depth of the hole should be equal to the height of the root ball, never deeper. The planting hole should be two to three times wider than the root ball. Toss the excavated soil onto a piece of burlap or in a wheelbarrow to make planting and cleanup easy.

2 EXAMINE ROOTS
Carefully remove the tree from the pot. Examine the roots. If they are circling the outside of the root ball, cut four equally spaced 1- to 2-inch-deep vertical slices into the root ball. The severed roots will stop circling and, over time, grow outward into the surrounding soil. Gently place the tree in the planting hole. Or for a balled-and-burlapped tree, gently roll the root ball into the planting hole. Remove any twine or portions of a wire basket that might girdle the trunk.

3 CHECK DEPTH
The point where the roots flare out from the trunk should be even with or slightly above the surrounding grade. Ensure the tree is at the correct depth by placing a shovel handle across the hole. Using the handle as a guide, check the planting depth. Always err on the side of planting a tree a little higher than the surrounding grade, especially if the soil drains slowly.

4 BACKFILL
Fill the planting hole about halfway with the excavated soil, breaking up clods and lightly tamping the soil to prevent air pockets. The handle end of a spade works well for tamping. Fill the hole the rest of the way and lightly tamp again. Build a 3-inch-tall berm around the edge of the planting hole and spread a 2-inch-thick layer of mulch over the soil surface. The berm and mulch will aid in water retention.

5 WATER
Finish planting by watering the tree well. Using a hose or watering can, gently drench the new tree and surrounding soil. Deliver water slowly so as not to disturb the soil berm. The berm will corral water, preventing it from flowing away from the tree into the surrounding landscape.

How to plant shrubs

When planting balled-and-burlapped shrubs, pull the burlap away from the top of the root ball before backfilling the planting hole with soil.

Planting a shrub is much like planting a tree.

Depth is critical. The top of the root ball should be even with the surrounding soil. If the soil is clay or poorly drained, position the root ball so it is 2 inches above the soil line. Just as for trees, planting hole preparation for shrubs consists of digging a hole that is as deep as the root ball and two to three times as wide. Use existing soil as backfill and tamp the soil lightly while backfilling to eliminate air pockets.

Space smart

When planting shrub borders, foundation plantings, and hedges, the space between shrubs becomes important. When planted too close together, two shrubs will quickly overtake one another, and neither plant will develop a pleasing shape. Planting too closely also compromises plant health as the shrubs compete for limited resources. Exceptionally generous spacing creates a polka-dot effect in the landscape. The relationships between plants are lost in the expanses of open soil.

To create a full, lush landscape in short order, arrange plants so the outer edge of their current forms are 2 to 3 feet apart. When spaced closely, the plants will grow together in a couple of years. Regular pruning will be necessary to maintain the shrubs' good looks. The trade-off is that the planting will look nearly mature from the time it was planted.

Limit maintenance and save dollars by placing plants farther apart. Use their mature width as a guide. For example, if a viburnum has a mature width of 4 feet, plant another viburnum about 4 feet away.

Spacing near entryways, walkways, and windows is especially important. Plan for at least a 1-foot buffer between shrubs and high-traffic areas or structures.

Plant spacing in a hedge depends on how quickly you would like the plants to grow together. Site plants closer together than their mature width, and the hedge will fill in more quickly. You'll also need more plants. Space the shrubs based on their mature width, and the hedge will take several years to fill in to create a screen, but the cost will be lower because you'll need fewer plants.

TEST GARDEN TIP

Planting B&B

First remove all twine and wire around the trunk. Peel back the burlap to reveal the upper third of the root ball. If the root ball is circled by a wire basket, it can be left in place. Removing it can damage the root ball. However, use wire cutters to snip away portions of the basket that extend over the top of the root ball.

Easy weed control

Keep pesky weeds at bay around newly planted trees and shrubs with these easy tips. Weeds are not only unsightly, but they also absorb valuable moisture and nutrients, which are useful to the landscape plants.

MULCH
A 2- to 3-inch-thick layer of mulch is a great tool for suppressing weeds. When spread around plants right after planting, it will prevent weeds for several months. Shredded wood, chopped leaves, pine straw, and cocoa hulls are all excellent mulch materials. As they break down, they add nutrients to the soil. Plan to top planting beds or the area around trees with a 1-inch layer of fresh mulch annually.

HERBICIDE
Preemergent herbicides prevent weed seeds from germinating. These materials need water for activation. Sprinkle preemergent herbicide granules on the soil around plants prior to rainfall. The herbicide must be reapplied throughout the season. See the package label for more specific information. If trees or shrubs will benefit from additional nutrients, look for a preemergent herbicide that contains a slow-release fertilizer.

10 MINUTES A WEEK
Dedicate 10 minutes a week to eradicating weeds at the base of trees and around shrubs. It's a cinch to pull weeds in simple foundation plantings and around three or four trees in just 10 minutes a week. Stay on top of the weeding and not only will your plants thank you with robust growth, the weeds that emerge will be easy to pull because they'll be small.

After-planting care

The soil around newly planted trees and shrubs dries out quickly. Plan to water young plants at least once a week.

Caring for a new tree or shrub begins

as soon as it is planted. When new woody plants receive timely, regular care for 8 to 12 weeks after planting, they will establish a strong root system, increasing their drought tolerance and their ability to mine nutrients. Give your plants a strong start with these simple care tips.

Water deeply

The most important part of after-planting care is watering. Container-grown trees and shrubs are planted in fast-draining potting soil that dries out quickly in the landscape, especially in hot, windy conditions. Balled-and-burlapped plants are surrounded by field soil that retains water well, but they also require regular watering.

Differing soil conditions and weather patterns will affect the frequency and amount of water a plant needs. Check soil moisture by pushing your fingers into the soil 4 inches below the surface. If the soil is dry or just slightly moist at that depth, the plant needs water. It's important to note that overwatering causes just as much harm as underwatering. Be sure to check soil moisture in the root zone before watering.

A slow trickle of water from a garden hose or drip hose at the base of the plant is the best method to apply water. Slow watering like this ensures the entire root ball is moistened and promotes deep root growth.

Add a layer of mulch

Preserve soil moisture, suppress weeds, and add nutrients with organic mulch. Spread a 2- to 3-inch-deep layer of mulch around a tree or shrub to form a 3- to 6-foot-diameter circle around the plant. This wide mulch blanket will allow water to more easily seep into the root zone. Keep the mulch away from the tree trunk or shrub stems to prevent moist mulch from rotting the bark. Shredded wood, bark chips, and cocoa hulls are good mulching materials.

No need to fertilize

Newly planted trees and shrubs do not need fertilizer. Excessive nutrients while the plants are getting established in the landscape can lead to growth of excess leaves and stems that the limited root system cannot support.

After one growing season, pull away the mulch from around the plant and spread a 1-inch-thick layer of well-rotted compost under the plant canopy. Replace the mulch. The compost will be pulled into the root zone by earthworms and soil insects, providing valuable nutrients to plant roots.

Pruning

Good news—pruning is rarely needed after planting. Reputable nurseries prune plants prior to sale. At planting, the tree or shrub should be free of limbs that rub against each other, broken branches, narrow-angle branches, and co-dominant leaders. If a new plant is affected by any of these troubles, prune it to correct the problem. For pruning tips and techniques see Chapter 6 beginning on page 90.

TEST GARDEN TIP

Rarely stake

Most container-grown and balled-and-burlapped trees do not need staking. Poor, shallow soils or excessively moist conditions at planting time call for short-term staking. If a tree must be staked, position the stakes as low as possible. Materials used to tie the tree to the stake should be flexible to allow the trunk to move slightly. Remove all staking material within a few months.

Far left: **Protect the trunks of new trees from deer and rabbit damage by surrounding them with a length of drainage tile shortly after planting. The drainage tile can be left in place for several years as the trunk expands.**

Left: **A 2- to 3-inch-thick layer of organic mulch offers many benefits to newly planted trees and shrubs; the most important is preventing soil moisture loss.**

Seasonal care summary

Trees and shrubs require minimal care to produce cooling shade, attractive flowers, and intriguing structure in the landscape. Use this quick checklist to keep your easy-care plants in top form.

SPRING

RENEW MULCH Organic mulch slowly decomposes. Refresh the mulch around trees and shrubs by topdressing with a new thin layer of shredded bark, cocoa hulls, or other mulch. For optimum soil improvement and weed suppression, blanket the entire area under the drip line of trees and create a circle that extends about 1 foot beyond the outer branches of shrubs. Keep mulch away from the base of the plant. Excess mulch near the base has the same effect as planting the tree or shrub too deep.

SPREAD PREEMERGENT HERBICIDE If you decide to use a weed killer, spread preemergent herbicide granules over shrub beds as soon as shrubs begin to leaf out. Be sure to follow package directions. Preemergent herbicide prevents weed seed germination for several weeks. It does not affect weeds that have already taken root; be sure to eradicate established weeds by hand.

REMOVE WINTER DAMAGE As trees and shrubs leaf out in spring, prune stems and branches that were damaged in winter. Candidates for pruning include branches broken from ice and snow as well as those killed by cold temperatures.

PLANT Plant trees and shrubs early in the season to take advantage of seasonal rains and cool soil temperatures, which promote root growth. See pages 74–75 for details about when to plant.

SUMMER

COMBAT DROUGHT Established trees and shrubs tolerate drought with ease. The plants will slow their growth to wait out the dry season. Young plants—those that have been on the site less than two years—benefit from supplemental watering during drought. To thoroughly soak the root ball, water with a drip hose or a slow trickle from a garden hose.

PRUNE Summer is a good time to prune most spring-blooming shrubs. Shortly after the shrub finishes flowering, prune away excessive growth, crossing branches, and any dead or diseased wood.

FALL

WRAP TRUNKS OF YOUNG TREES Young, thin-barked trees, such as maples, are especially prone to sunscald. Similar to sunburn, sunscald is caused by bark heating by winter sun during cold weather and rapid refreezing, causing ice crystals to develop. It results in sunken, dried, or cracked bark. Prevent sunscald by wrapping the trunks of young maple and honeylocust trees with commercial tree wrap from the base of the trunk up to the first branch. Commercial tree wrap is commonly available at garden centers.

PREVENT ANIMAL DAMAGE In winter, hungry mice and rabbits may gnaw through bark, girdling stems. Deer may eat stems and evergreen foliage as well as rub their antlers on young plants, causing extensive damage. If any of these destructive animals plague your area, refer to the Pest Patrol section beginning on page 86 and take appropriate steps to prevent winter damage.

PLANT Several months of cool soil temperatures and occasional rainfall make fall a great time for planting. Be sure to water new plants thoroughly, because they will continue growing in early winter.

WINTER

PRUNE Late winter is the optimal time to prune many trees and some shrubs. Leafless branches make the plant structure easy to assess. Learn more about pruning beginning on page 90.

CONSIDER REPELLENTS Commercial spray repellents are an effective means of protecting a large number of trees and shrubs from deer and rodents in winter. The repellents must be reapplied periodically. See package directions for details.

Opposite, top left:
Magnolias and other spring-blooming trees are candidates for pruning in early summer after their flowers fade.

Opposite, top right:
Variegated hydrangeas debut long-lasting flowers in early summer. Water plants deeply during drought for robust flowers and foliage.

Opposite, bottom left:
'Pink Champagne' smoke tree lights up the fall landscape as soon as temperatures drop.

Opposite, bottom right:
Trees and shrubs with long-lasting fruit comprise decorative elements of the winter landscape and important food sources for wildlife.

In fall, wrap vulnerable tree trunks with wire mesh or drainage tile to prevent damage caused by deer, rabbits, and mice. Wire mesh or drainage tile can be left in place for several years.

Pest Patrol

Trees and shrubs are some of the easiest plants to grow because pests rarely trouble them. Bark, extensive root systems, and large quantities of energy-producing foliage give them the ability to shrug off most diseases and occasional nibbling by insects. If pests do penetrate a plant's natural defenses, combat them with the tips on the next few pages.

Deer The most rapidly spreading urban pest, deer browse foliage in spring and summer. They are notorious for munching emerging flowers and soft, succulent new growth. In fall and winter deer rub their antlers against the trunks of young evergreen and deciduous trees. Deer will also eat evergreen foliage and small twigs when food is scarce in winter. Look for hoof prints in snow or soil to help determine whether damage is caused by deer.

DAMAGE

Because deer lack upper incisors, browsed twigs and stems develop a rough, shredded outline. Bark scraped away from one side of a tree 2 to 4 feet above ground level is an indication of antler rubbing.

CONTROL

Protect plants from deer rub in fall and winter by enclosing the trunks of young deciduous trees with corrugated drain tile. Slit the tile down one side and wrap it around the tree. Wrapping the trunk with wire mesh is also effective. Protect individual plants by surrounding the plant with a fence that is at least 5 feet tall. Liquid repellents work for short periods. Change them often, because deer get used to the scent of nearly any product. Plant deer-resistant species. See the examples on pages 67 and 69.

Rabbits Rabbits are troublesome in winter when food is scarce. They gnaw on tender twigs, bark, and foliage. Damage is particularly costly when they chew off a complete ring of bark around a trunk. This is called girdling and usually kills the plant.

DAMAGE

Damaged twigs and bark at ground level or a few inches above the snow line indicate rabbit damage. The twigs are usually cut off the plant at a neat and sharp 45-degree angle. Trees and shrubs with smooth bark are damaged more often than those with rough bark. The bark might be scraped off the trunk all the way around the tree or in one 3- to 4-inch-high section.

CONTROL

Wrap the trunks of young deciduous trees with a cylinder of ¼-inch-mesh hardware cloth. The cylinder should be at least 2 feet tall and extend at least 1 foot above the expected snow line. Be sure the cylinder is a couple of inches wider than the tree trunk. Remove the cylinder in spring. Hardware cloth is an investment, but it can be reused for many years. Keep rabbits out of shrub beds with a 2-foot-tall hardware cloth or chicken wire fence. Repellents also work for a short time. Reapply them often.

Japanese beetles Adult Japanese beetles feed on flowers and leaves of various trees and shrubs, such as linden, crabapple, birch, and rose. When the beetles find a food source, they release a scent that attracts more beetles. Females lay eggs in the soil, which hatch into grubs, a major lawn pest.

DAMAGE

Japanese beetles eat leaf tissue between the veins, creating a skeletonized effect. They may also eat large holes in flower petals and buds.

CONTROL

Treat for grubs in your lawn and you'll reduce the number of Japanese beetles (unless your neighbor doesn't control grubs, in which case beetles will invade your garden). A fungus called milky spore controls grubs but may take a few years to build up an effective concentration. Adult beetle traps may lure more beetles than you already have in your garden. Plant trees and shrubs that beetles don't like to feed on. Arborvitae, lilac, hemlock, holly, juniper, pine, red maple, red oak, rhododendron, and yew are a few plants that Japanese beetles rarely attack.

Caterpillars

Assorted caterpillars feed on tree and shrub leaves. Caterpillars are the larvae of moths, which lay eggs on host plants from early spring to midsummmer, depending on the species. Larvae feed singly or in groups on buds or leaves. Certain caterpillars web leaves together as they feed. In some years, damage is minimal because of unfavorable environmental conditions. When conditions are favorable, caterpillars can defoliate an entire plant.

DAMAGE

Caterpillars chew on or skeletonize leaves. They may attack one section of a plant and then move on, or they may overtake the entire canopy.

CONTROL

Caterpillar damage to less than 50 percent of a plant's foliage is rarely a cause for concern, especially if the plant is receiving adequate moisture and nutrients. Healthy trees and shrubs can even overcome compete defoliation. If defoliated in summer, a plant may or may not produce new foliage in the current growing season. It will likely leaf out the following spring. Repeated defoliation will quickly weaken a plant and is cause for control. Spray affected plants with *Bacillus thuringiensis* (*Bt*) when the caterpillars are small. Horticultural oil and insecticidal soap also control young caterpillars.

Bagworms

Bagworms eat leaves of many trees and shrubs. Larvae hatch in May or June and immediately begin feeding. Each larva constructs a bag that covers its entire body. Larvae pupate in the bags. When adult males emerge from pupal cases, they fly to find females and mate. After mating, the female lays eggs in the bag and it overwinters on a tree or shrub. Larvae emerge in spring to continue the cycle.

DAMAGE

Leaves are chewed and branches or entire plants may be defoliated. Brown, 1- to 3-inch-long "bags" hang from the branches.

CONTROL

Spray with *Bacillus thuringiensis* (*Bt*) between late May and mid-June to kill young worms. Handpick and destroy bags in winter to reduce the number of eggs and young the following year.

TEST GARDEN TIP

Top 4 Pest Control Tips

1. Think before you treat. Pest damage is often cosmetic. A pest creates tattered foliage or spotted leaves for a short time, but then environmental conditions change and the pest is no longer present. The plant will cast off the damaged leaves and continue to thrive. A healthy ecosystem makes this possible.

2. Plant diverse species. Pests tend to prey on particular plant groups. Plant a mix of species, and pest damage that does occur will be confined to a few plants instead of spread through the entire landscape.

3. Choose plants that are well-suited to your site. Healthy, thriving plants will naturally overcome many pest attacks.

4. More is not always better in gardening. More water, more fertilizer, and more mulch can all lead to disease and pest problems.

Pest Patrol

Leaf rust When you see orange, gold, or reddish spots rupturing leaf surfaces, you're dealing with rust. While it rarely kills plants, rust fungus makes leaves unsightly and weakens the plant by interfering with photosynthesis, the process a plant uses to make food. Each plant that is susceptible hosts a particular rust species that may vary from other rusts in appearance.

DAMAGE
Leaves are discolored or mottled yellow to brown. Powdery fungal clusters appear on the leaves. The powdery material can be scraped off. Leaves may become twisted and distorted and may dry and drop off. Twigs may also be infected.

CONTROL
Many rust fungi are usually harmless to the plant and rarely require control measures. Where practical, remove and destroy leaves in fall. Several fungicides are available that can control rust fungi. Check with your local extension service for current recommendations.

Fire blight Aptly named, fire blight gives trees and shrubs the appearance that portions of their branches have been scorched by fire. Blossoms and leaves of some twigs suddenly wilt and turn brown or black. Fire blight is caused by bacteria that are particularly active in warm, moist weather. Bees, rain, and infected pruning tools spread the disease.

DAMAGE
Tips of infected branches may hang down. The bark at the base of the blighted twig takes on a water-soaked appearance, then looks dark, sunken, and dry. Fire blight attacks a few twigs at a time to create a flaglike effect of dead foliage on different areas of the plant.

CONTROL
Prune out infected branches about 12 inches beyond any discoloration and destroy them. Disinfect pruning tools by dipping after each cut in a solution of 1 part chlorine bleach and 9 parts water. Avoid excess nitrogen fertilizer in spring and early summer. It forces succulent growth, which is more susceptible to fire blight infection.

Powdery mildew Powdery mildew forms a white coating on leaf surfaces during dry, cloudy weather with high humidity. It is caused by any one of several fungi. Plants growing in shaded areas are often the most affected.

DAMAGE
Leaves are covered with a thin layer or irregular patches of a powdery, grayish-white material. Leaves may become distorted. Infected leaves may turn yellow or red and drop. In late fall tiny black dots are scattered over the white patches like grains of pepper.

CONTROL
When planting new trees and shrubs, choose resistant varieties. Some groups of highly susceptible plants, such as crape myrtles, crabapples, and lilacs, have cultivars selected for resistance to powdery mildew. Several fungicides are available that will control this mildew.

Garden Doctor solutions

Some woody plant problems are caused by environmental conditions. Extreme temperatures, excessive or limited moisture, and a host of other adverse conditions hinder plant growth and occasionally cause unsightly damage or long-term injury. Here are a few of these common plant problems along with simple solutions.

Few or no flowers
There are several reasons why trees and shrubs may fail to flower. Here are a few of the most common.

JUVENILITY. Plants must reach a certain age or size before they can flower. Some shrubs must be at least three years old before they begin flowering, and trees often require 10 years of growth. Young crabapple, flowering cherry, and tulip trees commonly don't bloom when they are young.

WARM WINTER. Many plants must undergo a period of cooling during winter to spur flower development. If the cooling requirement isn't met, plants don't bloom.

IMPROPER PRUNING. If a plant is pruned too severely, flower production can be reduced. Flowering is also reduced if flower buds are pruned off. See the encyclopedia beginning on page 108 for specific pruning advice for a species.

TOO MUCH NITROGEN. Plants that are overfertilized with nitrogen produce a flush of green growth and few flowers. Fertilize plants carefully.

SHADE. Plants grown in inadequate light for their species produce few flowers. Prune nearby plants to allow more light to reach the nonblooming plant.

Cracks in bark
When patches of bark crack, it's important to determine the source of the problem and prevent future problems if possible. Bark is an essential protective layer for every woody plant. Once bark is damaged it cannot be repaired, but if action is taken, further damage can be prevented.

SUMMER SUNSCALD. Bark exposed to intense summer heat occasionally cracks, and a sunken area called a canker develops. This is most common on bark that was once shaded and is suddenly exposed to intense sunlight. Protect vulnerable bark by wrapping it with tree wrap, available at garden centers.

WINTER SUNSCALD. Bark injury occurs in winter when temperatures swing widely from cold nights to sunny days. Exposed bark becomes much warmer than the air during the day but cools rapidly after sunset. This rapid temperature change often results in bark cracking. Young trees with smooth, thin bark are most susceptible to winter sunscald. Protect them with tree wrap in winter. Remove the wrap in spring and reapply in late fall.

Wilting
Droopy leaves and sagging branches are a sign of wilt. Although dry conditions are the most frequent cause of wilting, there are several other possibilities. Investigate the cause of the wilt symptoms to find a solution.

DRY SOIL. Roots are not able to pull water from dry, crumbly soil. Sandy or rocky soil does not hold water well. Use a small spade to dig a hole 8 to 12 inches below the soil surface. If the soil is dry at this level, water the plant immediately. Apply water slowly to ensure it filters down to the root level. Help conserve soil moisture by spreading a 1- to 2-inch layer of mulch over the plant's root area.

WET SOIL. Excessively wet soil can lead to wilting. Soil moisture displaces oxygen. When soil oxygen is nearly depleted, some plants show signs of wilting. If the plant is small, dig it up and transplant it to well-drained soil. Large plants often overcome wilting induced by waterlogging.

EXTREME HEAT OR WIND. If a plant is wilting but pests and waterlogged soil are ruled out, extreme heat or wind is likely the cause. It is most common in young plants with limited root systems. Wind and heat accelerate water loss from leaves, causing the plant to wilt. The plant will usually recover when the temperature drops or the wind subsides.

all about pruning

Pruning is as simple as removing dead and damaged wood and crafting a pretty plant form. Take the guesswork out of trimming trees and shrubs with step-by-step pruning advice.

All about pruning

ASK THE GARDEN DOCTOR

I pruned my lilac shrub early this spring. It didn't bloom later in the season. What happened?

ANSWER: You pruned off the flower buds. Expect your shrub to produce plenty of blooms next year. Pruning plants shortly before they bloom often results in few flowers, especially on shrubs that produce flowers at their branch tips. The best time to prune lilacs is early summer, after their blooms fade and before new flower buds develop.

Pruning is simply the removal of unwanted material.

So why does the thought of pruning cause trepidation in many people from newbie gardeners to green thumbs? Misinformation and lack of factual pruning knowledge is likely the root cause. This chapter is full of basic pruning facts that will dispel the myths that make you avoid wielding the pruning shears. Armed with helpful tips and straightforward advice, you'll prune with confidence and your plants will thank you for it.

Dead, diseased, damaged

Dead, damaged, and diseased wood—known as the "three Ds" of pruning—are always candidates for clipping. Often noticed after a particularly harsh winter or a violent storm, dead and damaged wood are entry points for pests. Insect pests, fungi, bacteria, and viruses make their way into a plant through the weakened wood. Prune away dead and damaged wood as soon as you notice it to prevent further damage.

Diseased plant parts call for inspection before pruning. Powdery mildew, which creates a white substance on leaves, does not cause harm and will often disappear on its own. Pruning away twigs and leaves covered with powdery mildew is an aesthetic choice. Fire blight, on the other hand, is a destructive disease that

can be controlled with pruning. Bottom line—determine the cause of the disease before making any pruning cuts.

Too big

Trees and shrubs are constantly growing and occasionally, even with the best planning, they outgrow their planting place. When you have to bat the butterfly bush out of the way to get to the front door, it's beyond time to prune. Many shrubs can be pruned to a small size with little effect on flowering and form. With regular pruning you can maintain a lovely, healthy Japanese barberry at 2 feet tall and wide. A flowering quince, on the other hand, thrives when it is allowed to grow 4 to 5 feet tall and wide. Limit pruning by choosing plants with an appropriate mature size for the space.

Mature size is especially important when selecting and caring for trees. A crabapple or Callery pear tree that grows 20 feet tall and 15 feet wide is just right for a small residential lot, but a sycamore that will reach a lofty 80 feet will quickly overwhelm the space. Pruning is often not practical for limiting the size of trees. If a limb begins to encroach on a roof or low branches obscure a walkway, pruning is a good solution. But it is not a viable solution for long-term height and width control.

Strong structure

Narrow branch angles and multiple central leaders weaken the structural integrity of a woody plant. Strong wind or a heavy snow load is likely to snap weakly attached branches. Damage extends when the broken branches snap other limbs as they careen to the ground. Thoughtful annual pruning when plants are young creates trees and shrubs with strong branching.

Above left: **Simply enjoy the brilliant foliage hues in fall and resist the urge to prune. Fall pruning produces tender growth that is damaged in winter.**

Above right: **Deadwood, like the branch on this shrub rose, is best pruned away as soon as you notice it.**

Opposite: **Shade-loving and slow-growing azaleas and rhododendrons develop a pleasing form with little or no pruning.**

Types of pruning cuts

1

2

3

4

Pruning removes stems and branches and influences new growth. **How you prune is just as important as when and why you prune. Some pruning cuts cause plants to produce a flush of succulent new growth, but other methods reduce the overall size of a plant for several seasons. Use the best pruning technique for the desired outcome and you'll promote healthy growth and limit future pruning.**

The first step in choosing the right pruning cut is to learn about each one. Each technique has specific results. Be confident. If you choose the wrong cut, the most serious consequence is that your plant will not look as you intended and will require another round of pruning. As long as you don't remove more than one-third of the growth, deciduous trees and shrubs readily forgive pruning mistakes.

1. THINNING

Keep plants at the same height and width for many years with selective thinning. This is a great pruning technique for maintaining a plant's natural shape.

THE CUT Thinning involves removing lateral branches back to the main stem, the trunk, or the ground. Unlike shearing, which removes the terminal buds (the buds on branch tips that control growth) and promotes rapid succulent growth, thinning results in moderate growth.

WHEN TO THIN Thinning is a good solution for trees and shrubs with excessively dense interior growth. Use a thinning cut to remove crossing or rubbing branches. For shade trees, promote the growth of a strong central leader by thinning out competing upright branches.

2. PINCHING

A quick and easy method for producing a compact plant, pinching is typically reserved for needled evergreens or herbaceous plants.

THE CUT No equipment is involved in pinching. With your thumb and forefinger, gently remove the tip of a plant's soft new growth.

WHEN TO PINCH To promote a compact plant, pinch needled evergreens in late spring as the new shoots elongate but before they become stiff. Pinching is not necessary for most species, because they will produce a relatively dense habit naturally, but a few minutes of pinching will encourage young plants to create a strong structure.

3. HEADING

A common pruning cut that produces poor results, heading involves removing the terminal buds (the buds on the branch tips) at no particular point along the stem. When the terminal buds are removed, the plant produces many side branches near the pruning point. The new branches shade the interior of the plant and create weak branching structure.

THE CUT Heading is as simple as removing the branch tips. Unlike shearing, heading does not reduce the plant to a uniform size. Instead, varying amounts of branches are removed.

WHEN TO HEAD Heading cuts are undesirable. They are particularly destructive to shade trees. The surge of new growth spurred by heading cuts creates weak branching that is especially susceptible to storm damage. Heading cuts on shrubs are similar to shearing and create a dense outer canopy and woody base, which is rarely desirable except for hedges.

Instead of using a heading cut, employ a thinning cut. Remove branches back to a main stem or ground level for healthy growth.

4. SHEARING

Shearing creates a formal appearance that gives boxwood orbs and neatly clipped junipers their good looks. Shearing must be repeated often and regularly to be effective.

THE CUT Using shears or an electric trimmer, shorten all stems by a certain amount. Robust new growth occurs just below the pruning cut.

WHEN TO SHEAR Shearing is effective for hedges and topiary but not for most shrubs or trees. The dense outer shell of leaves and stems blocks light to the inside of the plant, killing off leaves and stems in the interior. The best time to shear hedges is after the spring flush of growth and again in late summer. Avoid pruning within a month of the expected first fall frost date. The succulent new growth is susceptible to frost damage.

TEST GARDEN TIP

Pruning guidelines

Make quick decisions about pruning branches based on their size with the help of these handy guidelines from the US Forest Service. If the branch is less than 2 inches in diameter, go ahead and remove it. If the branch is between 2 and 4 inches in diameter, think twice. Finally, if the branch is greater than 4 inches in diameter, have a good reason for removing it.

Whack it back **Most multistemmed shrubs prove quite resilient after severe pruning. Don't be afraid to remove overgrown stems to within a few inches of the soil line in late winter or early spring before the shrubs begin new growth. For more on renewing overgrown shrubs, see pages 106–107.**

The right tool for the job

Sharp, sturdy pruning tools make pruning chores a breeze.

High-quality tools last a lifetime and are always a good investment. Visit your local garden center or home center to check out the many styles of pruners, loppers, and saws. You'll find that today's tools are lighter and more thoughtfully designed than tools of the past. Ergonomic design gives many tools the ability to produce stronger action with less effort. Look for slip-resistant handles, cushioned grips, and gear or ratchet mechanisms.

Taking care of tools will keep them in good shape and make them last longer. Clean them after each use and rub them with a few drops of oil to prevent rust. Occasionally oil the moving parts so they'll operate smoothly. Always store pruning tools in a dry place.

Pruners: best for branches up to ¼ inch in diameter Also called hand shears, pruners are the most important pruning tool. The majority

Loppers extend your reach and cutting power. Use loppers to prune branches up to 1½ inches in diameter.

of annual pruning is done with a hand pruner, so take time to look at many different brands and find the best pair for your hand. Look for bypass pruners, as opposed to pruners with straight anvil or scissor action. Bypass pruners have one sharp blade and one hooked anvil. They make clean cuts.

Loppers: best for branches up to 1½ inches in diameter Strong but lightweight handles are critical for a great pair of loppers. Loppers, or lopping shears as they are sometimes called, give good leverage and allow you to reach into the base of an overgrown shrub. Look for a model with bypass pruning action—the cutting end should have one straight blade and a hooked anvil. Ratcheted or geared models provide more power with less effort. When buying loppers, make sure there is enough space between the handles so your fingers don't get pinched as the handles close.

Saws: best for branches greater than 1 inch in diameter Traditional pruning saws have coarse teeth for clean cuts. Japanese-type saws have smaller teeth and cut quickly and neatly. Most saws cut on the pull stroke for easier, safer use.

A folding saw is handy because it can be carried in a pocket. Use it for cutting smaller branches. Be certain the locking mechanism

works well, or the saw can collapse while you're cutting. Most folding saws have a curved blade, which is convenient when branches are crowded.

A pole saw is mounted on a 4- to 6-foot-long pole. It is useful for cutting overhead limbs up to 2 inches in diameter.

Hedge shears: best for branches up to ¼ inch in diameter Manual hedge shears are best for pruning hedges. Look for notched or wavy blades, which do a good job of keeping the foliage from slipping out of your grasp. A lightweight handle and some kind of shock absorption are important if you do large quantities of hedge trimming.

Electric trimmers, which have a blade that oscillates, make fast work of shearing the top of a hedge evenly, but you have to be careful not to cut the cord. Gas-powered models are also available, as are battery-powered shears. Always hold power shears with both hands while cutting.

Chain saws: best for large branches A chain saw is not necessary in the average residential landscape. Made for large pruning jobs that are often best left to professionals, chain saws are challenging to maneuver if you have not used one before. A lightweight 12- to 16-inch chain saw is the most convenient size for homeowners.

TEST GARDEN TIP

Favorite pruners

Quality materials and construction coupled with thoughtful design make Felco brand pruners a favorite in the Test Garden. There are several different styles of the red-handled beauties. Choose the style that best fits your hand.

Safety first
A little common sense goes a long way toward ensuring safety during pruning. Keep these basic tips in mind.

Call a professional for large trees or jobs for which you lack the proper equipment.

Keep all equipment sharp and in good repair.

Be conscious of power lines. Don't prune trees that are near or touching power lines.

Never climb a tree without a safety rope, with or without a ladder.

Although cumbersome at times, a hard hat and safety glasses provide valuable protection when pruning.

Always take time to consider where a branch will fall when you cut it or drop it from the tree. Make sure no one will be hit and that it will not knock over the ladder.

When to prune

Timing is an important aspect of smart pruning.

Just as *how* a branch is pruned influences future growth, *when* a branch is pruned has a similar effect. Thoughtful timing can promote growth and quick recovery from severe pruning, or suppress growth on a fast-growing hedge.

Generally, late winter or early spring is the best time to prune. By pruning just before spring growth starts, fresh wounds are exposed for only a short length of time before new growth begins the wound-sealing process. Also, pruning decisions are made easier thanks to the leafless branches—plant structure is readily evident on deciduous plants in late winter.

Of course there are many exceptions. For best results, use the type of plant as a guide to when to prune. Some pruning chores can be done anytime, no matter the type of plant. For example, cut off dead, diseased, or damaged branches and remove suckers (vigorous shoots growing from the roots or trunk) and water sprouts (vigorous shoots arising from the branches) any time you spot them.

Spring-flowering shrubs
Determine when to prune spring-flowering shrubs based on their condition. Old, neglected spring-flowering shrubs often require extensive

Above: **Timing is not critical when it comes to dead, diseased, or damaged wood. Remove these branches any time you notice them.**

Opposite: **Branch structure is readily apparent in winter, making it a great time to prune.**

pruning to spur them to bloom prolifically. The best time to rejuvenate these overgrown plants is late winter or early spring. While heavy pruning in late winter or early spring will reduce or eliminate flowering for a few years, the long-term health of the shrubs is worth it.

If a spring-flowering shrub needs only light pruning or shaping, prune it shortly after the blooms fade. Pruning after flowering ensures the annual bloom display is unaffected and provides ample time for the plant to set flower buds for next season.

Summer-flowering shrubs

Late winter or early spring is the best time to prune summer-flowering shrubs. These plants produce flower buds on new growth. If they are pruned before growth begins in spring, they'll bloom with gusto in summer.

Deciduous shrubs with nonshowy flowers

Deciduous shrubs grown primarily for their pretty foliage, fruit, or bark should be pruned in late winter or early spring before growth begins. Do not prune shrubs in late summer. Pruning near the end of the growing season may encourage a late flush of growth. The new growth may not harden sufficiently before cold winter temperatures arrive, making it susceptible to winter injury.

Evergreen shrubs

Junipers, yews, and other evergreen and needled shrubs are best pruned in mid-spring before new growth begins. Light pruning may also be done in late June or early July to limit plant size.

Deciduous trees

Late winter or early spring is the best time to prune deciduous trees. Branching structure is readily visible on the leafless woody plants. Some trees, such as maples and birches, produce a large amount of sap in late winter and "bleed" heavily when pruned in late winter or early spring. The heavy bleeding doesn't harm the trees. If you are concerned about the bleeding, instead prune these trees in late spring or early summer after their leaves are fully expanded. Never remove more than one-quarter of the foliage.

Oak wilt and fire blight are two diseases that are more prevalent in oaks, crabapples, Callery pear, European mountain ash, and hawthorns pruned in mid-spring. Prevent oak wilt and fire blight by pruning in December and January in warm climates and in January, February, and March in cold areas.

Evergreen trees

Evergreen trees rarely require pruning. If branching structure needs to be corrected, the best time to prune is late winter or early spring. Expect pruned plants to produce vigorous new growth. Whenever possible, avoid pruning evergreen trees in late summer or early fall. Pruning late in the growing season can produce new growth that may not harden off before winter. The tender growth may be damaged by cold temperatures, making the plant more susceptible to disease.

TEST GARDEN TIP

Forcing branches

No need to wait for spring to enjoy sweet-scented colorful flowers of spring-flowering woody plants. Follow these simple steps to force pruned branches into bloom indoors.

1. When temperatures rise above freezing in late winter, select and cut branches of redbud, crabapple, forsythia, magnolia, dogwood, and other spring-blooming trees and shrubs. Look for branches with lots of plump buds.

2. Use pruners to carefully make a 4-inch-long slit in the cut end of the branch to help it absorb water.

3. Place the branches in water and remove any buds and twigs that are under water.

4. Place the container of branches in indirect light in a warm room. Change the water every few days.

Pruning broadleaf trees

A small investment of time and effort in pruning young trees will pay generous dividends in the form of strong, spreading branches that withstand storms and provide ample shade. Pruning young plants also promotes a pleasing plant form.

Large, established broadleaf trees demand little pruning. When pruning is required, perhaps after a storm or in preparation for a building project nearby, leave the heavy-duty work to tree care professionals who have specialized equipment. When discussing the project with a professional, emphasize that a natural plant form and overall tree health are of utmost importance when making pruning decisions. An experienced tree care professional will ensure a newly pruned established tree is structurally sound after pruning.

The graceful trunks of this small maple, revealed when low side branches were pruned away, add a sinuous vertical element to the garden scene.

Late winter or early spring is the best time to prune most broadleaf trees. For further discussion of timing see pages 98–99. Follow these quick and easy tips and you'll promote lovely, strong trees.

Remove broken or damaged branches as soon as you notice them. Damaged bark offers a portal for pests to invade. Removing the damaged plant material with a clean pruning cut allows the tree to quickly seal the wound, preventing pest infestation.

Prune off suckers and water sprouts. Suckers are vigorous upright stems that arise from the roots or the main trunk, near ground level. Some trees, such as crabapples, are prone to suckering. Snip suckers away by pruning at ground level. Water sprouts are vigorous upright growths that are weakly attached to branches. They rob valuable nutrients from the tree and are not structurally sound. Remove them by pruning at the base of the water sprout.

Prune narrow-angle branches, leaving branches with wide, and therefore strong, angles. Trees with upright forms are an exception; they naturally include many narrow branch angles. Instead of pruning away branches with narrow angles on upright trees, focus on creating well-spaced branches.

Remove crossing branches or ones that rub against another branch. **Remove lower branches gradually** as young trees grow, to raise the crown. Low branches encourage strong, sturdy trunk development, also called trunk taper. Leave low branches in place for as long as possible.

Skip the wound dressing. Trees naturally close wounds in short order. Oaks are an exception. Where oak wilt is a problem, wound dressing in the form of latex paint applied to the pruning cut will create a barrier that helps to prevent disease transmission.

ASK THE GARDEN DOCTOR

Should I paint tree wounds after pruning?

ANSWER: No, unless you are pruning an oak. Trees naturally seal wound sites quickly. Paint or sealants only hinder the tree's process. Oaks are an exception. Prevent destructive oak wilt from invading a healthy tree by sealing wounds on oak trees with a thin coat of latex paint.

Step-by-step: three-part pruning cut

Ideal for removing branches that are greater than 1½ inches in diameter, the three-part pruning cut ensures a tree is not damaged as the branch is removed. Using a sharp handsaw, follow these steps to easily prune large branches.

1 CUT A NOTCH
About 12 inches from the tree trunk, cut a notch on the underside of the branch. Cut one-third to halfway through the branch. This cut will prevent the falling branch from tearing the bark on the tree trunk as it drops from the tree.

2 MAKE A SECOND CUT
A couple of inches beyond the notch cut make a second cut, slicing all the way through the branch this time. A short branch stub will remain on the tree.

3 REMOVE THE STUB
Remove the stub just beyond the branch collar—the slightly swollen area where the branch attaches to the trunk.

Pruning needled trees and shrubs

One of the greatest attributes of needled trees and shrubs

is their ability to develop pleasing, strong forms with little or no pruning. If you select the right-size cultivar for an area, you'll need to prune only to combat storm damage. When needled trees and shrubs do require pruning, it's important to prune carefully because, unlike deciduous plants, needled evergreens cannot outgrow an errant pruning job. Once an evergreen is disfigured it will likely display that appearance for life.

Don't let the limited growth of needled plants stop you from caring for your trees and shrubs. Keep these easy-to-follow tips in mind, and the job will be straightforward.

Watch for co-dominant trunks. Some needled plants are prone to producing multiple trunks when they are young. Annually inspect the tree and remove any competing trunks by selecting the largest and most vertical trunk and removing all others.

Maintain natural shape by thinning. Cut large branches back to the ground or the tree trunk. Don't shear plants. Not only does shearing produce a contrived shape, it requires frequent maintenance.

Reduce shading. Dense upper branches shade lower branches, causing them to lose needles and die. The plant then has green growth at the top and bare, woody branches near the ground. Prevent shading dieback by selectively thinning branches back to ground level or the main trunk to allow light to filter down into the plant. Prune the plant so that it is wider at the bottom than it is at the top.

Pinch candles. Pines, spruces, and firs produce new growth at branch tips. The new growth first emerges as "candles" or condensed shoots. To encourage dense growth, cut or pinch the candles back by half when they are about 2 inches long. It is important to reduce the candles before the needles unfold. Cutting the shoots after the needles develop results in a misshapen plant.

Avoid late summer pruning. When pruned late in the growing season, the plants will produce a flush of tender new growth that is susceptible to cold damage. Winter or early spring is the best time to prune.

Opposite: **Most needled trees and shrubs develop pleasing shapes naturally. Use thinning cuts to reduce plant size when necessary.**

TEST GARDEN TIP

Leader repair

The tender upright leaders of pines, firs, and spruces are susceptible to breakage from wind and large birds perching on the soft growth. Remedy a broken leader by selecting a replacement from the nearest branch. Use masking tape or string to tie the branch upright. Check the new leader the next growing season. It should be growing strongly upright. Remove the string or tape.

Evergreen shrub solutions

Avoid shearing needled evergreen shrubs. While shearing is quick and easy, it is detrimental to plant growth and form. Shearing encourages dense foliage on a plant's exterior. The dense growth shades the interior branches and the plant develops a thin shell of foliage.

Because most needled evergreen shrubs produce new growth only from the branch tips, the result is bare, brown branches topped with tufts of green foliage. Instead of shearing evergreen shrubs, thin plants by pruning overgrown branches back to main stems or ground level. Selectively reduce the length of overgrown branches by pruning them back by half their length; be sure to work carefully to maintain the plant's natural form.

Pruning broadleaf shrubs

Unlike trees, which can get by without pruning, broadleaf shrubs generally grow best when pruned annually. If you put off pruning an oak for three or four years, there will be few repercussions. If you skip pruning a mature burning bush, the shrub will likely outgrow its planting space and become a dense mass of twigs and foliage.

Before picking up your pruners, make a pruning plan. What is your goal? Are you pruning to reduce the size of the plant? Or maybe you're pruning to encourage flowering or promote sturdy growth? Perhaps you're pruning to create or maintain a hedge? Choose pruning cuts based on the desired outcome.

Prune to control size
When shrubs grow too large, use thinning cuts to reduce their size without changing the natural branching habit. (Reminder: A thinning cut removes an entire branch back to a main stem or ground level.) First, remove excessive twiggy growth and crowded, weak, and misshapen

stems, as well as suckers and water sprouts. Next, use loppers to cut the longest stems back to ground level or a main branch. This opens the plant to sunlight, which encourages new growth and gives it a graceful shape. When thinning shrubs, do not remove more than one-third of the live stems.

If more drastic size control is needed, think about rejuvenation. Learn all about rejuvenation on pages 106–107. Be sure to take age and vigor into consideration when deciding to prune a shrub. Older, less vigorous, or actively growing shrubs should be pruned more lightly than younger ones, unless you are pruning to rejuvenate them.

Opposite: **Occasional thinning maintains the pleasing form of the blooming azaleas and rhododendrons near this entryway and keeps their growth in check.**

Prune to encourage dense growth

A shrub that screens an unsightly view needs to be dense, not loose and open. In this situation, greater branching and thicker growth are what you want. Shearing or pruning off a few inches of the branch tips will encourage the plant to produce dense growth at the growing points. Create dense growth in the interior of a plant by shortening long branches by about half their length. New growth will emerge near the pruning cut.

Prune to promote flowers

When a shrub isn't blooming as well as it did in the past, the first thing to check is whether it's still receiving enough sunlight. As surrounding trees grow, they gradually shade an area. If the light hasn't become too dim to support healthy plant growth, thinning the shrub's older branches can help. Thinning lets light into the interior of the shrub to help stimulate growth and improve flowering.

If light is not the problem, make sure you're pruning the shrubs at the correct time. For example, trimming a weigela or other spring bloomer in September removes most of the buds that would flower the following spring. Prune weigela in early summer right after the plant finishes blooming. See plant entries in the Encyclopedia of Shrubs beginning on page 168 for specific pruning advice.

How to create a hedge

Formal and informal hedges have different pruning requirements. Formal hedges—those with straight sides and a flat top or other geometric shapes—call for frequent light shearing. Informal hedges, which have a natural habit, can be trimmed infrequently.

FORMAL HEDGE

ABOUT A MONTH AFTER PLANTING, cut young plants back by about one-third. This extreme pruning at a young age will create strong, dense growth.

IN SPRING OF THE PLANT'S SECOND and third years, level the top and sides of the hedge. Each time new growth elongates by 2 to 3 inches, clip it back just above the previous trimming.

ALWAYS AIM TO CREATE A SHRUB that is wider at the bottom than it is at the top. If the top of the shrub is allowed to shade the bottom branches, those bottom branches will die back.

SHEARING LONG HEDGES is easiest with a gas or electric power trimmer.

INFORMAL HEDGE

LET PLANTS GROW WITHOUT PRUNING through their second season, except to remove broken or diseased branches.

USE THINNING CUTS to reduce the size of the shrub.

HAND PRUNERS OR LOPPERS are great for pruning shrubs growing as informal hedges.

Rejuvenating overgrown shrubs

Overgrown lilacs produce copious foliage and few flowers. Rejuvenate a lilac by cutting it back to 4 to 6 inches above the ground in early spring.

Bring an overgrown shrub back to its youthful glory

with rejuvenation pruning. A result of years of neglect, overgrown shrubs are landscape eyesores. Their bloom show is often reduced to a few clusters of flowers, and their massive size overwhelms nearby plants, walkways, and everything else in their reach.

Without annual pruning, many broadleaf shrubs become overgrown in three or four years. There are a couple of easy ways to rejuvenate a shrub; each method will produce a lovely, right-size shrub in about three years.

Gradual renewal

This rejuvenation method takes place over a three-year period. Begin by removing one-third of the largest, oldest stems at ground level in late winter or early spring. One year later remove one-half of the remaining old stems. Also, thin the new growth by cutting closely spaced branches back to ground level. Finally, in late winter or early spring of the third year, remove all the remaining old stems. Thin the new shoots so the renewed shrub has several well-spaced, vigorous stems.

Severe pruning

Aptly named, severe pruning is drastic, but some shrubs tolerate it with ease. Note, not all shrubs are candidates for severe pruning. See the chart below for the shrubs that are best adapted to this method of renewal. Severe pruning begins by cutting a shrub back to 4 to 6 inches above the ground in early spring. Timing is essential, as the plant will begin regrowth during the cool, moist days of spring. The plant will produce many shoots during the growing season. In late winter of the following year, select several strong healthy shoots to keep and remove all others at ground level. Cut back the retained shoots by about one-third to encourage branching.

Annual maintenance

Keeping a renewed shrub healthy and within bounds is as easy as annually thinning it in late winter or early spring. Cut one-quarter to one-third of the oldest branches back to ground level each year, and the plant will continue to produce new, vigorous shoots. Expect it to bloom prolifically and produce plenty of healhty foliage.

Needled evergreens

Large, overgrown evergreen shrubs present a challenge because, unlike broadleaf shrubs, most needled shrubs don't have the ability to sprout new growth on bare or severely pruned branches. The best course of action for remedying an overgrown needled evergreen is to remove it and plant a new small shrub.

TEST GARDEN TIP

Rejuvenating treelike shrubs

Some shrubs are more like small trees. They have one or a few stout trunks that support small branches and leaves. Several species of viburnum, as well as smoke tree and some forms of rhododendron, fall into this category of treelike shrubs. Do not rejuvenation-prune these plants. Reduce their size by thinning instead.

Candidates for severe pruning

Prune these shrubs back to within 4 to 6 inches of the ground in late winter and they will produce a flush of new growth during the growing season. Expect spring-flowering shrubs to commence blooming two to three years after severe pruning. Summer bloomers (indicated with * below) will bloom the same year that they are pruned.

AZALEA

*BUTTERFLY BUSH

CAMELLIA

DOGWOOD

FORSYTHIA

HYDRANGEA

LILAC

HEAVENLY BAMBOO

*POTENTILLA

PRIVET

encyclopedia of broadleaf trees

Providing shade, valuable habitat for wildlife, and a seasonal burst of color from flowers or foliage, broadleaf trees are a great landscape asset. Use the detailed entries in this encyclopedia to choose the best trees for your yard.

OUTDOOR ROOMS
Trees are essential components of most outdoor rooms. Employ their canopies as a colorful, shade-giving ceiling.

FLOWERS AND FOLIAGE
From sweetly scented flowers to magnificent fall foliage, trees have many unique features.

EASY-CARE
Trees require little maintenance after they become established with a strong root system.

American holly
(*Ilex opaca*)

Lustrous evergreen foliage is a lovely backdrop for American holly's glistening red berries in winter. A small to medium tree with a pyramidal shape and low branches, it makes a great screen. Be sure to plant several plants to ensure pollination and fruit set.

Best site
Plant American holly in full sun or part shade and average, moist, well-drained soil. Plants do not tolerate clay or other poorly drained soils. Zones 5–9.

Growing
Most cultivars grow 15 to 30 feet tall and wide. A slow-growing plant, American holly increases in height just a few inches a year, making it a good choice for small gardens. Plant one male for every two to three female plants for good fruit set. Plant tags will denote plant sex.

Prune holly, if necessary, in late winter or early spring. Numerous pests plague holly but healthy plants are rarely susceptible to pests.

Names to watch for
'Croonenburg' has a compact habit with heavy fruit set every year. **'Jersey Princess'** is a female cultivar with abundant fruit set. Pair it with **'Jersey Knight'** for good fruit set.

Ash
(*Fraxinus* species)

Once a popular landscape tree, ash is plagued by emerald ash borer. This destructive pest decimated mature plantings in Michigan and is spreading across the country. New plantings of ash are not advised while scientists learn about the pest and its control.

Best site
Ashes grow well in full sun or part shade and adapt to many types of soil, including clay and sandy soil. Zones 3–9.

Growing
Ash trees grow 40 to 60 feet tall and about 30 feet wide. Their medium green foliage turns bright yellow or purple in fall, depending on the species and cultivar. Prune ash in late winter.

Emerald ash borer is the most significant pest of ash trees. There is no known cure once trees are infected. Signs of infestation include significant branch dieback in the top of the tree. If emerald ash borer is in your region, contact your local cooperative extension service for pest protection suggestions.

Names to watch for
All ash species are susceptible to emerald ash borer. Until the pest is eradicated or a resistant species is found, do not plant ash trees.

Beech
(*Fagus* species)

A stately, elegant tree, beech is beloved for its massive stature and pyramidal outline with dense branching from crown to ground level. Particularly striking in winter, beech has smooth gray bark and a captivating silhouette. In fall its golden bronze foliage is spectacular.

Best site
Beech grows well in full sun or part shade. It thrives in moist, well-drained soil. Do not plant beech where soil is hard, sticky, or poorly drained. It does not tolerate these types of soil. Beech is also intolerant of extreme heat. In Zones 8 and 9 plant it where it will receive afternoon shade. Zones 4–9.

Growing
American beech (*F. grandiflora*) reaches 50 to 70 feet tall and wide, and European beech (*F. sylvatica*) 50 to 60 feet tall and about 30 feet wide. Transplant container-grown plants in spring and be sure to water well after planting. Spread a 2-inch layer of mulch around the base of the tree to conserve moisture and prevent weed growth. It is often difficult to grow grass under a beech's dense canopy. Opt for a layer of mulch instead. Not only will the mulch suppress weeds, but it will also decompose and enrich the soil.

Prune beech trees, if necessary, in late winter or early spring. Beech tolerates pruning well, although its pleasing natural habit will be hindered if it is molded into a geometric form. Beech has few pest problems.

Names to watch for
AMERICAN BEECH is a native plant and there are no cultivars available. **EUROPEAN BEECH** has many excellent selections. **'Asplenifolia'** has finely cut foliage that gives it a fernlike texture. **'Fastigiata'** is an elegant, upright selection that is columnar. Use it to make a strong vertical statement. Look for upright cultivars with purple or yellow foliage too, such as **'Dawyck Gold'** and **'Dawyck Purple'**. **'Tricolor'** is a unique variegated form with green-and-white leaves with pink margins. Use a weeping cultivar, such as **'Purple Fountain'**, as a garden focal point.

Far left: **'Tricolor' beech is an understory tree, thriving in part shade. It grows 20 to 30 feet tall.**

Left: **'Purple Fountain' beech's foliage has the most intense color in spring. The leaves occasionally fade in the heat of summer. It is 25 feet tall and 15 feet wide.**

Birch
(*Betula* species)

North American natives, river birch and paper birch are grown for their adaptable nature and intriguing peeling bark. Count on birch to tolerate a variety of soil conditions. Often grown in multistemmed clumps, a cluster of birch trees is a great focal point in a landscape.

Best site

Birch grows best in moist, well-drained soil and full sun or part shade. River birch (*B. nigra*) tolerates moist to swampy soil, as its name implies. Plant river birch in slow-draining soil or near an area that floods occasionally, such as a rain garden. Paper birch (*B. papyrifera*) is less tolerant of waterlogged soil and should be planted in moist, well-drained soil. Zones 3–9.

Growing

Birch trees grow 40 to 60 feet tall and wide. They have a pyramidal outline and delicate arching branches that extend toward the ground. Plant container-grown or balled-and-burlapped birch trees in spring. Water plants well the first season after planting and also during excessive drought.

When purchasing a clump of birch trees— three-stem clumps are the most common—each tree in the clump should be similar in size and vigor. If one member of the clump is small compared to the others, choose another clump. In an unbalanced clump, the larger trees will likely overtake the smaller tree and a three-tree clump will become a two-tree planting.

Prune birch trees in summer after the leaves have expanded. In spring, sap flows freely out of pruning cuts, making for a messy and sometimes unsightly situation. Trim trees in early summer to avoid excessive sap.

The bronze birch borer is a destructive pest of birch trees. Healthy vigorous trees are less susceptible to borer attack than environmentally stressed trees. Sufficient watering is the best way to promote a healthy birch. Water plants deeply during drought and spread a 2-inch layer of mulch over the plant's root system to help preserve soil moisture. Several cultivars have

shown good resistance to bronze birch borer. When possible, choose a resistant cultivar.

Names to watch for

Heritage river birch is a tough, easy-to-grow tree with rich yellow fall color and papery exfoliating bark. The young stems are white, turning a dark bronze hue as they age. **Dura-Heat** is another popular river birch with good yellow fall color. It has glossy dark green leaves with a pleasing fine texture. Both cultivars have good resistance to bronze birch borer.

Renaissance Series paper birch trees are highly resistant to bronze birch borer. They all have magnificent exfoliating white bark. **Compact** is a tight pyramidal form that grows 30 feet tall and 15 feet wide. **Reflection** is a fast-growing borer-resistant form that grows 50 feet or more tall and about 25 feet wide.

White-bark birches are especially susceptible to bronze birch borer attack. Be sure to choose a borer-resistant cultivar.

Bark begins to curl and peel away from the trunk of birch trees at a young age. This is a normal, healthy process.

Black gum
(Nyssa sylvatica)

Also called tupelo, black gum is a native tree that lights up in fall. Its glossy dark green foliage becomes fluorescent yellow and orange, then scarlet and purple as the nighttime temperatures drop. Use this medium tree to cast valuable shade over an outdoor room.

Best site
Black gum grows best in full sun and moist, well-drained soil. It thrives in deep soil where its roots can expand. Zones 4–9.

Growing
Black gum grows 30 to 50 feet tall and about 20 to 30 feet wide. It has a rounded outline with graceful spreading branches that arch toward the ground. Plant container-grown or balled-and-burlapped trees in spring. Black gum has a deep taproot that occasionally makes it challenging to establish in the landscape. Move plants carefully.

Black gum rarely needs pruning. Remove low-hanging branches in early spring. The tree has no notable pest problems.

Names to watch for
'Autumn Cascades' has a pronounced weeping habit and brilliant fall color. **Forum** has a strong pyramidal habit and bold red fall color.

Black locust
(Robinia pseudoacacia)

A solution for sandy, infertile soil, black locust is a tough tree. It is decorated with ropelike strands of fragrant white flowers in late spring. Black locust is an upright tree with a rounded crown. It is invasive in some areas; plant with caution.

Best site
Adaptable to a variety of soils and climates, black locust grows best in moist, rich soil, but it will easily root in sandy, infertile soil that is common along seaside areas and in parking strips. It does best in full sun. Zones 4–8.

Growing
Black locust grows 30 to 50 feet tall and 25 to 30 feet wide. It begins flowering at a young age. The flowers are especially popular with bees.

Prune black locust in summer. It bleeds heavily when pruned in spring. Several pests trouble black locust but none are especially notable. Vigorous, fast-growing specimens often thwart potential pests.

Names to watch for
'Purple Robe' has pink flowers and bronzy-red new leaves that turn green. **Twisty Baby** is a dwarf black locust that has contorted branches.

 YOU SHOULD KNOW
Black gum produces blue-black fruit in late summer. Many species of birds and mammals dine on these tasty morsels in September and October, when other food sources are becoming less plentiful. Because the fruits can be messy in high-traffic areas, plant black gum in an open lawn where the fruit will not be troublesome.

Buckeye
(*Aesculus* species)

Buckeyes have a bold presence in the landscape. They add color with tropical-looking spring flowers and pumpkin-orange to yellow or brown fall foliage. Use large buckeyes, also called horse chestnuts, as shade trees in medium to large yards.

Best site

Buckeyes grow best in full sun or part shade. Plants tolerate shade better than many other tree species. Moist, well-drained, deep, fertile soil is best for buckeyes. Most do not adapt well to difficult growing conditions and are likely to balk at slow-draining clay soil or urban situations.

Most buckeyes develop into large, stately trees. Be sure to plant them where they will have plenty of space to grow. Zones 3–8 depending on species.

Growing

There is great variety within the buckeye group. Some selections top out at 15 to 20 feet tall while others rise to more than 70 feet. Most trees have a rounded, spreading habit with a hint of horizontal branching.

Buckeyes bloom in late spring in shades of white, yellow-green, or red. The 6- to 8-inch-long flower clusters appear after the leaves have expanded. Smooth round fruit, often called buckeyes, ripen inside hard seed coats in fall. In autumn buckeye foliage varies from dull brown to shades of yellow and pumpkin orange. Fall color is variable from year to year.

Plant container-grown or balled-and-burlapped plants in early spring. Spread a 2-inch layer of organic mulch under the tree canopy to aid in soil moisture retention. Water regularly for two to three months after transplanting.

Prune buckeye in late winter or early spring. Various leaf diseases affect these trees. Leaf blotch is common in summer. It appears as small brown spots on the leaves. The spots expand to create large blotches, and eventually the leaves fall. Drought contributes to leaf blotch as well as makes trees susceptible to other pests such as Japanese beetle, bagworms, and canker. Water buckeyes deeply and infrequently during extended periods of drought.

buckeye species:

1. **OHIO BUCKEYE** (*A. glabra*) does not have prominent flowers. It is troubled by leaf diseases. 20 to 40 feet tall and wide. Zones 3–7.
2. **RED BUCKEYE** (*A. pavia*) thrives in light shade. It has dark green leaves, rich red flowers, and a round habit. Moist soil is essential. 15 to 20 feet tall and wide. Zones 4–8.
3. **RED HORSE CHESTNUT** (*A. × carnea*) has a rounded outline and a dense canopy. Rose-red flowers cover the tree in late spring. Red horse chestnut is adaptable to a wide range of soils. 30 to 40 feet tall and wide. Zones 4–7.
4. **YELLOW BUCKEYE** (*A. flava*) is a native horse chestnut that is notably trouble-free. It has yellow flowers and is adaptable to most conditions. 60 to 75 feet tall and 30 to 50 feet wide. Zones 4–8.

Callery pear
(*Pyrus calleryana*)

Resembling a cottony cloud, callery pear, also called flowering pear, is covered with white flowers in spring. One of the most reliable small flowering trees, callery pear also has brilliant fall color. Its glossy green leaves turn scarlet and purple in fall.

Best site

Callery pear grows best in moist, well-drained soil, but it tolerates a wide variety of difficult growing conditions including slow-draining clay and infertile, sandy soil. It demands full sun. Callery pear is a popular street tree because it has an upright oval habit. It is also useful near buildings thanks to its upright form. Its dense growth makes it a good informal hedge or screen plant during the growing season. Zones 5–9.

Growing

Callery pear grows 20 to 40 feet tall and 10 to 20 feet wide. Many cultivars exist; choose the best size for your landscape. Container-grown or balled-and-burlapped plants are easy to establish in spring. Callery pear grows quickly. Water plants regularly for at least eight weeks after planting to encourage them to develop a strong root system.

Prune callery pear in late winter or early spring. Plants have a tendency to develop narrow branch angles. Such branch connections are weak and prone to breaking in wind and snowstorms. Prune away branches that are weakly connected to the tree.

Fire blight is a troublesome problem on callery pears. Some cultivars have notable fire blight resistance; choose among those. Few other pests trouble these easy-to-grow trees.

Names to watch for

'Chanticleer' has a narrow, upright form with profuse flower production. It has red-purple fall color. It is about 30 feet tall and 15 feet wide. **'Aristocrat'** grows about 30 feet wide and 15 feet tall and is a good choice for small spaces such as along a driveway or parking strip. **'Cleveland Select'** is another excellent narrow cultivar.

 YOU SHOULD KNOW

'Bradford' was once a popular and widely planted callery pear. It was overplanted in the 1990s and many of the now-mature trees are splitting apart due to weak branch angles. Still popular with some nurseries, 'Bradford' is available but should be avoided. Choose a healthier, more attractive cultivar such as 'Chanticleer' or 'Jack'.

Far left: **Blooming in spring before leaves debut, callery pear blossoms are pleasingly fragrant.**

Left: **Callery pear's glossy green summer foliage turns shades of yellow, red, and orange in fall.**

Camphor tree
(*Cinnamomum camphora*)

Ideal for use as a shade tree in tropical climates, camphor tree has a large, spreading form similar to the stately live oak. It produces small black berries that are favored by wildlife but can be troublesome in traffic areas. Plant it where the fruit will not cause a problem.

Best site

Camphor tree grows best in full sun and a variety of soil conditions from sand to clay loam. It will tolerate drought. Zones 9–11.

Growing

Fast-growing camphor tree reaches 40 to 60 feet tall and wide. It is easy to transplant in spring. Camphor tree has a tendency to develop large roots near the soil surface. These surface roots combined with dense shade cast by the leaves make it tough to grow grass under the canopy. Blanket the area with a 2-inch layer of organic mulch instead.

Prune trees annually to prevent multitrunked specimens. When pruning, aim to develop sturdy branches that are spaced about 18 to 30 inches apart on the trunk.

Names to watch for

'Monum' has large, rich green leaves.

Carolina silverbell
(*Halesia tetraptera*)

A small native tree perfect for planting in a mixed shrub border or in front of an evergreen backdrop, Carolina silverbell is adorned with bell-shape white or pale pink flowers in spring. It grows best in part shade, making it an adaptable tree for a variety of landscapes.

Best site

Carolina silverbell thrives in part shade and well-drained, moist soil that is high in organic matter. Zones 4–8.

Growing

Carolina silverbell grows 30 to 40 feet tall and 20 to 30 feet wide. It has a rounded outline with branches that arch toward the ground. A low-branched tree, it will often develop multiple trunks. Transplant container-grown plants in spring. Carolina silverbell does not establish well from balled-and-burlapped specimens; choose container-grown plants instead.

Prune plants in late winter or early spring as needed. No significant pests trouble this easy-to-grow native plant.

Names to watch for

'Arnold Pink' has rose pink flowers. **'Wedding Bells'** grows 20 feet tall and has white flowers.

Catalpa
(*Catalpa bignonioides*)

A long-lived tree with a rugged, irregular outline, catalpa has massive heart-shape leaves and showy white flowers in early summer. Best for an open area, it is a good candidate for growing along a property line or in a large grassy expanse where its outline can be admired.

Best site
Catalpa grows best in sun or part shade and moist, well-drained soil. It tolerates a variety of soil conditions and is known for its ability to adapt to tough sites, especially those that are hot and dry. Zones 4–9.

Growing
Catalpa is a large tree growing 30 to 40 feet tall and wide. It is fast growing. Transplant balled-and-burlapped or container-grown plants as young trees. Young catalpa plants have few branches and a very irregular appearance. Their branching will improve as they age.

Prune catalpa in late winter. Plants have brittle wood and lose branches easily in strong wind. There are no notable pests of catalpa.

Names to watch for
'Aurea', also called yellow catalpa, has chartreuse foliage.

Chinese tallow tree
(*Sapium sebiferum*)

A fast-growing tree that will create quick shade around a deck or patio in warm climates, Chinese tallow tree has dark green leaves that turn yellow to red in fall. It is easy to grow, but its planting is restricted in some areas where it has become a nuisance.

Best site
Chinese tallow tree grows in moist to dry soil. It tolerates flooding by either fresh or salt water. Best in full sun, it will tolerate part shade with ease. Zones 8–10.

Growing
Count on Chinese tallow tree to grow about 25 feet tall and 15 feet wide. It has an upright, mounded shape. Ropelike yellow-green flowers in spring are followed by seeds that open to resemble popcorn—hence another common name for this plant, popcorn tree.

Prune the tree to promote a strong central leader. It has no notable pests. Planting Chinese tallow tree is restricted in some areas. Check with your local extension service before planting.

Names to watch for
There are no noteworthy cultivars of Chinese tallow tree.

YOU SHOULD KNOW Some plants are simply too easy to grow. They self-seed and grow so readily that they overtake natural vegetation. Chinese tallow tree is one of those plants. It is classified as an invasive plant in some areas and should not be planted. Government agencies monitor the invasive nature of plant species and restrict their planting when appropriate. Prevent invasive species from choking out native plants by adhering to all planting regulations for your area.

Citrus
(*Citrus* species)

Landscape trees and food sources, citrus trees are grown for their lush evergreen foliage, fragrant blossoms, and tasty fruit. Plant these easy-to-grow small to medium trees for fruit production and reliable, year-round shade. Group several citrus trees for a living screen.

Best site

Citrus trees are easy to grow and thrive in a multitude of subtropical and tropical landscapes. They grow best in full sun but will tolerate some shade. They grow well in moist, well-drained soil. Useful as both landscape plants and food sources, citrus trees grow rapidly and produce plentiful shade. Zones 8–11.

Growing

Citrus trees range from small trees that grow just 5 to 10 feet tall to 30- to 40-foot-tall trees. Many citrus species produce the most fruit when planted alongside a compatible plant for cross-pollination. Read plant tags closely when purchasing plants to learn about cross-pollination requirements.

Plant container-grown citrus trees year-round. Build a soil basin around the planting hole to aid in moisture retention. Water newly planted citrus trees at least once a week for eight weeks.

Regular watering is one of the most important aspects of caring for citrus trees. Lack of moisture during the growing season causes fruit and sometimes foliage to drop. Water citrus trees deeply during dry periods.

Citrus trees must be fertilized regularly. They are typically fertilized from February to September with a complete general-purpose fertilizer, such as an 8-8-8 product. The number of applications depends on the region. Citrus in Florida and along the Gulf Coast are usually fertilized three to four times a year while citrus in California, Arizona, and Texas are fertilized two to three times a year.

Citrus trees generally do not require regular pruning. Lemon trees and other vigorous types of citrus can be pruned annually to control size. Prune trees as needed in late winter or early spring. Vigorously growing citrus trees usually have few pest problems.

citrus species and varieties:

1. **ORANGE** trees have delightfully fragrant blossoms. Navel oranges are popular for fruit production. Try **'Cara Cara'** and **'Washington'**. 15 to 20 feet tall.
2. **LEMON** trees are some of the most vigorous citrus trees. Prune the plants regularly to ensure the fruit is within reach for harvest. Lemons have attractive light green foliage. Try **'Improved Meyer'**. 10–20 feet tall.
3. **MANDARIN ORANGES** are also known as tangerines and are complex hybrids of different types of citrus. Try **'Clementine'** and **'Satsuma'**. 10 to 15 feet tall.
4. **GRAPEFRUIT** is impressive in the landscape. The large fruit decorates trees for months. **'Marsh'** is an excellent cultivar. 20 to 30 feet tall.

Corktree
(*Phellodendron amurense*)

Handsome, corklike bark is the hallmark of this tough tree. Its spreading limbs reach 30 to 45 feet tall and are cloaked with dark green leaves that turn yellow in fall. Plant it where its lovely bark can be admired. Corktree is an excellent shade tree.

Best site
Corktree, also known as amur corktree, grows in full sun or part shade and does well in many types of soil. It is remarkably drought-tolerant. Zones 4–7.

Growing
Growing 30 to 45 feet tall and equally wide, corktree has a rounded outline. When purchasing a corktree, search out a male cultivar. Female corktrees produce fruit that is more of a liability than an asset. The fruit has a strong odor when bruised and litters and stains walkways.

Prune as needed in late winter. Corktree does not have any notable pests.

Names to watch for
'Macho' is a male cultivar with leathery dark green foliage. **Shademaster** is another male cultivar with dark green foliage and vigorous, healthy growth.

Cottonwood
(*Populus deltoides*)

Common in the Plains states, cottonwood is known for its tufted seeds that regularly take flight in early summer. This large tree has an irregular outline and tolerates boggy sites well. It will grow in waterways and other places that are too wet for most trees.

Best site
Cottonwood grows best in moist soil, but it will tolerate dry and very wet soils. It prefers full sun and deep, rich soil. It is very adaptable to pollutants and salty soil conditions. Zones 3–9.

Growing
Cottonwood is a large tree, growing 75 to 100 feet tall and 50 to 75 feet wide. It develops a broad vase shape with age. This species is easily transplanted and grown. Trees over 70 years old deteriorate rapidly.

Prune plants in late winter or spring. Cankers trouble cottonwood trees. Trees growing in dry conditions are especially susceptible.

Names to watch for
Many cottonless forms of cottonwood have been selected. **'Siouxland'** is one such selection. **QUAKING ASPEN** (*P. tremuloides*) is a fast-growing relative. See page 149.

Crabapple (*Malus* species)

Essential elements of spring for gardeners in northern states, crabapples are decorated with thousands of delicate flowers in colors ranging from sparkling white to deep crimson. Sweetly fragrant, the blossoms last for a week to 10 days and are followed by petite round fruit. Many crabapples have brilliant fall color. Small cultivars are perfect for adding color to a front yard garden bed or foundation planting. Use large cultivars throughout the landscape, including as small shade trees.

Best site

Crabapples flower and fruit best in full sun. They are adaptable to a variety of soil conditions but grow best in deep, rich, well-drained soil. Heavy loam produces excellent results. Crabapples are popular in northern states thanks to their extreme cold hardiness.

From streetside planting strips to perennial gardens and mixed tree borders, crabapples are at home throughout the landscape. Pair them with evergreens for a color-rich privacy screen 12 months a year.

One of the few reliable spring-blooming trees for northern climates, crabapples are a prized landscape plant. Crabapples are not widely planted in southern states, but they thrive in Zones 7 and 8 when provided adequate moisture. Zones 3–8.

Growing

Most crabapples reach 15 to 25 feet tall and wide at maturity. There are hundreds of crabapple cultivars and their mature sizes vary greatly, as do their growth habits.

These flowering trees range from moundlike low plants to narrow upright types. There are also cultivars with branches that arch toward the ground. Crabapple's branching habit provides valuable architecture in the winter landscape, especially when the branches are decorated with red, yellow, or green fruit.

Birds, squirrels, and other wildlife dine on crabapple fruit throughout the fall and winter months. If fall and winter food sources are abundant in your area, crabapple trees will often be decorated with colorful fruit through winter. If food is scarce, birds will strip fruit from the trees in short order.

Plant container-grown or balled-and-burlapped trees in spring or fall. Water plants well during the first season after planting. Crabapples are generally easy to establish and grow at a moderate rate.

Crabapples require little pruning. If it is done, it should be completed shortly after flowers fade. Most crabapples form flower buds for the following year in mid-June. Pruning in mid-June or later will likely reduce the number of flowers the following year. Pruning may be done anytime, however, to remove suckers and cut off out-of-place or broken branches.

Crabapples are susceptible to many pests, but resistant cultivars are available and they are generally pest-free and easy to grow. Some of the most common crabapple pests include fire blight, cedar apple rust, powdery mildew, apple scab, canker, and Japanese beetles.

As with any tree or shrub, a healthy plant is less susceptible to pests. Water crabapples deeply during prolonged periods of drought. Prevent trunk injury on young trees by wrapping the trunk with drainage tile if deer or rabbits are prevalent and destructive in your area. Male deer will rub their antlers on the trunks of young trees. Rabbits will eat the bark when food is scarce in winter.

Names to watch for

While there are hundreds of crabapple cultivars in commerce, only a small number excel at flower production, plant form, hardiness, and disease resistance. The cultivars on the following page are a handful of the best crabapples available today. Inquire about great cultivars for your area at your local nursery.

crabapple varieties:

1. **CENTURION** is a very cold-hardy selection with pink flowers and cherry red fruit in fall. Its disease-resistant foliage emerges reddish green and matures to bronze-green. 25 feet tall and 15 to 20 feet wide. Zones 4–8.

2. **'DONALD WYMAN'** has rich red buds that open to white flowers. Its glossy red fruit persists into winter. It has good disease resistance and grows 25 feet tall and wide. Zones 4–8.

3. **INDIAN MAGIC** is known just as much for its fruit as it is for its showy flowers. Deep rose pink flowers are followed by large fruit that turns bright red in late summer and hangs on the tree through winter. Trees have red-orange fall color. 15 to 20 feet tall and wide. Zones 4–8.

4. **'PRAIRIFIRE'** is a highly disease-resistant cultivar with deep pink flowers and red-purple fruit. It flowers prolifically and grows about 20 feet tall and wide. Zones 4–8.

5. **'PROFUSION'** produces hundreds of small pink flowers that are followed by red fruit. It's an excellent choice for small landscapes. 12 to 15 feet tall and 15 to 20 feet wide. Zones 4–8.

6. **RED JEWEL** is a wonderful petite tree for small spaces. It has white flowers and bright red fruit. 15 feet tall and wide. Zones 4–8.

7. **ROYAL RAINDROPS** is full of color. Bright red fruit follows pretty single pink flowers. The finely cut foliage is deep purple in summer, orange-red in fall. 20 feet tall and 15 feet wide. Zones 4–8.

8. **SCARLET BRANDYWINE** has dark rose pink flowers and a pleasing round outline. The flowers are followed by pumpkin-orange crabapples that ripen in fall and provide winter interest. 15 to 20 feet tall and wide. Zones 5–8.

9. **SUGAR TYME** is a very disease-resistant cultivar with pink buds and white flowers. It has red fruit and a pleasing oval outline. 18 feet tall and 15 feet wide. Zones 4–8.

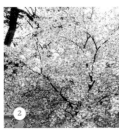

Crape myrtle (*Lagerstroemia indica*)

Affectionately called the summer lilac of the South, crape myrtle is a year-round tree or shrub for landscapes ranging from tiny patio gardens to expansive suburban yards. In spring its fresh green to bronze, red, or purple foliage emerges and is followed by cloudlike, long-lasting flower clusters in shades of white, pink, purple, or red that last for weeks in summer. In fall the foliage takes on warm hues, and peeling bark reveals silky smooth inner bark, adding interest to the plant in winter.

Best site

Crape myrtle grows best in full sun and moist, well-drained soil. Because there is great variety in mature size, crape myrtles are useful throughout the landscape.

Grow small or dwarf cultivars in containers and enjoy their beauty on a deck or patio. Petite varieties are also valuable for foundation plantings and mixed shrub borders. Call on 10- to 15-foot-tall varieties to anchor garden beds or frame a walkway or garden entrance. Often planted in groups, a crape myrtle grove is a striking sight. Underplant it with an easy-care groundcover for a low-maintenance planting.

Crape myrtles are hardy in Zones 7 to 10, but recent introductions have expanded their growing Zone north to Zone 5 in some cases. Bolster cold hardiness in cold Zones by limiting summer pruning to prevent a flush of tender growth and by sheltering the plants from cold winter winds.

Growing

Crape myrtle usually grows 15 to 25 feet tall and about 10 to 20 feet wide. Available cultivars range from 3-foot-tall patio-size plants to lofty 45-foot-tall shade trees. Crape myrtles are commonly sold as multistemmed trees or shrubs. Plants typically have a cloud of pretty foliage and graceful bare trunks.

When purchasing a multistemmed crape myrtle at a nursery or garden center, look for a plant that has a collection of similar-size stems. If one or more of the stems is noticeably smaller than the others, look for another plant. In time, small trunks will likely die as the large stems overtake them. Plants with like-size trunks will maintain their pleasing form for years.

Plant crape myrtles as container-grown or balled-and-burlapped plants in winter or spring. Newly planted trees thrive when watered regularly. Maintain moist, but not waterlogged, soil for the first eight weeks after planting.

These flowering trees thrive when fertilized while they are young. Fertilize them in spring as the new leaves are emerging. Use an all-purpose, slow-release fertilizer. Mature plants thrive without fertilizer. Spread a 2-inch-thick layer of organic mulch, such as shredded bark, around the base of mature plants to help conserve soil moisture and replenish nutrients.

Prune crape myrtles lightly in winter if needed. Remove crossing or rubbing branches and branches with wayward growth habits. Generally crape myrtles require very little pruning and develop a pleasing shape with no help from the gardener.

In Zones 5 and 6 provide protection from cold winter temperatures and drying winds by wrapping small crape myrtle trees and shrubs with burlap. If possible, plant a natural windbreak nearby to deflect winter winds.

Japanese beetle, powdery mildew, and aphids are common pests. Many disease-resistant crape myrtle cultivars have been developed to combat powdery mildew. Proper siting—planting in full sun and moist, well-drained soil—will help plants overcome other pests.

Names to watch for

There are hundreds of crape myrtle cultivars available at nurseries and garden centers. The cultivars on the following page are a few of the best performers. Be sure to match the mature size of the plant with the available growing space in your yard.

YOU SHOULD KNOW Crape myrtles are easy to grow provided they are planted in full sun and fertile soil and receive plenty of air circulation. The top causes of poor flowering include too much nitrogen fertilizer, not enough sunlight (less than six hours per day), and severe pruning.

crape myrtle varieties:

① DAZZLE SERIES Members of this group include fuchsia-flowered **Berry Dazzle**, red **Cherry Dazzle**, and reddish-pink **Strawberry Dazzle** among others. All members of the series have good disease resistance, a dense compact habit, and rich-colored flowers. Plants grow 5 to 10 feet tall. Zones 6–10.

② HOPI has a shrublike habit and clusters of pink blooms. 7 feet tall. Zones 7–10.

③ 'NATCHEZ' is a striking white bloomer with cinnamon-brown exfoliating bark. Its glossy green leaves turn vibrant orange-red in fall. 20 feet tall. Zones 6–9.

④ PINK VELOUR has crimson buds that open to reveal deep pink flowers. Its new foliage is burgundy and turns purple-green and finally dark green. 10 to 12 feet tall. Zones 7–10.

⑤ RED ROCKET is grown as a tree or shrub and is covered with ruby-red flowers. It has pleasing bark and dark green foliage turns bronze-red in fall. 15 to 20 feet tall. Zones 5–9.

⑥ 'SIOUX' is a dark-pink-flowering cultivar with excellent fall color. Its leaves turn light pink to dark red in autumn. 15 feet tall. Zones 7–10.

Dogwood
(*Cornus* species)

Prized for their profuse blooms and horizontal branching pattern, dogwood trees are a pleasing complement to strong vertical elements such as buildings, fences, and upright trees. Valuable multi-season plants, they are excellent trees for residential landscapes.

Best site

Ever popular flowering dogwood (*C. florida*) is an understory tree preferring to grow in dappled shade. It thrives in moist, rich, well-drained soil and is a great choice for the north or east side of a structure. It will also grow well in the shade of existing trees, provided that the soil is moist and well-drained. Zones 5–9.

Kousa dogwood (*C. kousa*) is more tolerant of intense light and grows well in full sun or part shade. Moist, rich, well-drained soil is ideal. Zones 5–8.

Pagoda dogwood (*C. alternifolia*) grows as a large multistemmed shrub or a small tree. It grows best in moist, acidic, well-drained soils and partial shade. Its horizontal branches give it a layered appearance. Its showy white flowers are held above the foliage for several days in May or June. Zones 5–7.

Growing

Flowering and kousa dogwoods grow 20 feet tall and wide. Usually multistemmed trees, they are often low-branched and grow slowly. Many other forms of dogwood have shrublike habits. Dogwoods bloom in mid-spring and their glistening red fruit ripens in September. Birds often devour the juicy fruit. Medium green summer foliage turns shades of yellow, red, and orange in autumn.

Plant container-grown or balled-and-burlapped dogwoods in spring. Plant flowering dogwood in partial shade; plants growing in full sun quickly fail. Spread a 2- to 3-inch-deep layer of compost or organic mulch over the soil under the canopy to prevent moisture loss.

Prune dogwoods lightly, if needed, in late spring after flowers fade. Pruning is rarely required. Several pests, including powdery mildew and borers, infect dogwoods. Thwart pests by promoting plant health.

dogwood varieties:

1. **'CLOUD 9'** is a prolific bloomer that begins flowering at a young age. 15 feet tall and wide. Zones 5–9.
2. **CHEROKEE BRAVE** has unique pink flowers and bronze-red new foliage that turns green. 20 feet tall and wide. Zones 5–9.
3. **'WOLF EYES'** has variegated leaves and great pink to red fall color. It tends to be more of a shrub than a tree. 6 feet tall and wide. Zones 5–8.
4. **'SATOMI'** is a slow-growing cultivar with pink flowers. 20 feet tall and 15 feet wide. Zones 5–8.
   CHEROKEE SUNSET has pinkish-red flowers and foliage that does not scorch in summer sun. 20 feet tall and wide. Zones 6–9.

Elm
(*Ulmus* species)

New disease-resistant selections of this graceful beauty are making it possible to enjoy the vaselike form and fine texture of this large shade tree once again. Adaptable and easy to grow, elm trees have lovely exfoliating bark and yellow to burgundy fall color.

Best site

Elms thrive in full sun and a wide range of soils, from slow-draining clay to fast-draining sand. They are prized for their ability to tolerate tough growing conditions in urban settings and disturbed sites. Lacebark elm (*U. parvifolia*) is the most common elm today; it thrives from Iowa to Florida and from the Atlantic Coast to the Pacific.

Elms mature to large trees requiring ample space for their extensive root systems and large canopies. Use elms as shade trees in the landscape or as a natural screen along a property line. Narrow upright forms make good streetside trees in many locations. Zones 5–9.

Growing

Elms grow 40 to 80 feet tall. Medium to fast growers, they will provide shade relatively quickly. Researchers are continuously developing new and improved varieties of elms. Look for new, small to medium cultivars for residential landscapes. A 20- to 40-foot-tall elm will complement most yards.

Plant container-grown or balled-and-burlapped trees in spring. Very easy to establish, elms require little post-planting care other than regular watering until they establish a strong root system—usually within one growing season. Aim to keep the soil moist, but not waterlogged. Blanket the soil under the canopy of young trees with a 2-inch-thick layer of organic mulch to prevent soil moisture evaporation.

Prune elms in late winter or spring. Trees rarely need pruning. Remove crossing or rubbing branches or those that are damaged.

Dutch elm disease devastated plantings of American and European native species in the 1950s. Scientists have used disease-resistant Asian species to develop resistant cultivars with the pleasing arching habit characteristic of American elms. Dutch elm disease aside, elms in the landscape today are rarely troubled by pests.

YOU SHOULD KNOW
Until about 1950, American elms lined boulevards in hundreds of cities across the United States. Dutch elm disease wiped out elms of American and European origin, leaving streets devoid of shade. Lesson learned: Diversity is key. A mix of species is more likely to weather pest problems. If one species falls victim to a pest, other trees will continue to thrive and uphold the general look of the landscape.

elm varieties:

1 HOKKAIDO is a dwarf elm that is grown as a bonsai tree or in rock gardens where its petite leaves and tiny branches can be admired. 2 feet tall and wide. Zones 5–9.

2 DYNASTY is a fast-growing lacebark elm with a rounded habit and orange-yellow fall color. 40 feet tall and wide. Zones 5–9.

ACCOLADE has glossy dark green foliage that turns yellow in fall. It has arching limbs and a graceful vase shape like that of American elm. It has excellent disease resistance. 60 feet tall and 40 feet wide. Zones 4–7.

FRONTIER has glossy green foliage that turns burgundy in fall. It has a narrow upright form. 40 feet tall and 30 feet wide. Zones 4–9.

European mountain ash
(*Sorbus aucuparia*)

Grown for its stunning orange-red fruit clusters, this medium tree has equally brilliant fall foliage. The fruit ripens in early fall and is devoured by birds. It's a great tree for mixed borders and small landscapes in cool climates.

Best site

European mountain ash thrives in full sun and moist, well-drained soil. It does not tolerate poorly drained, infertile soil or any type of stressful situation. Zones 2–7.

Growing

European mountain ash grows 30 feet tall and 20 feet wide. Its leaves are composed of many small leaflets, giving the plant a fine, airy texture. Transplant container-grown or balled-and-burlapped plants in spring.

Prune as needed in late winter. The plant is susceptible to many pests including fire blight, canker, scab, and aphids. The best line of defense is a vigorous, healthy, actively growing tree.

Names to watch for

Cardinal Royal has a tidy oval shape. 35 feet tall and 20 feet wide. **Coral Fire** has red stems and red-bark branches.

Flowering cherry
(*Prunus* species)

Synonymous with spring, fragrant blossoms decorate the branches of flowering cherry trees in mid-spring. Plant daffodils and tulips under the canopy of one of these small to medium trees and enjoy the beauty of spring from ground level to the tree's uppermost branches.

Best site

Flowering cherries thrive in full sun and moist, well-drained soil. They tolerate tough growing conditions, such as drought and infertile soil, with relative ease. They do not pair well with clay or slow-draining soil. Plant flowering cherries in mixed shrub borders, where they will add a vertical element with impressive spring color. Small cultivars anchor a foundation planting, and large specimens act as shade trees in small landscapes. Highlight the springtime flowers by planting the trees in front of an evergreen backdrop. Zones 4–8.

Growing

Many species of flowering cherry are available. Although their mature size varies greatly—from 10 to 15 feet tall to more than 30 feet tall—they are alike in that they all flower before their leaves emerge, making for a magnificent springtime flower display. Flower colors range from white to deep pink. Flowering cherries produce small fruit that is valuable food for wildlife. Fall color varies from orange to deep burgundy. Some species are long-lived; others thrive for only 15 to 20 years.

Plant container-grown or balled-and-burlapped trees in spring. Flowering cherry trees are easy to establish provided they receive ample water when they are forming a new root system.

In late spring after blooms fade prune as needed to correct rubbing or crossing branches. Remove broken or damaged branches along with suckers and water sprouts anytime.

Several pests attack flowering cherry. For this reason, most flowering cherries should not be viewed as long-term landscape plants. Instead, plan for 10 to 15 years of excellent growth. Longevity beyond this span is a gift.

 YOU SHOULD KNOW Don't forget to consider summer and fall leaf color when selecting a flowering cherry cultivar. Some species are renowned for their reliable vibrant fall foliage. Others shine in summer with glossy green or purple leaves.

flowering cherry species and varieties:

1 SARGENT CHERRY (*P. sargentii*) is one of the most prolific-flowering members of the group. Sargent cherries have an upright, rounded canopy and shiny red-brown bark. Pink flowers open before leaves unfurl in spring and are followed by fruit that ripens to dark purple in midsummer. The red-tinged new leaves become shiny dark green in summer and bronze-red in fall. Unlike most other flowering cherries, Sargent cherries often surpass the typical 15-year life span. 25 feet tall and 15 feet wide. Hardy to Zone 4. **'Accolade'** has large blush-pink flowers with many petals. 20 to 25 feet tall and wide. **Pink Flair** has single pink flowers and is one of the most cold-hardy Sargent cherries.

2 JAPANESE FLOWERING CHERRY (*P. serrulata*) is another popular flowering cherry. Its springtime flowers are followed by lustrous dark green leaves that turn bronze-red in fall. Flower colors vary by cultivar. A notably short-lived group, Japanese flowering cherries usually thrive for 10 to 15 years. Hardy to Zone 5. **'Mount Fuji'** has clusters of fragrant snowy white flowers. 20 feet tall and 25 feet wide.

3 YOSHINO CHERRY (*P. × yedoensis*) is the cherry that flowers with fanfare in Washington, D.C. Its showy flowers are followed by yellow-bronze leaf color in fall. 15 feet tall and 20 feet wide. Hardy to Zone 6. **'Shidare Yoshino'** is a weeping white-flowered selection.

Fringe tree
(*Chionanthus* species)

In late spring, fringe tree debuts showy, lacy clusters of fragrant white flowers. One of the best flowering small trees, it is perfect for anchoring a foundation planting, striking in a shrub border, it also makes an enchanting shade tree for small spaces.

Best site

Fringe tree is easy to grow. It thrives in full sun to part shade. Fringe tree is adaptable to a wide range of soils. Zones 4–9.

Growing

Chinese fringe tree (*C. retusus*) is the best choice. It grows 15 to 20 feet tall and 20 to 25 feet tall. Its broad, spreading outline is useful in the landscape. Plant container-grown plants in spring and water well.

Pruning is rarely needed. If necessary, prune in early summer after flowers fade. Pests do not trouble fringe tree.

Names to watch for

Chinese Fringe Tree has upright branches and a domed shape. It flowers prolifically in June and grows 15 to 20 feet tall. Cultivars of Chinese fringe tree include **'China Snow'**, **'Ivory Tower'**, and **'Arnold's Pride'**.

Ginkgo
(*Ginkgo biloba*)

An ancient tree with timeless appeal, ginkgo has unique fan-shape leaves that turn a warm shade of golden yellow in fall. Young ginkgos have an open form, but they become dense and full as they age. It's a great shade tree and eye-catching landscape focal point.

Best site

Ginkgo grows best in full sun and moist, well-drained soil. It readily adapts to a variety of soil conditions except waterlogged sites. It is slow growing, but in time ginkgo reaches a massive size. Zones 4–9.

Growing

Ginkgo grows 35 to 60 feet tall and wide. Always purchase male selections. Female plants produce odiferous fruit that litters the neighborhood. Plant container-grown or balled-and-burlapped plants in spring. Water well after planting.

Ginkgos rarely require pruning. If needed, do so in late winter or early spring. No notable pests attack ginkgo.

Names to watch for

'Autumn Gold' is a nonfruiting strain with magnificent fall color.

Golden rain tree
(*Koelreuteria paniculata*)

An underused tree, golden rain tree has stunning yellow flowers in midsummer, handsome fruit, and a rounded habit with age. A fast-growing, medium-size tree, it makes a fine shade tree or specimen plant in the landscape.

Best site
Golden rain tree grows best in full sun and moist, well-drained soil. It tolerates tough growing conditions with ease and responds by not growing as vigorously but still performing well. Zones 5–9.

Growing
Golden rain tree grows 20 to 40 feet tall and wide. Size varies greatly by cultivar. Count on plants to produce their sulfur-yellow flowers in June and July. The plants' large leaves with many leaflets turn yellow to orange in fall.

Plant container-grown or balled-and-burlapped trees in spring and water well. If needed, prune in late winter. No notable pests attack golden rain tree.

Names to watch for
'Fastigiata' has a distinct upright, narrow habit. 25 feet tall and 4 to 6 feet wide.

Goldenchain tree
(*Laburnum × watereri*)

Ropelike clusters of flowers flow over the canopy of this small tree, dripping toward the garden in late spring. A spectacular sight in bloom, goldenchain tree is best for cool, moderate climates. Use it as a focal point in a mixed border.

Best site
Goldenchain tree grows best in full sun and moist, well-drained soil. It prefers a moderate climate where temperatures do not rise to scorching levels in summer nor dip to frigid levels in winter. It is a challenging plant to grow. Zones 6–8.

Growing
This small, rounded tree grows 20 feet tall and 15 feet wide. Plant container-grown or balled-and-burlapped plants in spring. Spread a 2-inch layer of organic mulch under the canopy.

Prune plants as needed in late winter. Goldenchain tree is a short-lived plant in most areas. Plan for 10 to 15 years of good growth. It has no notable pest problems.

Names to watch for
'Vossii' has a dense habit and pretty yellow flower clusters that are more than 24 inches long.

YOU SHOULD KNOW
Deadheading, the practice of removing spent blossoms, is common on perennial plants. Flowering trees and shrubs rarely require deadheading for great bloom. This easy-care characteristic adds to their low-maintenance landscape appeal.

Gum tree
(*Eucalyptus* species)

A tough, adaptable tree for warm climates, gum tree has color-rich, silky bark, large leaves, and impressive stature. A good shade tree or windbreak plant, it also makes an excellent privacy screen. It is a fast-growing plant and is invasive in some areas.

YOU SHOULD KNOW

Gum tree hails from Australia. Unlike many trees, gum tree has distinct juvenile and adult phases visible in its leaf development. Leaves on a young plant are often vastly different from leaves on a mature one.

Best site

Gum tree grows best in full sun and well-drained soil. It is adaptable to a wide range of soil conditions, from sand to slow-draining clay. Gum tree is very sensitive to cold temperatures. Although it is listed as hardy in Zone 9, it does not grow well in the climate extremes and humidity of the Southeast. It performs well in the more consistently warm temperatures of the Southwest. Plants that freeze often resprout from ground level. Zones 9–10.

Growing

Gum tree can reach lofty heights. Site plants where they have plenty of space to grow. Some cultivars grow 50 to 70 feet tall and about 40 feet wide. Others top out at 20 to 30 feet tall. Choose the best size for your landscape.

Plant container-grown trees in winter or early spring. Prune in winter if needed. Avoid pruning from spring through fall to discourage eucalyptus longhorn beetle infestation. Gum tree is susceptible to many pests. A vigorous, healthy, actively growing tree will overcome most pest problems with ease.

Names to watch for

There are more than 60 species of gum tree. Here are a handful of plants for the landscape.

CIDER GUM (*E. gunii*) is a large tree, at least 70 feet tall in time, with bicolor pale green-and-white bark. Juvenile leaves are nearly circular. Yellow flowers are showy in autumn. It is easy to grow in many landscape situations.

SNOW GUM (*E. pauciflora niphophila*) is a slow-growing, wide-spreading, open small tree that reaches 20 to 25 feet tall. The trunk often turns and bends, creating an interesting effect. Spear-shape silvery blue foliage contrasts gracefully with the peeling bark.

SILVER DOLLAR GUM (*E. polyanthemos*) is a fast-growing medium tree with a slender upright growth habit. Mottled, flaking bark adds to its visual and textural appeal. A hardy and tolerant tree, it thrives in dry conditions.

gum tree species:

1. **ARGYLE APPLE** (*E. cinerea*) grows 50 feet tall with reddish bark, graying on older trees. Young leaves are silvery blue. 'Pendula' is a weeping form with silver leaves.

2. **LEMON-SCENTED GUM** (*E. citriodora*) grows 70 feet tall in time and has powdery white, pink, or gray bark. Its mature leaves are lemon-scented when crushed.

3. **RED-FLOWERING GUM** (*E. ficifolia*) grows 25 feet tall and does well in coastal regions. When in full flower, its bright red blossoms are attractive against its large dark green leaves.

4. **BLUE GUM** (*E. globulus*) is potentially a very large tree but is excessively fast growing and weak-wooded. It is likely to be seriously damaged by occasional freezes in Zones 8 and 9. 'Compacta' is a dense and useful landscape tree.

Hackberry
(*Celtis occidentalis*)

A tough tree that is rapidly gaining popularity, especially as ash trees decline, the best hackberry selections have a graceful form that is similar to the dignified American elm. Use it as a low-maintenance shade tree in suburban landscapes where it has room to expand.

Best site

Hackberry thrives in full sun and moist, well-drained soil. It also grows well in challenging landscape sites. Dry, heavy, sandy, or rocky soils are no problem for hackberry. It stands up to drought, wind, and moderately wet sites too.

Hackberry is an excellent choice for the climate extremes in the Midwest and parts of the South. The tree grows with little care through periods of extended drought and intense moisture. It stands strong in fierce wind and intense urban conditions.

Use hackberry as a shade tree in the landscape or employ it as a street tree that will tolerate hot, dry planting strip areas. Zones 3–9.

Growing

Hackberry grows 40 to 60 feet tall with a similar spread. Young trees have a rough pyramidal outline. Mature trees develop a dense, full crown composed of arching, ascending branches. Plants have light green foliage. Trees produce fruits that ripen in September and October and are favored by wildlife. In fall, hackberry reliably develops golden yellow fall color. Leaves often fall quickly after turning color.

Plant container-grown or balled-and-burlapped trees in spring. Hackberry is also easy to establish from bare-root plants. Prune hackberry in late winter or early spring.

Galls commonly disfigure hackberry foliage. They appear as small growths on the leaves. No treatment is necessary for these benign but unsightly pests. Witches'-broom, caused by a combination of mites and mildew, is also common. These clusters of twiggy growth give some selections an odd appearance.

Names to watch for

'Prairie Pride' has glossy foliage and no gall or witches'-broom. Its round to oval outline resembles the form of an ash tree. It grows 50 feet tall and about 40 feet wide. **Prairie Sentinel** is an upright columnar form that grows 45 feet tall and just 12 feet wide. It is a great tree for narrow streetside planting areas.

Hackberry's yellow-green foliage is a bright spot in the fall landscape.

Hawthorn
(*Crataegus* species)

A wonderful small tree, hawthorn has creamy white springtime flowers that develop into glossy red fruits in fall. Hawthorn species have sharp spines on their branches, making the tree a good barrier or screen. Thornless varieties are useful in mixed borders.

 **YOU SHOULD KNOW**
Hawthorn trees have sharp spines. When purchasing a cultivar, read the plant tag closely. Look for a cultivar that has no thorns if you intend to plant the hawthorn in a high-traffic area.

Best site

Hawthorns grow best in full sun and well-drained soil. They tolerate a wide range of soil types and fertility levels—from infertile sandy soil to nutrient-rich loam. Hawthorns also grow well in the rigors that exist in busy urban areas.

Beware of their thorns. Sometimes exceeding 3 inches in length, the thorns pose a danger. For this reason, plant thornless cultivars in outdoor living areas and locate thorny plants away from high-traffic areas as well as away from areas where children play. Zones 4–7.

Growing

Hawthorns grow 15 to 30 feet tall and wide. They have a rounded, mushroomlike outline with mostly horizontal branching. Many selections are densely branched, giving substance to their winter silhouette. Expect plants to bloom in late spring. Glossy dark green summer foliage turns shades of orange, red, and purple in fall.

The trees' glossy, round red fruit is rarely messy because birds, squirrels, and other wildlife consume it shortly after it ripens. Fruits of Washington hawthorn hang on the tree well into winter.

Transplant container-grown or balled-and-burlapped plants in spring. Hawthorns are easy to establish and require little more than supplemental watering for two to three months after transplanting.

Prune hawthorns as needed in late winter or early spring. Hawthorns rarely require regular pruning because they develop a pleasing shape on their own. Several diseases including fire blight and cedar hawthorn rust affect hawthorns. Plant resistant cultivars and space plants to provide plenty of air circulation.

Names to watch for

ENGLISH HAWTHORN (*C. laevigata*) has abundant white flowers in spring and small red fruit in fall. Its fruit display is not as showy as cockspur hawthorn's. 15 to 20 feet tall and wide. **'Crimson Cloud'** has red flowers with white centers and good disease resistance.

hawthorn species and varieties:

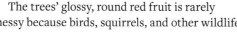

① COCKSPUR HAWTHORN (*C. crus-galli*) has shiny dark green leaves and bronze-red to purple-red fall color. Exceptionally tolerant of hot, dry conditions, it is popular in the Midwest and East. **Crusader** is a thornless variety. 20 to 30 feet tall and wide.

② WASHINGTON HAWTHORN (*C. phaenopyrum*) is the most popular landscape hawthorn thanks to its dark green foliage and long-lasting red fruit. It is one of the best hawthorns for the South. Its leaves turn orange, scarlet, and purple in fall. 25 to 30 feet tall and wide.

③ LITTLEHIP HAWTHORN (*C. spathulata*) is a small tree or large shrub reaching 20 to 30 feet tall. It has small spoon-shape leaves and peeling, exfoliating bark.

Honeylocust
(*Gleditsia triacanthos inermis*)

Large leaves composed of many petite leaflets create lovely filtered shade under a honeylocust canopy. A North America native, this large shade tree is easy to grow in northern climates and adapts to a wide range of soils. It has intense gold fall color.

Best site
Honeylocust grows best in full sun and moist, well-drained soil. It tolerates a wide range of soils as well as tough urban conditions. Most honeylocust varieties do not grow well in the Southeast. Zones 4–9.

Growing
Honeylocust grows 30 to 60 feet tall and wide. The species has sharp thorns. Choose a thornless cultivar. Transplant in spring or fall. Once established, honeylocust has good drought tolerance. Honeylocust has abundant sap flow in spring. Prune plants in summer or fall to avoid messy sap.

Honeylocust is riddled with pest problems brought about by overplanting.

Names to watch for
'Shademaster' is a vigorous plant with dark green leaves. It is considered one of the best cultivars. 45 feet tall and 35 feet wide.

Hornbeam
(*Carpinus* species)

A diverse group of small to medium trees, hornbeams have clean green foliage and a refined elegance. Use these easy-to-grow plants as screens, as hedges, or in groups to soften the side of a building. In fall their foliage reliably turns a pleasing shade of yellow-brown.

Best site
Hornbeams grow best in full sun but tolerate light to moderate shade. Plants thrive in well-drained soil. Zones 5–7.

Growing
European hornbeam (*C. betulus*) is an excellent choice for residential landscapes. It grows 30 to 40 feet tall and wide. American hornbeam (*C. caroliniana*) grows 20 to 30 feet tall and wide and is well-suited to naturalized planting areas.

Hornbeams tolerate pruning so well that small trees can be sculpted into long-lasting hedges. Prune plants in late winter or early spring. Hornbeams have no notable pests.

Names to watch for
EUROPEAN HORNBEAM 'Columnaris' has closely spaced upright growth, making it a good hedge or screen plant. **AMERICAN HORNBEAM Native Flame** has an oval outline and red fall color.

Jacaranda
(*Jacaranda mimosifolia*)

A tropical tree, jacaranda has delicate, fernlike foliage and clusters of trumpet-shape lavender flowers in spring. Its fine-textured foliage creates filtered shade, making the tree perfect for planting near outdoor living areas. Pair it with bold plants for a pleasing effect.

Best site
Jacaranda grows best in full sun and well-drained soil. This forgiving plant adapts to many soil types. Once established, it has high drought tolerance. Zones 9–11.

Growing
Jacaranda grows 25 to 40 feet tall and wide. It has an open, vase-shape habit, giving it an informal appearance. It is deciduous to semi-evergreen, depending on the cultivar and region. Plant container-grown plants in winter or early spring.

Jacaranda benefits from annual pruning. Prune side branches regularly so they remain less than half the diameter of the trunk. Branches that exceed half the diameter of the trunk often break away from the plant. No pests are of major concern.

Names to watch for
'Alba' is a white-flowered cultivar.

Japanese snowbell
(*Styrax japonicus*)

A splendid small tree to plant by a patio, near a pathway, or as a centerpiece in a border, Japanese snowbell has bell-shape pure white flowers in spring and rich red and yellow foliage in fall. Its horizontal branching adds to its graceful, elegant appearance.

Best site
Plant Japanese snowbell in full sun in moist, well-drained, humus-rich soil. Moist soil is key to good growth. In Zones 7 and 8, plant it where it will receive afternoon shade. Zones 5–8.

Growing
Japanese snowbell grows 20 to 30 feet tall and wide. The fragrant flowers in spring, dark green summer foliage, and colorful fall leaves make it an excellent small tree.

Plant container-grown or balled-and-burlapped plants in spring and water regularly until they develop a strong root system.

Prune Japanese snowbell as needed in early summer after blooms fade. It has no notable pest problems.

Names to watch for
'Fragrant Fountain' has graceful arching branches and white flowers. **'Pink Chimes'** has good heat tolerance and light pink flowers.

Japanese tree lilac
(*Syringa reticulata*)

A unique member of the lilac family, this small tree is decorated with frothy clusters of white flowers in May or June. Incredibly easy to grow, it adapts to many situations and is a good focal point in a foundation planting or mixed border, or it can stand alone in the yard.

Best site

Grow Japanese tree lilac in full sun and moist, well-drained soil. This late spring-flowering tree thrives in areas with cool summers. For that reason, it commonly doesn't perform as well in Zone 7. Zones 3–7.

Growing

Japanese tree lilac grows 20 to 30 feet tall and 15 to 25 feet wide. Its white flowers debut several weeks after common purple-flowering lilacs bloom. They have a light fragrance that is unlike common lilac, but the two plants share the same heartlike leaf shape.

Plant container-grown or balled-and-burlapped plants in spring. Prune plants after the flowers fade in spring or summer. No notable pests trouble Japanese tree lilacs.

Names to watch for

'Ivory Silk' flowers abundantly at a young age.

Japanese zelkova
(*Zelkova serrata*)

A tough, easy-to-grow tree, Japanese zelkova is a small to large shade tree, depending on the cultivar. The tree adapts to a variety of sites. It is a good tree for drought-prone regions and high wind areas. Its medium green foliage turns yellow to bronze-red in fall.

Best site

Japanese zelkova grows best in full sun and moist, well-drained soil. It thrives in fertile, deep soil but tolerates a variety of conditions with ease. Once established, the tree is wind- and drought-tolerant. Zones 5–8.

Growing

Japanese zelkova grows 25 to 70 feet tall and 15 to 50 feet wide. Be sure to choose a variety that fits the space in your yard.

Plant container-grown or balled-and-burlapped plants in spring. Prune in late winter. The tree has no notable pest problems.

Names to watch for

City Sprite grows 24 feet tall and 18 feet wide. **Green Vase** has upright, arching branches and foliage that turns orange-bronze in fall. 60 to 70 feet tall and 40 to 50 feet wide. **'Masashino'** is a narrow, upright tree that is good for tight planting spaces. 45 feet tall and 15 feet wide.

YOU SHOULD KNOW Small landscape trees, such as Japanese tree lilac and Japanese zelkova, are valuable in beds and borders, near outdoor rooms, and in large foundation plantings. Additional excellent small trees include Japanese maple, flowering crabapple, crape myrtle, and Japanese snowbell.

Katsura tree
(*Cercidiphyllum japonicum*)

With a fashion sense unsurpassed by nearly any other tree, katsura tree is an elegant species for landscapes large or small. Young leaves emerge bronze-purple, mature to blue-green, and finally turn rich yellow to apricot in the fall. It is an excellent shade tree.

Best site
Katsura tree grows best in sites with full sun and moist, well-drained soil. Ample moisture is key to good growth. Zones 4–8.

Growing
Katsura tree grows 25 to 60 feet tall and wide. Several small cultivars are well-suited to mixed borders and to large foundation beds, as well as growing near patios and along driveways.

Plant container-grown or balled-and-burlapped plants in early spring. Katsura tree can be difficult to transplant so care for it thoughtfully after planting to ensure that it establishes a strong root system.

Prune in late winter or early spring. Protect the trunks of young trees (those less than 10 years old) by wrapping them with commercial tree wrap in fall and removing it in spring. Katsura tree is relatively pest-free.

Names to watch for
'**Morioka Weeping'** grows upright with cascading branches.

Lemon bottlebrush
(*Callistemon citrinus*)

A hummingbird favorite, lemon bottlebrush is a small tree or large shrub with fuzzy bright crimson blooms. Crush a leaf from a bottlebrush plant and you'll enjoy a citrus aroma. Plant this nearly year-round bloomer in mixed borders and containers.

Best site
Lemon bottlebrush grows best in full sun and moist, well-drained soil. It tolerates a wide range of soil conditions and is an excellent choice for hot, dry locations. Zones 8–11.

Growing
Lemon bottlebrush grows 10 to 25 feet tall and wide. Petite cultivars reach just 3 to 5 feet tall and wide. Plant container-grown plants in spring and water well during the first growing season. Lemon bottlebrush does well in dry conditions after it establishes a deep, strong root system.

Prune in summer. The plant tolerates shearing well and can be sculpted into a large screen or hedge. If an upright, single-stem tree form is desired, stake the plant at planting time and remove low branches. Lemon bottlebrush has no notable pest problems.

Names to watch for
'**Little John'** is a compact, bushy plant with narrow blue-green leaves and rich red flowers. 3 to 5 feet tall and 3 feet wide.

Linden
(*Tilia* species)

A neat and tidy tree suitable for northern landscapes, linden has shiny, heart-shape dark green leaves and a defined pyramidal outline. An easy-care shade tree, it turns yellow in fall. Avoid linden where Japanese beetles are prevalent. The destructive pests will decimate the tree's foliage.

Best site

Linden grows best in full sun and moist, well-drained soil. It is legendary for tolerating soil conditions ranging from clay to dry, sandy soil. With its strong structure, linden stands up to wind- and snowstorms well and is a good candidate for planting near streets, driveways, and homes. Linden grows best in cool climates. While it tolerates Zone 7, it does not develop a pleasing form and color in the heat. Zones 3–7.

Growing

Lindens grow 20 to 80 feet tall and 15 to 40 feet wide. Dense branching and foliage give most plants a pronounced pyramidal outline. Linden trees have small yellow flowers in June or July. The flowers are not showy, but they have an intense fragrance that will perfume the landscape for a week or more.

Plant container-grown or balled-and-burlapped plants in spring or fall. Plants transplant readily and thrive when watered regularly during the first growing season.

Prune linden in late winter or early spring. Japanese beetles are the chief pests of linden trees. They will devour leaf tissue of a mature tree in a week or less, leaving a nearly defoliated, sad-looking tree in their wake. If Japanese beetles are a problem in your region, do not plant linden. Aphids and sooty mold can also trouble lindens. Vigorous, healthy plants put up the best defenses against disease.

Names to watch for

LITTLELEAF LINDEN (*T. cordata*) is the most popular linden for the landscape. Its dark green leaves turn a warm yellow in fall. Tolerant of urban conditions, it is an excellent shade tree. **SILVER LINDEN** (*T. tomentosa*) has shiny, dark green foliage with a silver backing. It has reliable yellow fall color. Ample moisture is essential for establishment of silver linden. It has better disease and Japanese beetle resistance than littleleaf linden.

linden species and varieties:

1. GREENSPIRE is a littleleaf linden with a strong central leader and uniform branching habit. 40 to 50 feet tall and 30 to 40 feet wide.
2. AMERCAN LINDEN (*T. americana*) has large heart-shape leaves that turn golden in autumn. It is also commonly called basswood. 80 feet tall.
3. SATIN SHADOW is a new selection of silver linden that grows 50 feet tall and 40 feet wide. SUMMER SPRITE is a littleleaf linden that is good for small spaces. 20 feet tall and 15 feet wide.

Magnolia (*Magnolia* species)

A shining star of the garden year-round, magnolia reigns supreme in spring. Its large cup-shape flowers in shades of white, pink, or yellow have a sweet perfume that is never overwhelming and always a welcome sign of warmer days to come. Ranging from medium shrubs to massive, long-lived trees, there is a magnolia for nearly every landscape. Magnolias are spectacular plants for mixed borders and outdoor rooms where you can enjoy their beauty and fragrance up close.

YOU SHOULD KNOW
Sweetbay magnolia (*M. virginiana*) thrives in wet, even swampy soil. Most magnolias would quickly succumb in boggy environments, but sweetbay thrives and has magnificently fragrant flowers.

Best site

Magnolias thrive in full sun or partial shade. In warm climates, plant them where they will receive a few hours of shade in the heat of the afternoon. They thrive in moist, well-drained soil that is rich in organic matter. Some varieties tolerate heavy, poorly drained soil.

Be sure to site large magnolias where they have plenty of space to expand. With a height of nearly 80 feet and a width approaching 50 feet, species like the stately Southern magnolia require a large open space. Small species can be grown in pots. With annual pruning, star magnolia (*M. stellata*) will happily reside in a container for many years.

Freezing temperatures in spring are most detrimental to magnolias. Even a brief flash of freezing weather will damage or kill fleshy flower buds or newly opened flowers. Protect susceptible plants from spring frost by planting them near a shrub border, hedge, or building that will block chilling winds. Zones 4–9, depending on the species.

Growing

From shrubs 10 to 15 feet tall and wide to 80-foot-tall trees, there are many sizes of magnolias available at garden centers. Small plants have a dense, shrublike habit with a rounded outline. Count on the medium to large trees to have an oval shape and low branching. Some species are evergreen while others drop their leaves in fall. Magnolia leaves are generally large, dark green, and thick with a waxy upper surface. Some plants bear leaves that have a fuzzy covering on the underside.

Plants bloom from early spring to summer, depending on the species. When selecting a species or variety for your region, be mindful of its bloom time. Select a plant that blooms after the last spring frost date for your area. Or inquire with neighbors, local botanic gardens, or garden center professionals about reliable blooming cultivars for your region.

Flower colors range from white to pink to yellow. Some plants have petite flowers just a couple of inches wide while other plants, such as Southern magnolia, have massive 12-inch-wide blossoms.

Plant magnolias in spring in the North and late winter or early spring in the South. Occasionally tough to transplant, young magnolias have many large roots and few fine roots to aid in water absorption. Transplant young plants carefully so as not to disturb the fine roots, and water plants regularly during the first growing season. Build a soil basin around the planting hole to contain water and direct it toward the root ball. After planting, blanket the soil with a 2-inch-thick layer of shredded wood mulch or pine straw to prevent soil moisture loss.

Enrich the soil around plants by spreading a 2-inch layer of compost or organic mulch under the canopy every spring.

Prune magnolias in spring or early summer after the blooms fade. These moderately fast-growing trees rarely require pruning and develop a pleasing structure on their own.

Magnolias are nearly pest-free when grown in rich, moist, well-drained soil and full sun or part shade. They are one of the easiest flowering trees to care for in home landscapes.

magnolia species and varieties:

1 CUCUMBERTREE MAGNOLIA (*M. acuminata*) is prized for its yellow-green flowers. This large shade tree looks like it has yellow canaries on its branches when in flower. Zones 4–8. **'Butterflies'** has deep yellow flowers 3 to 4 inches across. 18 to 20 feet tall. **'Elizabeth'** has a tidy pyramidal outline and pointed buds that open to reveal primrose-yellow flowers. 30 to 50 feet tall.

2 LOEBNER MAGNOLIA (*M. × loebneri*) is a small tree with pink or white flowers in spring. It grows 20 to 30 feet tall. Zones 5–9. **'Leonard Messel'** is frost-tolerant and has flowers with purple-pink on the outside. 15 to 20 feet tall. **'Merrill'** is a densely branched tree with white flowers. 25 to 30 feet tall.

3 SAUCER MAGNOLIA (*M. × soulangeana*) is a common and popular small flowering tree. It is beloved for its reliable bloom. Its 5- to 10-inch-wide white to pink flowers open in mid-spring on leafless branches. The fragrant flowers last for several days. Dark green leaves follow the flowers and last into fall. 20 to 30 feet tall and wide. Zones 5–9. **'Alexandrina'** has flower petals that are dark pink on the outside and white on the inside.

4 STAR MAGNOLIA (*M. stellata*) is a dense, twiggy large shrub or a small tree if the lower branches are removed. Star magnolia blooms have numerous soft, delicate petals. The bloom season lasts for 10 to 20 days because not all the flowers open at once. Leaves turn pleasing yellow in fall. Adaptable to various soil conditions and heat- and cold-tolerant, star magnolia is a great landscape plant. Zones 4–9. **'Pink Stardust'** has pretty pink flowers and grows 10 to 15 feet tall. **'Royal Star'** is an early-flowering white cultivar. It has exceptional cold hardiness. 10 to 12 feet tall.

5 SOUTHERN MAGNOLIA (*M. grandiflora*) is a mainstay in southern gardens and full of year-round charm. Its white flowers are intensely fragrant and 8 to 12 inches wide. The tree begins blooming in late spring, extending well into summer. The flowers are set off by glossy dark green evergreen foliage with fuzzy brown undersides. Zones 6–9. **'D.D. Blanchard'** is an open-branched tree with a strong pyramidal form. 50 feet tall and wide. **'Bracken's Brown Beauty'** retains its dark green leaves with cinnamon brown undersides longer than other varieties. It has 6-inch-wide creamy white flowers. 30 to 50 feet tall and wide. **'Greenback'** has green leaves with unique green undersides. Its 10-inch-wide flowers are exceptionally fragrant. 25 to 40 feet tall and 10 to 15 feet wide.

Maple (*Acer* species)

Essential shade trees and often glorious spectacles in fall, many maples are native to North America. They have a slow to fast growth rate depending on the species. For quick shade, plant a red maple. For a slow-growing, easy-care screen, plant an amur maple. Maples are generally adaptable to a variety of soils and tolerate pruning with ease.

YOU SHOULD KNOW

It's tough to grow turf under maple trees. Their dense foliage casts heavy shade, and surface roots take up much of the available water from the soil. For the best lawn under a maple tree, overseed the area with a shade-tolerant turf species. Or mulch the soil under the canopy with a 2-inch layer of organic mulch. The mulch suppresses weeds, prevents soil moisture loss, and enriches the soil as it decomposes.

Best site

Maples grow best in full sun or light shade. Large shade tree forms, such as red maple, Norway maple, and sugar maple, demand full sun for best fall coloration. The small maples, such as Japanese maple, hedge maple, and paperbark maple, thrive in full sun or dappled shade. Their leaves will develop the most intense fall color in full sun.

Maples grow best in moist, well-drained soil that is rich in nutrients, but they are exceptionally tolerant of a wide range of soils. Boxelder thrives in moist, swampy sites; red maple grows surprisingly well on dry sites.

There is a maple for nearly every size of planting space. Japanese maple thrives in containers on balconies or patios. It's also great for small-space gardens. Hedge and paperbark maples grow just 20 or so feet tall and 10 to 15 feet wide, making them great choices for small suburban landscapes. Zones 3–9, depending on species or variety.

Growing

Plant container-grown or balled-and-burlapped plants in spring or fall. Summer planting is common in some areas, but avoid planting then if possible. The heat of summer stresses a plant and could prevent it from developing a strong root system before winter. Water regularly for the first growing season after planting.

Prune maples in early summer. They produce large quantities of sap (the origin of maple syrup) from late winter to early spring, making for messy pruning at that time. Maples are rarely troubled by pests. Leaf scorch, leafhoppers, and borers attack stressed plants. Promote vigorous, healthy growth by watering plants deeply in times of extended drought and spreading a 2-inch layer of mulch under the canopy.

Japanese and related maples

(*A. palmatum*) is one of the most artistic maples. It has a broad outline with a layered branching structure similar to flowering dogwood's. Its lobed foliage is often finely cut, giving the plant a lacy appearance. Leaves may emerge chartreuse, turn blue-green, and then red, purple, or bronze in fall. Red-leaf cultivars will have green leaves if grown in the shade and red leaves if grown in the sun.

Japanese maple is a slow-growing small tree. Use it as a focal point or specimen plant in foundation plantings, mixed borders, or the lawn in small landscapes. It tolerates light shade well and thrives when planted in moist, humus-rich, well-drained soil.

Japanese maples are excellent small trees for shade gardens and borders near outdoor rooms. Their intricate foliage and brilliant fall color adds interest to the garden and is most appreciated when viewed at a close distance.

Hundreds of cultivars exist. Cultivars vary by size, leaf color, leaf texture, sunlight requirements, and hardiness. Be sure to choose a cultivar that is hardy in your area.

Promote strong growth by planting Japanese maple in moist, humus-rich soil where it will receive full sun or partial shade. Note: In Zones 7 and 8, most Japanese maples perform best when they receive afternoon shade. Choose a few and enjoy the unique character of each. Zones 5–9.

FULL MOON MAPLE (*A. shirasawanum*) is closely related to Japanese maple and used interchangably with Japanese maple in the landscape. Full moon maples are small trees with intense fall color. Like Japanese maples they are slow growing and thrive in part shade or full sun. Zones 5–7.

japanese and full moon maple varieties:

1 **'AUTUMN MOON'** is a full moon maple with rich fall color. Plant in full sun. 6 to 10 feet tall and wide. Zones 5–7.

2 **'BENI KAWA'** has light green leaves that turn yellow or orange in fall. It has bright coral red bark that is especially magnificent in the winter landscape. Grows best in full sun. The vase-shape tree grows 20 feet tall and wide. Zones 5–8.

3 **'SHISHIO IMPROVED'** has crimson-red leaves in spring that turn green in summer. A multistemmed tree or large shrub, its young stems are bright red. Fall color range is orange and red. 6 to 9 feet tall and wide. Zones 5–9.

4 **'VIRIDIS'** has a cascading mound shape. Its finely cut leaves have a lacy appearance and are bright green in summer and golden yellow in fall. Plant in part shade. 10 feet tall and wide. Zones 5–9.

5 **'BLOODGOOD'** has burgundy-red foliage that turns red-orange in fall. It has dark red bark. Plant in part shade. 15 to 20 feet tall and wide. Zones 5–8.

6 **'AUREUM'** is a full moon maple with bright yellow foliage in spring. The leaves darken to yellow-green in summer. 16 to 20 feet tall. Zones 5–7.

7 **'VILLA TARANTO'** has reddish-purple foliage in spring that turns green in summer and orange in autumn. It has a round, mounded habit and grows 6 to 10 feet tall and wide. Zones 5–8.

Large maples This group includes boxelder, Norway maple, red maple, sugar maple, and silver maple. Medium- to fast-growing trees, large maples are commonly employed as shade trees in the landscape. When planted in full sun and moist, well-drained soil, large maple trees will add 6 to 12 inches or more to their height each year. During periods of extreme drought, water plants deeply to encourage growth.

large maple species and varieties:

8 BOXELDER (*A. negundo*) is a fast-growing weak-wooded tree. Its best use is in tough growing conditions, such as swampy soil or dry, infertile sandy soil. Boxelder has medium green foliage and some cultivars have white leaf margins. It grows 30 to 50 feet tall. Zones 3–9.

9 SUGAR MAPLE (*A. saccharum*) is an excellent large shade tree. Count on sugar maple to light up the landscape with shades of red, orange, and yellow in early fall. 50 to 70 feet tall and 30 to 50 feet wide. Zones 4–8. **Green Mountain** has dark green, leathery foliage and orange to scarlet fall color. **'Legacy'** tolerates heat and is a good cultivar for the South.

10 NORWAY MAPLE (*A. platanoides*) is one of the most popular shade trees, but it is overplanted in many areas. It has a rounded canopy and dense foliage. Norway maple displays yellow fall color. An adaptable plant, it tolerates hot, dry conditions as well as a variety of soil types with relative ease. 30 to 50 feet tall and wide. Zones 4–7. There are many Norway maple cultivars. **'Crimson King'** is a commonly available cultivar with rich maroon leaves throughout the growing season. **'Deborah'** has dark green foliage and orange-yellow fall color. **Easy Street** is a narrow, upright plant that is good for streetside planting. 40 feet tall and 20 feet wide.

11 RED MAPLE (*A. rubrum*) is a tree that illuminates the fall sky in the Northeast and Midwest. Fall color varies from tree to tree, but most show fiery red color with hints of orange and yellow. A large shade tree, red maple is best for large, open lawns. Zones 4–9. There are many cultivars. **Red Sunset** has a pleasing pyramidal outline and red to orange fall color. **Autumn Blaze** is a cross between red and silver maple. Its rich, persistent fall color, strong branch structure, and dominant central leader make it a favorite tree.

12 SILVER MAPLE (*A. saccharinum*) is a fast-growing shade tree. It may grow 3 feet a year. Because of its fast growth, it has a tendency to break apart with age. Silver maple supplies quick shade, but it can become a liability as it ages. Most varieties have yellow fall color. 50 to 70 feet tall and 30 to 50 feet wide. Zones 3–9.

Small maples Easy-to-grow small trees for all types of landscapes, small maples have green summer foliage and good fall color. These 15- to 20-foot-tall plants are a valuable asset in mixed borders, as living screens, and near outdoor rooms.

small maple species and varieties:

13 **PAPERBARK MAPLE** (*A. griseum*) has beautiful cinnamon-brown to red-brown bark that peels and curls away from the trunk as the plant ages. It is especially striking in winter. It grows 20 to 30 feet tall and has good bronze-red fall color. It is adaptable and easy to grow. Zones 5–7.

14 **AMUR MAPLE** (*A. ginnala*) is a small maple with glossy, dark green summer foliage that turns shades of red and yellow in autumn. It is commonly grown as a multistemmed tree. Growing 15 to 20 feet tall and wide, it is a valuable plant for patioside plantings, small yards, and urban landscapes. It also makes a great hedge plant or focal point in a shrub border. Zones 3–8. **Red Rhapsody** has bright red fall color. **'Emerald Elf'** is a 5- to 6-foot-tall plant with red to purple fall foliage.

15 **HEDGE MAPLE** (*A. campestre*) is a small maple that accepts heavy pruning. It grows 15 to 30 feet tall and has a rounded outline and a tendency to branch all the way to the ground. As its name implies, it can be pruned into a hedge or used as a living screen. It has the best drought tolerance of all maples. Zones 5–8. **Queen Elizabeth** is a vigorous cultivar with good yellow fall color.

Mimosa
(*Albizia julibrissin*)

Mimosa, also known as silk-tree, has a tropical flair and fernlike foliage. Its fluffy pink flowers are fragrant for many weeks in early summer. Plant it near outdoor living areas where its flowers and foliage can be enjoyed up close. This small tree is short-lived.

Best site
Mimosa grows well in full sun or part shade and moist, well-drained soil. It produces the most flowers in full sun. Adaptable to a wide range of soils, it reseeds prolifically—to the point of becoming a nuisance in some areas. Plant with caution. Zones 6–9.

Growing
Mimosa grows 20 to 30 feet tall and wide. It grows fast and is often a multistemmed tree. Transplant container-grown plants in winter or spring and water them well to promote a strong root system.

Prune plants as needed in late winter or early spring. Unfortunately mimosa is quite susceptible to vascular wilt disease, which often kills plants to ground level. Webworm, leaf spot, and rust can also be destructive.

Names to watch for
'Summer Chocolate' and **'Merlot Majik'** have purple leaves. **'Rosea'** has pink flowers.

Oak (*Quercus* species)

Mighty and majestic, oaks add grace and elegance to a yard. This North American native is found from Maine to Florida with dozens of regionalized species. Long-lived plants with exceptionally strong structure, oaks have a moderate growth rate. Nearly pest-free, oaks are challenging to transplant, but once established they develop a pyramidal or broad, open form that is rarely surpassed in beauty by other trees.

> **YOU SHOULD KNOW**
> Oaks typically hold their leaves well into fall and even through winter in some cases. The leaves will likely display typical fall color for the species and then turn brown and flutter on the branches until they are blown away by strong winds.

Best site

Most oaks grow best in full sun and moist, nutrient-rich, well-drained soil. Where possible, allow the fallen leaves of deciduous species to collect below the canopy and decompose into the soil to add valuable nutrients. Zones 3–9, depending on species.

Growing

Oaks grow 30 to 80 feet tall and wide. Many plants have broad, open branching and develop contorted limbs with age. Other oaks, such as pin oak, have a strong pyramidal shape and a pronounced central leader. Be sure to plant an oak where it will have ample space to expand.

Some oaks have long taproots that make them difficult to transplant. Ease transplant shock by moving these species during winter. Water plants regularly during the first growing season. Spread a 2-inch layer of mulch over the soil under the canopy to aid in soil moisture retention.

Oak wilt is a destructive fungus that causes some oaks to wilt (and possibly die) within two to six weeks of infection. The fungus is spread by insects and enters trees through stem and trunk wounds as well as through root grafts of oaks planted close together. Limit the spread of oak wilt by pruning only when the tree is dormant, in January and February, and by spacing oaks widely. Sudden Oak Death is another destructive pest. Contact your area extension office if it is prevalent in your area.

oak species and varieties:

1 BUR OAK (*Q. macrocarpa*) is an adaptable oak that is more likely to thrive in tough urban conditions than other oaks. It is difficult to transplant. Move it in winter or early spring and water well after planting. 70 to 80 feet tall and wide. Zones 3–8.

CHINESE EVERGREEN OAK (*Q. myrsinifolia*) is a small oak for residential landscapes. Its evergreen leaves are lustrous green in summer. Transplant before buds break in spring. It is adaptable to tough soil conditions. 20 to 30 feet tall and wide. Zones 7–9.

ENGLISH OAK (*Q. robur*) is a large tree with an impressive, open canopy. Its branching structure is particularly striking in winter. A slow-growing tree, English oak is best suited for large landscapes where it has plenty of space to expand. 40 to 60 feet tall and wide. Zones 4–8. **Heritage** is a vigorous selection with leathery dark green foliage. **'Fastigiata'** is a narrow selection that grows about 50 feet tall and 15 feet wide. **Regal Prince** is another vigorous cultivar with a strong upright silhouette. It has good hardiness.

LIVE OAK (*Q. virginiana*) is the magnificent oak that graces plantations and old landscapes in the South. This spreading evergreen has horizontal branches and broad canopy. 40 to 80 feet tall and 60 to 100 feet wide. Zones 8–10. **Highrise** is an upright pyramidal form that is good for narrow spaces. 25 feet wide.

RED OAK (*Q. rubra*) is a fast-growing oak with shiny dark green foliage that turns russet red to bright red in fall. Red oak is easy to transplant and performs best in sandy loam soil. Use it as a shade tree or street-side tree. It develops a lovely silhouette, especially in winter. 70 to 80 feet tall. Zones 4–7.

CHINKAPIN OAK (*Q. muehlenbergii*) is an adaptable oak. It is well-suited to residential landscapes and grows 40 to 60 feet tall and wide. Zones 5–7.

PIN OAK (*Q. palustris*) is one of the fastest growing oaks, as well as one of the easiest to transplant. Pin oak thrives in moist, rich, well-drained soil. It is sensitive to pH; plant it in acidic soil to avoid leaf yellowing. It has a pyramidal habit and russet-bronze or red fall color. 50 to 70 feet tall. Zones 4–8.

SHINGLE OAK (*Q. imbricaria*) is an easy-care oak with a pyramidal habit and red-orange fall color. 40 to 60 feet tall and wide. Zones 5–8.

SWAMP WHITE OAK (*Q. bicolor*) is an excellent large tree for moist or swampy soil. It has medium yellow fall color and a broad, open outline. 50 to 60 feet tall and wide. Zones 4–8.

WHITE OAK (*Q. alba*) is a majestic and handsome oak with a broad, spreading canopy. Its fall color ranges from brown to wine red. It is difficult to transplant. Move it carefully and water well after transplanting. 50 to 80 feet tall and wide. Zones 4–9.

WILLOW OAK (*Q. phellos*) is a favorite oak for Zones 7 through 9. It has a pyramidal to rounded habit and a medium growth rate, unlike many of the slow-growing oaks. Fall color varies from yellow to yellow-brown to bronze-red. 40 to 60 feet tall and 30 to 40 feet wide.

Palm (Various species)

Exclamation points in the landscape, some palms serve as strong vertical accents. Other palms have a more shrublike appearance. Whether they are upright or spreading, palms have bold texture that adds instant drama to a space. Plant them in groups to form a grove or grow them singly as focal points with other tropical beauties. Be sure to choose plants that mature to a reasonable size for the planting location.

YOU SHOULD KNOW Newly planted large palms are susceptible to wind topple if the roots have not expanded into the native soil. Support large palms at planting time with three 2×4 lumber braces, placed at a 45-degree angle to the ground, and leaning against 1-foot-long pieces of 2×4s strapped vertically or banded around the palm's trunk. Protect the trunk with burlap where the 2×4s are secured. Remove the braces when the fronds are untied—about three months after planting.

Best site

Palms grow well in full sun, part shade, or full shade depending on the species. There are also palms with notable drought tolerance that thrive in dry, sandy soil as well as those that grow in boglike situations. Choose the best palms for the sunlight and soil conditions in your landscape. Zones 8–13, depending on species.

Growing

Container-grown palms are easiest to transplant. These 3- to 6-foot-tall plants are much easier to handle than massive balled-and-burlapped palms. Handle balled-and-burlapped plants with care. Take precautions to keep the root ball moist at all times. For transportation, use twine to tie the fronds together over the tender bud, or growth point, at the top of the trunk. Leave the twine in place for two to three months until new fronds begin to bulge out below the point at which the fronds are tied.

The best time to plant palms is late spring to early summer. They are actively growing at this time and they will quickly expand their root systems into the surrounding soil.

Palms require moist soil and deep watering in desert locations. In moist environments, nature provides most of the moisture, but an irrigation system is helpful to provide additional water when necessary.

Palms look their best when they have adequate nutrients. Apply a slow-release fertilizer every three months. Broadcast it around the palm's root zone.

Pruning palms is easier than many other woody plants. Simply remove fronds when they are completely brown. When removing a leaf, cut it as close to the trunk as possible.

Certain palms are susceptible to pests, but healthy, vigorous plants are generally pest-free.

palm species:

① CABBAGE PALM (*Sabal palmetto*), also called palmetto, has large, fan-shape leaves set on huge trunks, that often cross each other, giving the tree a loose, informal appearance. Cabbage palm is salt-tolerant and survives flooding well. 20 to 60 feet tall and 10 to 15 feet wide. Zones 8–10.

② CALIFORNIA FAN PALM (*Washingtonia filifera*) has large spiny leaves that hang down from the top of this tree, giving it a shaggy appearance. At nearly 100 feet tall, it has a commanding presence in the landscape. Zones 8–10.

③ CANARY ISLAND DATE PALM (*Phoenix canariensis*) is a stunning, tall, stiff-leaf feather palm that is even more exceptional when planted in rows. It is drought-tolerant and also tolerant of moist soil. A slow-growing plant, it takes many years to reach its mature size of about 60 feet. Zones 8–11.

④ MEDITERRANEAN FAN PALM (*Chamaerops humilis*) is one of the more cold-hardy palms. It can grow up to 20 feet tall with a crown reaching 15 feet wide. By the time it matures, it often has developed multiple smaller trunks surrounding a larger main trunk. It is a good palm for large containers. Zones 8–10.

⑤ NEEDLE PALM (*Rhapidophyllum hystrix*) has long, sharp needles nestled among its leaves, making it a good security hedge planting. It is relatively cold-hardy for a palm, but extended periods of cold winds may harm it. 5 to 10 feet tall. Zones 8–10.

⑥ PINDO PALM (*Butia capitata*) has 6- to 8-foot-long leaves gently arching toward the ground; this feather palm is wonderfully elegant. The trunk has a diameter of more than a foot across and nicely contrasts with the weeping fronds. Fairly cold-hardy, this palm needs protection in temperatures below 15°F to avoid damage to the leaves. It grows best in well-drained soil. 12 to 20 feet tall. Zones 8–10.

⑦ QUEEN PALM (*Syagrus romanzoffiana*) has gently drooping leaves that spread from the top of the tree in a pleasing fanlike shape. It is a very fast grower. 25 to 50 feet tall and 15 to 25 feet wide at the crown. Zones 9–11.

⑧ SAGO PALM (*Cycas revoluta*) is a slow-growing, long-lived plant that isn't a palm at all—it's a cycad. It has whorls of stiff, shiny leaves that resemble lovely feathers. It grows 20 feet tall but may take 100 years to reach that height. Zones 9–11.

⑨ WASHINGTON FAN PALM (*Washingtonia robusta*) is a lofty palm that easily grows 100 feet tall. A fast-growing plant, it is known for the collection of dead fronds that hang from the crown. It thrives in sandy soil and is very common in California. Zones 9–11.

⑩ WINDMILL PALM (*Trachycarpus fortunei*) is a single-trunk palm with massive fan-shape leaves that are symmetrically arranged around the trunk. It prefers partial shade in Zone 10. 25 to 40 feet tall with a crown about 8 feet wide. Zones 8–10.

Pepper tree
(*Schinus molle*)

An evergreen tree for hot, dry climates, pepper tree has a refreshing weeping habit when mature. It's a North American native with peeling cinnamon-color bark. Use it as an easy-to-grow shade tree in xeric landscapes.

Best site
Pepper tree grows best in full sun and well-drained soil. Once established, it needs only occasional watering, making it very drought-tolerant. It is also deer-resistant and an excellent tree for fire-resistant landscaping. Zones 8–11.

Growing
Fast-growing pepper tree grows 25 to 40 feet tall and wide. Its pleasing weeping habit develops with age. In fall and winter it has clusters of pinkish fruit that are favored by birds.

Transplant container-grown plants in winter or spring. Water new plants regularly during the first growing season to ensure they develop a deep, extensive root system. Prune plants in winter. No notable pests attack pepper tree.

Names to watch for
There are no commonly available cultivars of pepper tree.

YOU SHOULD KNOW

Xeriscaping is a common term in drought-prone areas. It is water-smart landscaping. Plants that require little water for establishment and good growth are considered xeric plants. These tough plants conserve water and often have the ability to withstand extended drought unscathed. Pepper tree is a xeric plant. Boxelder, catalpa, hackberry, and honeylocust are also water-smart plants.

Pistachio
(*Pistacia chinensis*)

Pistachio's bright orange-red to blazing red fall color makes it one of the most colorful trees for warm regions. This small to medium tree is just the right size for a front yard specimen or a streetside tree. It is easy to grow.

Best site
Plant pistachio in full sun and moist, well-drained soil. It's an adaptable species that tolerates a wide range of soils. Once established, it is drought-resistant. Zones 6–9.

Growing
Pistachio grows 30 to 35 feet tall and 25 to 35 feet wide. It has a broad rounded crown with a pleasing symmetrical form. Plant container-grown or balled-and-burlapped plants in spring. Young trees have a wayward habit and a tendency to produce multiple trunks. Remove suckers and competing leaders as soon as they are seen and stake plants to produce a sturdy upright tree.

Prune in late winter or early spring. Pistachio is not bothered by pests.

Names to watch for
There are no notable cultivars of pistachio.

Quaking aspen
(*Populus tremuloides*)

Quaking aspen gets its name from nearly circular leaves that flutter in the slightest breeze, creating a beautiful effect for both the eyes and the ears. Plant it in a grove of three or five or more to create a pretty focal point.

Best site

Quaking aspen grows well in full sun and moist, loamy sand to shallow, rocky soil and clay. It prefers cool growing conditions. Zones 1–6.

Growing

A fast-growing plant, quaking aspen attains heights of 40 to 50 feet tall and 10 to 15 feet wide. It is a short-lived tree, often killed before it reaches maturity. Quaking aspen has a long, narrow trunk and limited branching when young. As it ages it develops a rounded crown.

Plant container-grown or balled-and-burlapped plants in spring. Prune plants in late winter or spring. Many pests, including borers, cankers, various leaf spots, and powdery mildew, attack quaking aspen.

Names to watch for

There are no notable quaking aspen cultivars.

Redbud
(*Cercis canadensis*)

A graceful native tree, redbud is an early spring bloomer. Its bare branches are decorated with tufts of intense purplish-pink or bright white flowers. Plant redbud as a specimen in the landscape, in a group, or in a mixed shrub border.

Best site

Redbud grows best in full sun or part shade. It does well in the filtered sunlight of woodland-like situations. It prefers well-drained, moist, deep soil. Zones 4–9.

Growing

A small tree with a spreading, flat-topped crown, redbud grows 20 to 30 feet tall and 20 to 25 feet wide. Its trunk often divides close to the ground to give it a broad outline. Transplant container-grown or balled-and-burlapped young trees in spring or fall. Redbuds suffer from drought stress. Water plants deeply during extended dry spells.

Prune plants in spring after they bloom. Canker is the most destructive disease of redbud. It can cause stems to die. Vigorous, healthy plants are rarely affected by canker.

Names to watch for

'Alba' and **'Royal White'** have white blossoms.

Sassafras
(*Sassafras albidum*)

A native plant that displays a kaleidoscope of fall color, sassafras is a wonderful small tree for natural areas and mixed borders. Its purple-blue fruit ripens in fall and is a favorite of birds. Its thicketlike habit attracts birds to nest.

Best site
Plant sassafras in full sun or light shade and moist, nutrient-rich, well-drained soil. It grows best in acid soils. It is a great plant for naturalized areas because it will form a thicket if left unpruned, stabilizing soil and preventing erosion. Zones 4–9.

Growing
Sassafras grows 30 to 40 feet tall and 25 to 40 feet wide. It has a long taproot that makes transplanting challenging. Container-grown trees are easiest to establish. Transplant in early spring, and water regularly after planting to promote a deep, strong root system.

Prune sassafras in winter. For a single trunk, prune away suckers during the growing season. No notable pests affect the tree.

Names to watch for
There are no cultivars of sassafras.

Serviceberry
(*Amelanchier × grandiflora*)

Serviceberry is a small native tree with fragrant spring flowers, shiny blue fruit favored by birds, and spectacular fall color. Use this easy-to-grow plant in foundation plantings, mixed shrub borders, and naturalized plantings.

Best site
Serviceberry grows well in sun or partial shade. It is a common understory tree in woodlands and tolerates more shade than many other trees. It grows best in moist, well-drained soil but tolerates a wide range of soil conditions. Zones 3–9.

Growing
A small single-trunk or multistemmed tree or spreading shrub, serviceberry grows 15 to 25 feet tall and wide. It has a broad, flat-top habit. Fruit ripens in early summer; birds quickly devour it. Plant container-grown or balled-and-burlapped plants in spring.

Prune serviceberry in early summer after the plant blooms. This easy-to-grow plant has relatively few pest problems.

Names to watch for
'Autumn Brilliance' has bright red-orange fall color and clean, pest-free foliage.

Shagbark hickory
(*Carya ovata*)

A large native tree, shagbark hickory has rich golden yellow fall color. Its sweet nuts are edible and a favorite food source for squirrels. Because it has a long taproot, hickory is difficult to establish, but the effort is worth it.

Best site
Hickory grows best in full sun and moist, well-drained soil. Humus-rich soils are its preferred environment, but this common forest tree adapts to a wide range of soil conditions. Zones 4–8.

Growing
Shagbark hickory grows 60 to 80 feet tall and 50 to 70 feet wide. As it ages, its bark becomes loose and takes on a distinctive shaggy appearance. Count on its yellow-green summer foliage to turn golden in fall.

Plant container-grown or balled-and-burlapped plants in spring. Hickory has a long taproot, so take care in transplanting to limit disturbing the root ball. Prune in late winter. Hickory has no notable pests.

Names to watch for
PECAN (*C. illinoinensis*) is in the hickory family. Pecan trees grow 70 to 100 feet tall.

Stewartia
(*Stewartia pseudocamellia*)

Summer flowers and colorful fall foliage make this small to medium tree a great plant for residential landscapes. Its camellia-like white flowers have unique orange centers. It thrives in moist soil and is a great plant for rain gardens.

Best site
Stewartia grows best in full sun or part shade. In Zones 7 and 8 it grows best where it receives sunlight in the morning and shade during the hottest part of the afternoon. Moist to wet soil that is high in organic matter is essential for good growth. Zones 5–8.

Growing
Stewartia grows 20 to 40 feet tall and 15 to 30 feet wide. The plants are often difficult to establish so move them when they are small—still less than 5 feet tall. Transplant plants in early spring.

Stewartia rarely needs pruning. Prune in late winter or early spring if necessary. No notable pests attack stewartia.

Names to watch for
'Cascade' has arching, cascading branches. It is a small plant, growing just 15 feet tall.

YOU SHOULD KNOW Summer-flowering trees are less common than spring-flowering species. Stewartia is a lovely summer bloomer. Other trees that blossom in summer are littleleaf linden, catalpa, and golden rain tree.

Sweet gum
(*Liquidambar styraciflua*)

Grown for its glossy dark green summer foliage and deep purple, red, and yellow fall hues, sweet gum is a large native tree. Plant it in an open area where it has plenty of space to expand to become an impressive shade tree.

YOU SHOULD KNOW Sweet gum tree produces seeds enclosed in small round, spiny seed capsules. Smaller than ping-pong balls, the capsules can be a nuisance. The seeds are a good food source for wildlife

Best site
Sweet gum grows best in full sun and deep, moist soil. It adapts to many soil conditions, but is often slow to establish if the soil is dry or infertile. Zones 5–9.

Growing
Sweet gum grows 50 to 75 feet tall and 25 to 50 feet wide. Transplant balled-and-burlapped plants in spring. Water the plant regularly to encourage fibrous roots to develop.

Prune sweet gum in late winter or fall. It is not usually troubled by pests. Iron chlorosis can be a problem on high pH soils. It is sensitive to extreme cold in Zone 5 and occasionally shows winter injury.

Names to watch for
Cherokee is a hardy cultivar that has fall color ranging from deep burgundy to red. **'Palo Alto'** has foliage that turns orange-red in fall.

Sycamore
(*Platanus occidentalis*)

A massive and spectacular native tree in its natural habitat, sycamore is too large for the traditional residential landscape. It's by nature a messy tree, frequently dropping its large leaves, twigs, and fruits. Plant it in acreages or native areas.

Best site
Sycamore thrives in full sun and moist, rich soils commonly found alongside rivers and streams. Zones 4–9.

Growing
Sycamore grows 75 to 100 feet tall with a similar spread. Mature plants have massive trunks that display mottled bark.

Sycamore is easy to transplant in spring or fall. Prune plants in late winter or early spring. Several pests, including anthracnose, bagworm, leaf spot, sycamore lace bug, and a host of borers, attack sycamore.

Names to watch for
LONDON PLANETREE (*P. × acerifolia*) is a close relative of sycamore. It does not grow quite as tall as sycamore and is appropriate for large landscapes. It is exceptionally tolerant of tough urban conditions.

Tulip tree

(*Liriodendron tulipifera*)

Tulip tree is a massive, fast-growing tree with easy-to-identify tulip-shape flowers. It blooms in late spring. Plant it in a large landscape setting, grouping several plants together to create an impressive grove of yellow foliage in fall.

Best site

Full sun and deep, moist, well-drained soil is best for tulip tree. Zones 5–9.

Growing

Tulip tree grows 60 to 90 feet tall and 30 to 50 feet wide. Tulip tree blossoms are high in the tree canopy on mature plants.

Transplant balled-and-burlapped trees in spring. Tulip tree has a fleshy root system with few fibrous roots. Handle the root ball carefully to avoid damage, and water the plants regularly for the first growing season after transplanting.

Prune in late winter. Several pests attack tulip tree. Many can be avoided when plants are young by providing adequate moisture.

Names to watch for

'Arnold' is an upright tree for narrow spaces. It grows 25 to 50 feet tall and 8 to 10 feet wide.

Willow

(*Salix* species)

Trees for moist to wet soil, willows are beloved for their graceful, often weeping, habits. Although lovely to look at, willows demand frequent maintenance. They drop many branches, twigs, and leaves throughout the growing season.

Best site

Willows thrive in moist, rich soil. In nature they grow along streams and rivers. Zones 2–8.

Growing

Many species of willow are available. Most plants grow 15 to 50 feet tall and wide. Plant container-grown or balled-and-burlapped plants in early spring. If the soil is dry, blanket the area under the tree canopy with a 2-inch layer of organic mulch to help preserve soil moisture.

Prune plants in summer or fall. Numerous pests attack willows. Proper siting goes a long way toward ensuring a healthy, long-lived plant.

Names to watch for

GOLDEN WEEPING WILLOW (*S.* × *alba* 'Tristis') is one of the hardiest types. **PUSSY WILLOW** (*S. caprea*) is grown for its showy spring catkins. **CORKSCREW WILLOW** (*S. matsudana*) has contorted branches.

encyclopedia of conifer trees

Primarily evergreens, needled and needlelike trees add color and texture to the landscape year-round. Excellent living screens, the trees in this group block undesirable views and chilly winds to create an inviting outdoor oasis.

EASY TO GROW
Many conifers are nearly maintenance-free after planting. Simply choose an appropriate planting site and water plants well after planting.

SMALL TO LARGE
Conifers range from just a few inches tall to mighty 100-foot-tall trees. There's a conifer for every yard and garden.

RICH TEXTURE
Conifers add valuable texture to the landscape year-round. Choose stiff-needled spruce or soft-needled white pine or many other species with unique foliage.

Arborvitae
(*Thuja occidentalis*)

Soft foliage and dense growth make evergreen arborvitae a good screen or hedge plant. From globe-shape plants to tall trees, there is likely a form of this easy-to-grow plant for every landscape. Arborvitae is usually pest-free.

Best site
Arborvitae grows best in full sun, but it will tolerate partial shade. This evergreen thrives in fertile, moist, well-drained soil. Zones 3–11.

Growing
Arborvitae plants range from 1-foot-tall globes to 40-foot-tall trees. Many cultivars are fast growing. Plants are easy to establish in spring or summer. They need time to form a strong root system during the growing season, or winter browning of foliage may result. Avoid planting in fall in cold regions.

Prune arborvitae in spring or summer. Plants take pruning well and can be sculpted into intricate forms if desired. In general it is a tough evergreen and has few pest problems.

Names to watch for
'Emerald' is a compact pyramidal form with bright green foliage. 15 feet tall and 4 feet wide.

Atlas cedar
(*Cedrus atlantica*)

Don't let atlas cedar's open, awkward outline in youth dissuade you from planting this elegant tree. In time it develops picturesque horizontal spreading branches. It's a great specimen plant, and varieties with blue-hued needles are unique.

Best site
Atlas cedar grows best in full sun to partial shade. It prefers well-drained, moist, deep soil but will tolerate sandy soil or clay as long as there is no standing water. Zones 6–9.

Growing
Atlas cedar typically grows 20 to 50 feet tall and 10 to 30 feet wide. Transplant container-grown plants in spring. Spread a layer of mulch under the canopy to help preserve soil moisture.

Prune plants in spring. Atlas cedar rarely needs pruning because it develops a pleasing branch structure on its own. No significant pests attack the tree.

Names to watch for
'Glauca' has intriguing blue foliage. **'Glauca Pendula'** has a weeping habit. Its ropelike branches covered with blue needles look like water in a waterfall. 15 to 25 feet tall and wide.

Bald cypress
(Taxodium distichum)

Known for its changing colors, bald cypress debuts bright yellow-green needles in spring. The foliage becomes dark greenish blue in summer and then turns russet in fall. This big tree is best for large landscapes and moist soil.

Best site
Bald cypress grows well in full sun and moist, fertile soil. In the wild it is found in soil that is very moist or swampy. Research shows that bald cypress is very adaptable to wet, moist, or dry, soil. Zones 4–11.

Growing
This large deciduous tree grows 50 to 70 feet tall and 20 to 30 feet wide. It has a slender pyramidal habit with graceful ascending branches as it ages. Use it as a specimen in a large landscape or plant several trees together to form a grove.

Bald cypress is easy to plant from container-grown or balled-and-burlapped nursery stock. Prune in spring if necessary. The tree has no serious pest problems provided it is planted in full sun.

Names to watch for
'Shawnee Brave' has a narrow pyramidal form and deep sage green foliage in summer.

Canadian hemlock
(Tsuga canadensis)

One of the most graceful large evergreens, Canadian hemlock has drooping branches and soft, dark green foliage. Plant several hemlocks together for a lovely living screen. These long-lived plants tolerate shade very well.

Best site
Canadian hemlock grows best in full sun but it tolerates partial shade well. It thrives in cool, moist, well-drained soil. In Zone 7 plant it where it will receive afternoon shade. When planted in its preferred site, it will flourish. Zones 3–7.

Growing
This evergreen tree usually grows 40 to 70 feet tall and 25 to 35 feet wide. A young tree is easy to transplant in spring or summer.

Prune hemlock as needed in spring or summer. It tolerates pruning well and can be clipped regularly to form a hedge. Woolly adelgid is the most detrimental pest of hemlock. It is a tough pest to control and is especially prevalent in the Northeast.

Names to watch for
There are many cultivars of Canadian hemlock. Visit your local garden center to choose the best plants for your landscape.

YOU SHOULD KNOW
Plenty of evergreens are available in small or dwarf forms. These small plants have many of the characteristics of their lofty relatives, including year-round color and pronounced texture, but they are easy to integrate into small residential landscapes. Look for dwarf species of your favorite evergreens at your local garden center.

Dawn redwood
(*Metasequoia glyptostroboides*)

Dawn redwood is a stately tree that loses its needles in fall. Best for large landscapes, this pyramidal tree has a feathery appearance and makes an excellent screen. It is especially striking when planted in a group of three or five trees.

Best site
Dawn redwood grows best in full sun. It prefers moist, deep, well-drained soil but will tolerate soil that is wet or drains slowly. Dawn redwood is known to put on new growth late in the summer and into fall and that new growth is susceptible to early freezes. Zones 5–8.

Growing
A large tree, dawn redwood grows 70 to 100 feet tall and 25 feet wide. Container-grown or balled-and-burlapped plants are easy to transplant.

Pruning is rarely needed because plants develop a strong central leader and a neat and tidy branching structure. Dawn redwood rarely has pest problems.

Names to watch for
'**National**' and '**Sheridan Spire**' are narrow upright selections that grow about 60 feet tall and 20 feet wide.

Douglas fir
(*Pseudotsuga menziesii*)

A noble large evergreen that is well-adapted to northern regions, Douglas fir is commonly grown and sold as a Christmas tree but also makes a fine specimen tree. Or plant several trees together for a texture-rich small forestlike planting.

Best site
Douglas fir grows best in well-drained, moist soil. It quickly succumbs when planted in dry, poorly drained, or infertile soil. It thrives in humid environments and sunny, open growing spaces. Zones 4–7.

Growing
Douglas fir grows 40 to 80 feet tall and 12 to 20 feet wide. It has a pronounced upright habit that is spire-like. Plant a row of Douglas fir for an easy-care windbreak. It can be hard to find at garden centers, but balled-and-burlapped plants are easy to transplant and readily develop a new, strong root system.

Douglas fir rarely needs pruning. If pruning is needed, do so in spring. It has few pest problems.

Names to watch for
'**Glauca**' has blue-green needles.

YOU SHOULD KNOW Deer rarely browse Douglas fir. Other deer-resistant needled trees include several varieties of pine, spruce, and dawn redwood.

Eastern red cedar
(Juniperus virginiana)

An easy-to-grow evergreen with scalelike leaves, eastern red cedar is a pyramidal tree that makes an excellent hedge, windbreak, or screen. Cultivars with blue-tinged foliage are especially striking against a backdrop of green foliage.

Best site
Tolerant of adverse conditions, eastern red cedar grows well in infertile, gravelly soil and dry conditions. It thrives in deep, moist soil. Full sun is essential. Zones 4–9.

Growing
Eastern red cedar grows 15 to 50 feet tall and 8 to 20 feet wide. There are many cultivars available. Plants are easy to establish in spring or summer.

Eastern red cedar tolerates pruning well and can easily be sculpted into a topiary or hedge. Prune plants in summer. Cedar apple rust and bagworms attack eastern red cedar. Plants in very dry conditions are more likely to suffer.

Names to watch for
'Burkii' has gray-green foliage that develops a purple cast in winter. 35 to 40 feet tall. **'Emerald Sentinel'** has a pyramidal shape and dark green foliage. 20 to 25 feet tall.

False cypress
(Chamaecyparis species)

Dark green, blue-green, or chartreuse foliage makes this large group of evergreen trees and shrubs a valuable part of the landscape year-round. Use false cypress as a specimen plants in foundation plantings and mixed borders.

Best site
False cypress requires full sun and moist, well-drained soil. Humidity and cool conditions are preferred. Poor drainage and prolonged heat limit growth. Zones 5–9.

Growing
False cypress grows 40 to 60 feet tall and 15 to 25 feet wide. There are numerous tree and shrub forms. Some plants have a pronounced pyramidal habit; others are round or spreading.

Transplant container-grown plants in spring. False cypress tolerates pruning well. Prune plants in spring or summer. False cypress is occasionally troubled by a fungus called *Phytophthora lateralis*, which invades the root system and kills the plant.

Names to watch for
'Boulevard' has silvery blue-green foliage and a narrow pyramidal habit. It grows 20 feet tall.

YOU SHOULD KNOW Many needled and needlelike plants, such as false cypress, have foliage that is soft to the touch. Soft evergreen foliage is a great asset, especially in winter months when the bare branches of deciduous trees and inhospitable foliage of stiff-needled plants are prominent. Other plants with soft foliage include arborvitae, Canadian hemlock, and white pine.

Italian cypress
(*Cupressus sempervirens*)

Standing like a sentinel in the landscape, Italian cypress is prized for its uniform narrow, upright growth habit. It has a formal air about it and is a good choice for adding vertical interest to formal outdoor rooms.

Best site

Italian cypress grows best in full sun and well-drained soil. It thrives in hot, dry conditions where many other evergreen plants would suffer. It is fast growing. Zones 7–10.

Growing

Italian cypress grows 30 to 60 feet tall and 4 to 8 feet wide. Transplant container-grown or balled-and-burlapped plants in spring or summer. Italian cypress has good drought tolerance when it is established.

Prune plants as needed in winter. When planted in ideal conditions, Italian cypress is usually trouble-free.

Names to watch for

'**Glauca**' has blue-green foliage and grows 60 feet tall and 4 feet wide. '**Swane's Golden**' has golden yellow foliage on new growth.

Japanese cedar
(*Cryptomeria japonica*)

A great plant for a living screen, Japanese cedar is an evergreen with rich green needles that retain their intense hue through winter while many other evergreens take on a tinge of brown. It does not like extreme heat.

Best site

Japanese cedar grows well in full sun or partial shade. Choose a site that has deep, loose, nutrient-rich, well-drained soil for best growth. Japanese cedar grows best in cool climates. Zones 5–8.

Growing

Plants commonly grow 20 to 30 feet tall and 5 to 15 feet wide. Several shrubby forms exist, and they range from 2 to 10 feet tall and wide. Plant Japanese cedar in spring.

Prune plants in spring or summer. Leaf blight and leaf spot cause branch dieback on Japanese cedar. Plants in Zones 7 and 8 are most affected.

Names to watch for

'**Radicans**' has blue-green foliage and grows 20 to 30 feet tall and 7 to 10 feet wide. '**Taisho Tama**' has a pyramidal habit and good green color. It grows 15 to 20 feet tall.

Japanese larch
(*Larix kaempferi*)

A deciduous conifer, Japanese larch has grass green needles that turn yellowish gold in autumn. A large tree with graceful arching branches, it is best used in a large, open lawn where its form can be admired. It thrives in full sun and moist soil.

Best site

Full sun and moist, well-drained soil is the ideal site for growing Japanese larch. European larch, a close relative of Japanese larch, also thrives in these conditions. Zones 4–7.

Growing

Larches are known for their pyramidal outline. They grow 70 to 90 feet tall and 25 to 40 feet wide. Transplant container-grown or balled-and-burlapped plants in winter or early spring when they are dormant.

Prune larch as needed in late winter or early spring. Larch casebearer is a serious pest. This small insect eats its way into the needles, causing them to turn brown. Pesticide sprays have proved useful in combating them.

Names to watch for

'Pendula' is a weeping form that matures to less than 20 feet tall.

Leyland cypress
(× *Cupressocyparis leylandii*)

A noble evergreen that grows at a rapid clip, Leyland cypress is a quick solution for screening problem views and overcoming lack of privacy. Some members of the group grow to 100 feet tall and are best reserved for large landscapes.

Best site

Leyland cypress grows best in full sun and well-drained soil. It tolerates a multitude of adverse soil conditions from rocky to dry and sandy soil as long as the soil drains freely. Zones 6–10.

Growing

Leyland cypress can grow 100 feet tall and 20 to 25 feet wide. Transplant container-grown plants in spring and water well for at least eight weeks.

Prune in spring or summer if necessary. Plants put on as much as 3 feet of growth a year, so pruning is necessary to maintain a particular size or shape. Several pests, including bagworms, attack Leyland cypress. Root rot is a problem in poorly drained soils.

Names to watch for

'Castlewellan Gold' has handsome golden yellow foliage. **'Naylor's Blue'** has blue-green foliage and an open habit.

Pine (*Pinus* species)

A large group of evergreen plants with both tree and shrublike forms, pines thrive from frigid Zone 2 to subtropical Zone 10. Pines make valuable windbreaks, hedges, and specimen plants in residential landscapes. Needle colors range from green to blue-green to yellow-green and they are long and soft or short and stiff. More tolerant of adverse conditions than spruces or firs, pines grow in a wide range of soil conditions.

Best site

Full sun and moist, well-drained soil is optimal for growing pine. Clay soil and soil with limited nutrients challenge pines, but these tough plants usually survive, although they grow more slowly than they would if planted in optimum conditions. Scotch pine, loblolly pine, and Austrian pine are the most tolerant of tough growing conditions.

Take care when selecting a planting location for a pine. Tree forms need ample space to expand. Modern residential landscapes do not offer enough space for many pine tree species. Choose dwarf forms or large shrubs instead. Zones 1–10, depending on species.

Growing

From dwarf shrubs to massive trees, pines are available in a wide range of sizes and shapes. Many tree forms have a broad pyramidal shape in youth and then mature into a flat-topped tree with slightly arching branches and a wide trunk. Trees grow 30 to 80 feet tall and 20 to 50 feet wide. Shrub forms of pine are as small as 1 foot tall and wide.

Needle color adds diversity to pines. Some plants have medium green to dark green needles while others have needles that are blue-green or gold. Texture ranges from the soft, slender needles of Eastern white pine to the stiff, large needles of Austrian pine.

When purchasing container-grown pines, choose plants that are less than 3 feet tall. Small container-grown plants are easy to transplant and establish in the landscape. Large container-grown plants are challenging to establish because of their limited root systems. Pines larger than 3 feet tall should be field-grown and balled-and-burlapped for best establishment success.

Transplant container-grown or balled-and-burlapped plants in spring. Water plants regularly during their first growing season to ensure they develop a strong, vigorous root system. Spread a 2-inch-deep layer of mulch around plants to prevent soil moisture loss.

Pines withstand pruning well, if it is done at the right time. Prune plants in late winter or early spring before new growth begins. Pines generally require little pruning.

Pines can be sculpted into a hedge or a screen. To encourage dense growth, pinch the young growing tip (called a candle) back by half in late spring or early summer before the new needles expand. Carefully consider the result before pruning interor branches. Pines, like many conifers, produce new growth only at their branch tips. Plants will not generate new branches in the interior portions of the plant.

Pines are susceptible to many pests. Needle blight, twig blight, various rusts, and numerous weevils and aphids attack pines. The best defense against pests is prevention. Strong, healthy plants shrug off pests. Choose a planting site with well-drained soil and water plants deeply in drought to combat stress.

pine species:

① EASTERN WHITE PINE (*P. strobus*) has a graceful appearance thanks to its long, soft needles. The thin needles range in color from light green to dark green to blue-green. One of the fastest growing pines, it has many horizontal branches. 50 to 80 feet tall and 20 to 40 feet wide. Zones 3–7.

② AUSTRIAN PINE (*P. nigra*) is a very hardy tree that withstands the challenges of city growing more than many other pines. It has stiff needles and an upright habit, making it a good windbreak or living screen. 50 to 60 feet tall and 20 to 40 feet wide. Zones 4–7.

③ JACK PINE (*P. banksiana*) is a medium to large pine with dull dark green needles. It is valued for its extreme hardiness. Jack pine is a good choice for windbreaks in cold regions. 35 to 50 feet tall and wide. Zones 2–6.

④ JAPANESE BLACK PINE (*P. thunbergii*) has good heat and drought tolerance and transplants easily. It is especially useful in seashore plantings because it tolerates salt spray. Its dark green needles are lovely. This medium tree has an irregular pyramidal outline. It grows 20 to 40 feet tall and wide. Zones 6–8.

⑤ JAPANESE RED PINE (*P. densiflora*) has orange-red bark when it is young. The bark peels off in thin scales. This medium to large tree has many horizontal branches and a broad pyramidal outline. It needs plenty of space to grow. Dragon's-eye pine **'Oculis Draconis'** has yellow striped needles. 40 to 60 feet tall. Zones 4–7.

YOU SHOULD KNOW
Evergreen plants are not truly evergreen. Most plants keep their needles for two or three years. Needled evergreens generally shed one-third of their needles in autumn. The shed needles are quickly replaced, and gardeners rarely notice the needle drop. White pine is an exception. It tends to drop its needles in dramatic fashion. When viewed from a distance, the tree will have a pronounced yellow-green appearance when it is in the process of dropping needles. As soon as the old needles have dropped, white pine regains dark green coloring.

6

pine species cont.:

6 LACEBARK PINE (*P. bungeana*) has mottled, exfoliating bark that displays shades of brown, gray, russet, and green. It is a lovely specimen plant. 20 to 50 feet tall and 20 to 35 feet wide. Zones 5–7.

7 LIMBER PINE (*P. flexilis*) is a very adaptable species and one of the best pines for the Midwest and East. It is a small to medium tree with a horizontal branch habit. Limber pine is adaptable to adverse growing conditions, making it a good choice for planting sites with clay or sandy soil. 30 to 50 feet tall. Zones 4–7.

8 LOBLOLLY PINE (*P. taeda*) is easy to transplant and tolerant of difficult growing conditions. This fast-growing pine is a good choice for a living screen. It has a loose, open habit that is not particularly becoming, but it makes up for it by growing where other pines fail. 30 to 60 feet tall. Zones 6–9.

9 MUGO PINE (*P. mugo mugo*) is a popular shrubby pine. Its broad, spreading, bushy habit is useful in foundation plantings and mixed borders. Mugo pine is easy to transplant and thrives in moist, deep soil. See page 195 to learn more about mugo pine. Zones 3–7.

10 PONDEROSA PINE (*P. ponderosa*) is native to western North America and grows best in that region. It prefers deep, moist, well-drained soil and does not tolerate shade. Use this massive tree in large landscapes. 60 to 100 feet tall and 25 to 30 feet wide. Zones 3–7.

11 SCOTCH PINE (*P. sylvestris*) was once a popular species but pests have limited its use in recent years. There are many pines superior to Scotch at this time. Choose a more pest-resistant species. Zones 4–7.

12 SWISS STONE PINE (*P. cembra*) is a slow-growing pine that has an intriguing flat-top habit when mature. Its picturesque habit makes it a lovely specimen plant. 20 to 25 feet tall and wide. Zones 4–7.

7
8
9
10
11
12

Spruce *(Picea* species)

An evergreen staple in cool climates, spruce is grown for its dense, pyramidal habit. Many cultivars within the group develop graceful arching branches that complement their strong upright nature. A quick survey of your local garden center will reveal many cultivars that mature at 30 to 40 feet tall—a great size for small residential landscapes. Spruce is an ideal plant for a living screen and provides excellent wildlife habitat.

YOU SHOULD KNOW
Take time to carefully consider the repercussions of removing the lower branches of spruce and other pyramidal evergreens. Frequently, needled evergreens have the most pleasing habit when their lower branches extend to the ground. Once the branches are removed, new growth will not sprout along the bare trunk. After pruning, the tree's new look is permanent.

Best site

Spruce grows best in full sun and moderately moist, sandy, well-drained soil. It will tolerate average soil as long as it has adequate moisture and is well-drained. It grows poorly in clay. Spruces do not grow well in the heat and humidity of the Southeast. They also languish in the heat and intense dry conditions of the Southwest. Zones 2–7.

Growing

Spruces range from 1-foot-tall dwarf plants to massive 60-foot-tall trees. Take time to select a cultivar that, when it matures, will complement your landscape.

Spruce has an extensive shallow, spreading root system that makes it easy to transplant. Young plants that are more than 3 feet tall should be transplanted as balled-and-burlapped specimens. Smaller container-grown plants are easy to establish. Water plants regularly during the first growing season after transplanting to ensure they develop an extensive root system.

In early spring, prune spruce as necessary to groom and shape the plant. Pruning is rarely necessary except to develop a more dense habit on some species. To increase the density of a plant, prune the growing tips (called candles) by half shortly after they elongate but before the needles fully develop. Avoid pruning the central leader of spruce trees. Doing so can disfigure the tree's strong pyramidal shape.

Several pests attack spruce, but none are severe enough to limit planting the species. Mites, aphids, and bagworms are the most prevalent. Good cultural practices, including watering deeply in times of drought, promote healthy, vigorous growth that is resistant to pests. Rhizosphaera needle-cast disease may develop on mature spruces that are planted close together or in locations with poor air circulation. Allow ample spacing to prevent the problem. Cytospora canker can affect trees as well. Prune out affected limbs.

spruce species and varieties:

① **COLORADO SPRUCE** (*P. pungens*) is a popular spruce prized for its cultivars that sport blue foliage. An adaptable plant that tolerates dry conditions better than most other spruces, it develops into a large plant with stiff branches extending all the way to the ground. Its bulky habit overwhelms most residential landscapes. 30 to 60 feet tall and 10 to 20 feet wide. Zones 3–7. **'Glauca'** has pleasing blue-green needle color and matures at about 60 feet tall.

② **ENGELMANN SPRUCE** (*P. engelmannii*) is a large tree best adapted to cool climates and locations with well-drained soil. Like Colorado spruce, many selections have bluish needles. Mature trees reach 70 to 100 feet tall. Zones 2–5.

spruces species and varieties cont.:

③ NORWAY SPRUCE (*P. abies*) is an elegant medium- to fast-growing tree with a strong upright habit and lovely branches that become pendulous with age. It has dark green needles. Norway spruce develops into a massive plant and is challenging to integrate into residential landscapes. It is best reserved for acreages, commercial landscapes, and parks. 40 to 60 feet tall and 25 to 30 feet wide. Zones 4–7.

④ ORIENTAL SPRUCE (*P. orientalis*) is superior to Norway spruce and white spruce in most residential landscapes because of its lustrous dark green needles, slow growth rate, and upright habit with horizontal branching. Use Oriental spruce as a specimen in small landscapes. It needs protection from harsh winter winds and is not a good choice for a windbreak. 50 to 60 feet tall and 20 feet wide. Zones 4–7.

⑤ SERBIAN SPRUCE (*P. omorika*) has a pleasing pyramidal shape with short ascending branches, making it a great choice for most residential landscapes. It also makes a fine tree for planting along a street or boulevard thanks to its narrow upright form. An adaptable species, Serbian spruce tolerates urban environments but grows best in deep, rich soil that is moist and well-drained. 50 to 60 feet tall and 20 to 25 feet wide. Zones 4–7.

⑥ WHITE SPRUCE (*P. glauca*) is one of the most tolerant spruces of adverse landscape conditions. It withstands heat, wind, drought, and cold. Use it as a specimen, hedge, or windbreak in large landscapes. Count on white spruce to develop a dense pyramidal habit. 40 to 60 feet tall and 10 to 20 feet wide. Zones 2–6. There are many dwarf forms of white spruce. **'Conica'**, often marketed as dwarf Alberta spruce, is one of the most popular white spruce cultivars. It matures to 12 feet tall after about 25 years of growth.

White fir
(Abies concolor)

Also called concolor fir, white fir is the most widely adapted member of the fir family. It withstands drought, heat, and cold and has a rigid pyramidal outline in the landscape. Plant it along a property line or use it as a living screen.

Best site

White fir grows best in full sun and in deep, rich, well-drained soil. It quickly succumbs in clay soil. In general, firs grow best in cool regions and in moist conditions. Zones 4–7.

Growing

A slow-growing tree, white fir grows 30 to 50 feet tall and 15 to 30 feet wide. It is easy to transplant as a balled-and-burlapped specimen or a small container-grown plant.

Prune white fir as necessary in late winter or early spring. Keep pruning to a minimum. White fir takes on a ragged, unkempt appearance when its lower branches are removed. Few pests trouble white fir.

Names to watch for

'Candicans' has bright silver-blue needles and a narrow upright form. 30 to 40 feet tall and 20 feet wide.

Yew pine
(Podocarpus macrophyllus)

The shiny dark green needles of yew pine make this evergreen a great hedge or screen plant in warm climates. It is also useful along foundations because it is slow growing, tolerates some shade, and responds well to pruning.

Best site

Yew pine grows best in full sun and well-drained soil. It will grow in partial shade and poor soil but doesn't tolerate soggy growing conditions. It has excellent heat tolerance and is deer-resistant. Zones 8–10.

Growing

Both tree and shrub forms of yew pine are available. Tree forms grow 20 to 30 feet tall and 10 to 20 feet wide. Yew pine is easy to establish from container-grown plants. Transplant yew pine in spring.

Prune yew pine in spring or summer. Root rot is problematic in wet soil. Be sure to plant in well-drained soil.

Names to watch for

Icee Blue has gray-blue young foliage that matures to blue-green. It has a pyramidal habit and grows 15 to 25 feet tall and 15 feet wide.

encyclopedia of shrubs

Low-maintenance and bursting with flowers and colorful foliage, shrubs soften home foundations, lend structure to mixed borders, and create privacy around outdoor rooms.
Use this encompassing roundup of the best shrubs to choose the perfect plants for your landscape.

WEEKS OF COLOR
Add bloom power to your landscape with flowering shrubs. Many shrubs flower for several weeks in spring, summer, fall, or winter.

PLANT STRUCTURE
Call on shrubs to provide year-round form in planting beds. From foundation plantings to perennial beds, shrubs add structure.

LIVING SCREEN
Use shrubs to create a fence or visual backdrop. Always-changing shrubs make a dynamic living screen.

Arborvitae
(*Thuja occidentalis*)

A valuable shrub (or tree, depending on the cultivar), evergreen arborvitae is prized for vigorous growth in tough growing situations. It tolerates heat, cold, drought, and poor soil.

Best site

Arborvitae grows best in full sun or part shade and moist, well-drained soil. This fast-growing shrub tolerates a host of conditions including challenging urban environments. Zones 3–7.

Growing

Shrub forms of arborvitae are usually pyramidal or round. They range from 1 foot tall and wide to 20 feet tall and 10 feet wide. Foliage color ranges from chartreuse to deep green.

Transplant container-grown plants in spring or early summer. Water plants regularly for at least eight weeks after transplanting to promote an extensive root system.

Arborvitae tolerates pruning well. Prune in spring. Plants are susceptible to bagworms, spider mites, and deer browsing.

Names to watch for

'Golden Globe' has yellow foliage and a round habit. It grows 2 to 3 feet tall and wide. **'Little Gem'** is another round form. It has dark green needles and grows about 3 feet tall and wide.

Aucuba
(*Aucuba japonica*)

An easy-to-grow evergreen shrub for warm climates, aucuba thrives in shade. Its shiny dark green leaves add luster to foundation plantings and barren areas in shade.

Best site

Plant aucuba in part or full shade. Full shade is necessary in Zones 9 and 10; too much sun will make the plant's leaves turn black. Aucuba grows best in well-drained soil that is high in organic matter. Zones 7–10.

Growing

Aucuba is a slow-growing plant that usually grows 6 to 10 feet tall and 5 to 8 feet wide. It has an upright, rounded habit and a neat and tidy appearance. Its red, berrylike fruit ripens in autumn and persists until the following spring.

Transplant container-grown plants in spring. Aucuba transplants easily. Prune aucuba as needed in late winter or early spring. This easy-care shrub does not have any significant pests.

Names to watch for

'Picturata' has dark green leaves with bright golden yellow centers. Use it to light up a dark, shady location. It grows 4 to 6 feet tall and wide. **'Rozannie'** has bright red fruits and a spreading, compact habit. It grows 3 feet tall and wide.

Beautyberry
(*Callicarpa dichotoma*)

Abundant clusters of violet berries decorate beautyberry through fall. This medium shrub has attractive green foliage and is a perfect plant for mixed borders. Birds flock to the berries.

Best site

Beautyberry grows best in full sun and moist, well-drained soil. It will tolerate partial shade but does not produce as much of the colorful fruit. Zones 5–8.

Growing

Beautyberry grows 3 to 6 feet tall and wide. It tolerates pruning well and can be kept small with annual trimming. Container-grown plants are easy to transplant in spring or early summer. Water plants regularly for at least the first eight weeks after transplanting to encourage development of a strong root system.

Prune beautyberry in early spring. It can be sheared to create a sculpted appearance. Beautyberry does not have any notable pests.

Names to watch for

'**Profusion**' is prized for its copious berry production and bronze-tinged new foliage. '**Early Amethyst**' has striking yellow-bronze fall foliage that is a wonderful complement to its purple berries.

Beautybush
(*Kolkwitzia amabilis*)

A deer-resistant flowering shrub, beautybush has hundreds of arching branches decorated with clusters of bell-shape pink flowers in late spring or early summer.

Best site

Beautybush grows best in full sun and moist, well-drained soil. A fast-growing plant, it will quickly fill a planting space. Zones 4–8.

Growing

A medium shrub, beautybush grows 6 to 10 feet tall and about as wide. Its foliage turns dull yellow-red in fall.

Beautybush is easy to transplant as a container-grown plant in spring or early summer. Water plants regularly for at least the first eight weeks after transplanting.

Prune beautybush by removing about half of the oldest canes each year after the plant flowers. Cut the canes back to ground level. Or rejuvenate beautybush by cutting all the canes back to ground level in spring. Beautybush has no notable pests.

Names to watch for

Dream Catcher has golden yellow foliage in summer. In autumn the foliage becomes bright orange-red.

YOU SHOULD KNOW
Pair wildlife-friendly shrubs such as beautyberry with perennials that are valuable food sources, and your yard will likely become a gathering place for feathered and furry friends. Here are a few great perennials for wildlife:

Aster (*Aster* species)
Bee balm (*Monarda didyma*)
Coneflower (*Echinacea purpurea*)
Penstemon (*Penstemon*)
Sage (*Salvia* species)
Yarrow (*Achillea* species)

Bluebeard
(*Caryopteris × clandonensis*)

Blooming in mid- to late summer when many other plants are languishing in the heat, bluebeard adds cool blue-purple color to the garden. Cut this mounding shrub back to ground level each spring.

Best site
Bluebeard grows best in full sun and moist, well-drained soil. Plant it in loose, loamy soil for best results. Zones 5–9.

Growing
Bluebeard grows 2 to 3 feet tall and wide, and it has a neat, mounded habit. Plant it near patios, entryways, and other high-traffic areas where its long-lasting blue-purple flowers will be enjoyed. It attracts butterflies.

Bluebeard is easy to transplant as a container-grown plant in spring. Water new plants for at least eight weeks after planting.

Prune bluebeard back to within 6 inches of the soil each spring. It blooms on new wood and will send up new shoots with copious blooms. Pests rarely trouble bluebeard.

Names to watch for
Lil Miss Sunshine has yellow-green foliage that is an exciting contrast to its purple flowers. **Petit Bleu** is a popular selection with compact growth, many deep blue flowers, and dark green foliage. **Sapphire Surf** is a new compact introduction with numerous blue blooms.

YOU SHOULD KNOW Bluebeard is a popular shrub for perennial borders. Like most perennials, it too is cut back to ground level before the growing season starts. Very easy to care for, bluebeard blooms reliably year after year.

Bottlebrush buckeye
(*Aesculus parviflora*)

A native plant with a bold presence, bottlebrush buckeye is a spreading, multistemmed shrub with large leaves and 8- to 12-inch-long bottlebrush-like flowers in early summer. It's a great plant for mixed borders.

Best site
Bottlebrush buckeye grows well in full sun or part shade. Choose a site with moist, well-drained soil that has plenty of organic matter. Zones 4–8.

Growing
Growing 8 to 12 feet tall and wide, bottlebrush buckeye has an informal spreading habit that is especially striking when paired with upright needled evergreens and other plants with defined outlines.

Transplant container-grown or balled-and-burlapped plants in early spring. Water plants regularly for at least eight weeks after planting to ensure they develop a strong root system.

Bottlebrush buckeye rarely needs pruning because it is a slow-growing plant and naturally develops a graceful form. If necessary, prune in early spring. Rejuvenate plants by cutting stems back to ground level in early spring. This shrub has no significant pests.

Names to watch for
There are no notable cultivars of bottlebrush buckeye readily available.

Boxwood
(*Buxus* species)

One of the most popular hedge plants, boxwood has lustrous evergreen leaves. With regular pruning it can be sculpted into orbs, spires, cubes, and nearly any other shape you desire. A slow-growing plant, it has a pleasing shape when sheared just once a year.

Best site

Boxwood grows well in full sun or part shade and moist, well-drained soil. In warm climates it thrives when provided a few hours of shade during the hottest part of the day. Drying winter winds are problematic in cold regions. Site plants near other shrubs or buildings where they will be protected from harsh winter winds.

Create a formal edge along a garden bed with a neat and tidy row of nearly round boxwood. Or add easy-care structure to a mixed border with a pyramidal boxwood. Zones 4–9.

Growing

The height and width of boxwood varies greatly by cultivar. Plants range from 1 foot tall and wide to 10 feet tall and 5 feet wide. Choose a cultivar that has a mature size appropriate for the intended planting location. Leaf color also varies slightly. Some cultivars have dark green foliage while others have foliage that is medium green.

Transplant container-grown plants in spring. Water plants regularly for at least eight weeks after transplanting to promote a strong root system. Keep boxwood's root zone cool by spreading a 2-inch layer of organic mulch, such as cocoa hulls or shredded bark, over the area.

Prune boxwood anytime from spring to midsummer. Do not prune plants in fall because pruning will spur tender new growth that can be damaged by cold winter temperatures. Gas- or electric-powered shears make efficient work of pruning a boxwood hedge.

Canker, boxwood blight, leaf spots, and root rot are fungal diseases that affect boxwood. Yellow-tinged foliage in winter is a sign of winter burn. Foliage often returns to its lustrous green hue in spring. Prevent winter burn by protecting plants from drying winter winds.

varieties:

1. **CHICAGOLAND GREEN** is prized for keeping its green color through winter. 2 to 3 feet tall and wide.
2. **'GREEN MOUNTAIN'** is very hardy and has a pyramidal shape. 5 feet tall and 3 feet wide.
3. **'GREEN MOUND'** is a hardy cultivar that grows 3 foot tall and wide.
4. **'GOLDEN TRIUMPH'** is a low-growing mounded plant with showy golden yellow leaf margins. 3 feet tall and wide.

Burning bush
(*Euonymus alatus*)

Boasting one of the most consistent fall color shows, burning bush turns bright red in autumn. A slow-growing plant with a natural mounded habit, its unique corky-winged branches are delightful in winter.

YOU SHOULD KNOW
Pruning promotes blooms on butterfly bush. Prune away old, faded blooms and the shrub will produce new blooms. Spend five minutes a week pruning butterfly bush and you'll enjoy fresh, colorful flowers until the first frost.

Best site
Burning bush is easy to grow in full sun or partial shade. It is adaptable to a wide range of soil conditions. Moist, well-drained soil is preferred. Burning bush is an excellent choice for planting near a foundation or in a mixed border. Plant several of these shrubs together to form a colorful hedge. In some areas of the country it has become invasive. Zones 4–8.

Growing
Burning bush grows 8 to 12 feet tall and wide. It tolerates pruning well and is easy to maintain at a smaller stature. Transplant balled-and-burlapped or container-grown plants in spring. Drought stresses burning bush. Water plants deeply during times of drought.

Prune burning bush as needed in spring or summer. Burning bush has no serious pests.

Names to watch for
'Compactus' makes an excellent hedge or screen. It grows 10 feet tall. **'Cole's Compact'** grows 6 to 8 feet tall.

Butterfly bush
(*Buddleja davidii*)

A delightful source of nectar for butterflies and bees, butterfly bush blooms from early summer until fall. The showy flowers of this mounding shrub are an easy-care addition to beds and borders of all sizes.

Best site
This fast-growing shrub prefers moist, well-drained soil and full sun, but it grows in a variety of conditions. In Zones 5 and 6 the aboveground growth is killed in winter, but the plant regrows from its roots. Butterfly bush is invasive in some areas. Plant with caution. Zones 5–9.

Growing
If left unpruned, butterfly bush has an open, rangy habit and stands 10 to 15 feet tall and wide. Most often it looks best when pruned to 6 to 12 inches above the ground in early spring. Butterfly bush blooms on new growth. Bloom colors range from dark purple to shades of pink to yellow and white.

Butterfly bush is easy to transplant from container-grown plants in spring or summer.

It is rarely troubled by pests.

Names to watch for
'Honeycomb' has lovely yellow flowers with a sweet perfume. **Flutterby Petite Blue Heaven** grows just 30 inches tall and wide.

California lilac
(*Ceanothus* species)

A lovely shrub for the dry, moderate climate along the West Coast, California lilac is adorned with clouds of purple-hued blooms for weeks in spring. It is a great source of nectar for butterflies. Plant it near an outdoor living area and enjoy the winged visitors.

Best site

California lilac grows best in full sun and well-drained soil. It thrives in dry, arid climates and is an excellent plant for areas with water restrictions. California lilac quickly succumbs in the humidity and heavy soil of the Southeast. Zones 7–10.

Growing

California lilacs vary greatly in habit. Some plants are groundcovers. Other cultivars are mounded shrubs or small trees. Most cultivars have evergreen foliage.

Transplant container-grown plants in early spring. Monitor soil moisture carefully; plants are sensitive to excessive moisture. Do not water if the soil is moist 2 inches below the surface.

Prune plants in summer after blooms have faded. Remove dead, damaged, or crossing branches anytime. Aphids and whiteflies occasionally attack California lilac. Dislodge the pests with a strong spray of water.

Names to watch for

There are many California lilac cultivars. **'Julia Phelps'** has dark green leaves and indigo flowers. It is a long-blooming reliable plant. It grows 5 to 7 feet tall and 7 to 9 feet wide. **'Victoria'** is a tall upright cultivar that makes a fine hedge. It has deep blue flowers and grows 9 feet tall and 10 to 12 feet wide. **Dark Star** has arching branches and sapphire blue flowers. Its dark green leaves are almost black in winter. It grows 2 to 4 feet tall and 6 feet wide.

NEW JERSEY TEA (*C. americanus*) has misty white, pink, or blue flowers and is adapted to moist climates of the Midwest, Northeast, and Southeast. Small rounded cultivars of this native plant are excellent additions to mixed borders and foundations. **'Marie Simon'** has light pink flower clusters and a tidy rounded habit. It grows 2 to 3 feet tall and wide. **Marie Bleu** has misty blue flowers in spring that are followed by showy red seed heads.

California lilac varieties:

1 **'WHEELER CANYON'** has dark blue flowers and grows 6 feet tall when pruned regularly. It will grow 8 to 10 feet tall and wide if unpruned.

2 **RAY HARTMAN** has light blue flowers and glossy dark green leaves. It grows 20 to 25 feet tall and 15 feet wide.

3 **'JOYCE COULTER'** is a creeping California lilac. It grows 2 feet tall and 8 feet wide and has purple-blue flowers.

4 **'SNOW FLURRY'** is a tender California lilac with large white flower clusters. It is reliably hardy in Zones 9–10.

5 **EL DORADO** (*C. thyrsiflorus* 'Perado') is a variegated form of California lilac. It bears light blue flowers in spring and grows 8 feet tall and wide. Zones 7–11.

Camellia
(*Camellia* species)

Referred to as the rose of winter, camellia adds striking beauty to the sleepy winter landscape. Cup-shape, multipetaled flowers adorn small to medium evergreen shrubs for weeks. When not in bloom, camellia's glossy dark green foliage is a good backdrop for other plants.

Best site

Camellias grow best in moist, well-drained soil that is rich in organic matter. They languish in dry, sandy soil and should not be planted in such sites. Camellias prefer partial shade; a site with morning sun and dense afternoon shade is best. These slow-growing shrubs fare particularly well in the shade of pines. In Zone 7, site camellias in microclimates where they will be protected from extreme winter conditions. Protected areas along evergreen hedges, brick walls, and the side of a building will limit winter damage. Zones 7–9.

Growing

Camellias grow 5 to 15 feet tall and 4 to 10 feet wide. Very slow growing, they put on a few inches of new growth a year and are easy to maintain at a small stature. Camellia flower colors range from white to red and include variegated blossoms.

Transplant container-grown plants in spring. Water for at least eight weeks after transplanting to encourage plants to develop a strong root system. Spread a 2-inch-deep layer of organic mulch, such as pine straw, over the shrub's root zone to limit moisture loss and keep roots cool in the heat of summer.

If necessary, prune camellias after bloom. Because they are slow growing, they rarely need pruning. Leaf spot diseases and numerous scale insects attack camellias. The best defense against these pests is to promote healthy, vigorous growth. Water plants during extended dry periods and renew the mulch layer annually.

Names to watch for

There are more than 2,000 camellia cultivars. Many cultivars perform best in a specific region. Visit local botanic gardens and arboretums, talk with neighbors and garden center professionals, and inquire at your local extension service to learn which cultivars are best for your region.

varieties:

1. **'APPLE BLOSSOM'** has pearly white blooms that are edged with pink. It blooms in midwinter. Its dense habit makes it a good choice for a hedge. 10 feet tall and wide.
2. **'PEARL MAXWELL'** has double shell-pink blooms in late winter and glossy green foliage. 6 to 8 feet tall and wide.
3. **PINK PERFECTION** has cotton candy-pink blossons and dark green foliage. It blooms in mid- to late winter. 6 to 8 feet tall and wide.
4. **'YULETIDE'** has showy red blooms with bold yellow centers. It flowers in midwinter. 8 to 10 feet tall and wide.

Chaste tree
(*Vitex agnus-castus*)

Blue is elusive in the garden, but chaste tree annually serves up lush bouquets of purple-blue blossoms that are sure to catch your eye. Plant this large shrub or small tree in a mixed border or put it to work as a specimen plant.

Best site
Chaste tree grows best in full sun and moist, well-drained soil. After it is established, it will withstand drought with ease. Zones 5–9.

Growing
Fast-growing chaste tree grows 5 to 8 feet tall in Zones 5, 6, and 7. In Zones 8 and 9 it can be pruned into a tree form and grows 15 to 20 feet tall. White-, pink-, and purple-flowered cultivars exist. Transplant container-grown plants in spring.

Chaste tree has an open, irregular habit and benefits from pruning in most landscapes. There are several ways to prune chaste tree. For a refined habit, cut the entire plant back to 6 to 12 inches above the ground in late winter. Prune for a treelike form by selecting four or five main trunks and removing all side branches in early spring. Chaste tree is rarely troubled by pests.

Names to watch for
'Abbeville Blue' has large deep blue flowers.

Chokeberry
(*Aronia* species)

Grown primarily for its red or black berries that remain on the branches well into winter, chokeberry also has bold red-orange fall color. Plant this spreading shrub in mixed borders or natural areas, where it will provide valuable wildlife habitat.

Best site
Chokeberry is adaptable to a wide range of soil conditions. It grows well in moist, well-drained soil but also readily grows in dry, gravelly soil or wet planting locations. It prefers full sun but will grow in partial shade. Zones 4–9.

Growing
A multistemmed, suckering shrub, chokeberry spreads slowly to form a large colony. Plants grow 6 to 10 feet tall and spread 3 to 5 feet.

Transplant container-grown plants in spring and water regularly for eight weeks after planting. Prune chokeberry in late water to control its spread. Rejuvenate plants by pruning canes back to ground level. Chokeberry has no serious pests.

Names to watch for
RED CHOKEBERRY (*A. arbutifolia*) has glossy red berries.
BLACK CHOKEBERRY (*A. melanocarpa*) has purple-black berries and burgundy fall color.

varieties:
① **'MORTON'** is a black chokeberry that is also known as Iroquois Beauty. It has orange to deep-red fall color. It is compact and grows 2 to 3 feet tall and 5 feet wide.
② **'BRILLIANTISSIMA'** is a red chokeberry that has long-lasting berries and leaves that turn scarlet in autumn. 6 to 10 feet tall and 3 to 6 feet wide.

YOU SHOULD KNOW
Fresh chokeberries are so astringent that they are said to induce choking. Birds even find them disagreeable and stay away from them. When cooked, however, chokeberries lose their potency and are suitable for jams and jellies.

Cotoneaster
(*Cotoneaster* species)

Best adapted to the North and West, cotoneaster is a quick-growing plant with evergreen or deciduous foliage that often displays atractive red, yellow or orange fall color. Use it as a hedge or as a groundcover in a mixed shrub border.

Best site
Cotoneaster grows best in full sun and well-drained soil. Sandy loam or gravelly soil is best. Cotoneaster grows well in the North and West but succumbs to the humidity and wet soil conditions of the Southeast. Zones 4–10.

Growing
Groundcover types of cotoneaster grow 1 to 2 feet tall and spread 6 feet wide. Upright cotoneasters are typically grown as hedges and reach heights of 8 to 12 feet tall.

Transplant container-grown or balled-and-burlapped plants in spring. Prune cotoneaster as needed in late winter or early spring. Cotoneaster suffers from pests during drought. Water plants deeply during dry conditions.

Names to watch for
CREEPING COTONEASTER (*C. adpressus*) has dark green foliage and lustrous red fruit. It is a groundcover type and its leaves turn reddish purple in fall. Zones 4–8.

Daphne
(*Daphne* species)

Welcome winter or spring with daphne's sweetly fragrant flowers. Particular about its growing conditions, daphne demands moist, well-drained soil and partial shade. Grow it near an entryway or outdoor living area to enjoy its scent.

Best site
A great plant for partial shade, daphne thrives in moist, well-drained soil that is rich in organic matter. Daphne is notorious for being a short-lived shrub. Zones 4–9.

Growing
Semievergreen, evergreen, and deciduous, daphnes are mounded plants that usually grow 2 to 4 feet tall and wide. Some species small leaves add fine, airy texture to the landscape.

Transplant container-grown plants in spring. Spread a 2-inch layer of mulch over the root zone to keep soil cool and moist. Water plants regularly after planting and continue watering as needed during dry conditions.

Prune daphne in early summer. Plants respond well to annual pruning. Several pests attack daphne, but none are serious.

Names to watch for
'Carol Mackie' has pink flowers and variegated leaves. It is semievergreen and a great plant for foundation plantings. Zones 5–8.

Deutzia
(*Deutzia* species)

Add glorious elegance to spring with the flower-cloaked branches of deutzia. Plant this mounding shrub in mixed borders where it will anchor the spring bloom show. It is a low-maintenance medium shrub and it takes pruning well.

Best site

Deutzia grows in any well-drained soil. Plant it in full sun or very light shade for the best form and bloom production. Zones 4–8.

Growing

A medium shrub, deutzia grows 2 to 5 feet tall and wide. Plants have slender ascending branches that are particularly complementary to dense pyramidal plants such as needled evergreens. Transplant container-grown plants in spring and water regularly for at least eight weeks to encourage a strong root system.

Prune deutzia in late spring or early summer after flowers fade. Every few years, rejuvenate plants by cutting them back to 6 inches above ground level. Deutzia is generally pest-free.

Names to watch for

KALMIA-FLOWERED DEUTZIA
(*D.* × *kalmiiflora*) has light pink flowers and rich plum fall color. 4 to 5 feet tall. **'Nikko'** has white flowers and deep burgundy fall color. 2 feet tall and 5 feet wide.

Dogwood
(*Cornus* species)

Like its tree-form relatives, dogwood shrubs flower in spring and often sport colorful fall foliage. Bright red or yellow branches, which are outstanding in the winter, set these easy-to-grow shrubs apart in a mixed border.

Best site

Plant dogwood in moist, well-drained soil and full sun or part shade. Plants develop the best stem coloring in full sun. Shrub-form dogwoods are often quite vigorous and will overrun nearby plants if not pruned regularly. Zones 3–7.

Growing

Dogwood grows 3 to 10 feet tall and wide. The shrubs' white flowers blend in with the foliage. The flowers are followed by fruit, which is quickly eaten by birds.

Transplant container-grown plants in early spring. To promote best winter stem color, prune shrubs in late winter by removing one-third of the oldest stems. Or rejuvenate plants by cutting all the stems back to 6 inches above ground level. Dogwoods are rarely troubled by pests.

Names to watch for

RED-TWIG DOGWOOD (*C. alba*) is the most popular dogwood shrub. **'Siberica'** has bright coral red stems. **YELLOW-TWIG DOGWOOD** (*C. sericea* 'Flaviramea') has yellow stems.

False cypress
(*Chamaecyparis* species)

False cypress carries a shrub border through winter with style. Its soft evergreen foliage and upright, or mounding habit make a statement 365 days a year. Choose a variety with chartreuse foliage for a burst of easy-care color.

Best site

Plant false cypress in full sun and moist, rich, well-drained soil. Plants thrive in cool, moist environments where they are protected from drying winds. Zones 4–8.

Growing

False cypress shrubs grow 3 to 20 feet tall and 1 to 10 feet wide. Dwarf or compact varieties are often less than 3 feet tall and wide. They are well-suited for perennial borders, rock gardens, and small space plantings.

Transplant container-grown plants in spring. Prune false cypress in late winter or early spring as needed. Plants develop a pleasing form on their own and rarely need pruning. Plants are rarely troubled by pests.

Names to watch for

'Golden Charm' has golden yellow new foliage and feathery, stringlike clusters of foliage. It has a mounding habit. 5 to 6 feet tall and wide. 'Baby Blue' has bright silvery foliage and is ideal for a hedge. 6 feet tall and 4 feet wide.

Firethorn
(*Pyracantha coccinea*)

Spiny stems make firethorn an admirable barrier plant—would-be intruders will think twice about tangling with this evergreen. Its bright orange-red berries sparkle in the fall and winter landscape and provide food for wildlife.

Best site

Firethorn grows best in full sun and well-drained soil. It will grow in part shade but will produce fewer of its spectacular fruits. Zones 5–9.

Growing

A medium to large shrub, firethorn grows 6 to 18 feet tall and wide. Its stiff, thorny branches give it an open, wayward appearance. Prune it annually to maintain a good form and keep this fast-growing plant in bounds.

Transplant container-grown plants in spring. Choose the site carefully. Prune firethorn annually in late winter or early spring. Remove wayward stems and cut back overly vigorous stems to promote compact growth. Fire blight and scab are troublesome to firethorn. Choose resistant cultivars.

Names to watch for

'Kasan' has orange-red fruit. 'Lowboy' is a fast-growing groundcover type with orange berries. 3 feet tall and 5 feet wide.

Flowering quince
(*Chaenomeles speciosa*)

Flowering quince is a welcome sight when it blooms in winter or spring. Its vibrant white, pink, red, or orange flowers are a welcome sight after a long winter. Add it to a mixed border or pair it with spring-blooming bulbs.

Best site
Flowering quince grows best in full sun and moist, well-drained soil. It readily adapts to poor soil conditions, including dry, rocky soil. It is a good choice for low-water landscapes. Zones 4–8.

Growing
A medium shrub, flowering quince grows 3 to 6 feet tall and wide. It has a twiggy, spreading outline that is less than elegant. Leaves and debris collect in its rambling branches.

Plant container-grown plants in early spring. Prune plants in spring after flowers fade. For best bloom, rejuvenate plants every year by cutting stems back to 6 inches above ground level.

Flowering quince is troubled by leaf spot that results in the plant dropping as much as 75 percent of its foliage by midsummer. Excess moisture in spring is often the cause.

Names to watch for
'Pink Storm' has camellia-like large pink blossoms. **'Orange Storm'** and **'Scarlet Storm'** have similar large flowers.

Forsythia
(*Forsythia × intermedia*)

Forsythia's sulfur-yellow flowers illuminate the spring landscape. Plant this fast-growing shrub in groups to form an informal hedge or screen. Its awkward habit is ill-suited to foundation plantings and formal borders.

Best site
Plant forsythia in well-drained soil and full sun. It is drought-tolerant and grows well in infertile soil. Zones 5–8.

Growing
Forsythia grows 8 to 10 feet tall and 10 to 12 feet high. It is a popular shrub, but its upright and sometimes wayward stems coupled with its tendency to spread make it a challenging plant to integrate into the landscape. Use it as a low-maintenance hedge at the back of a property or carefully select a well-behaved cultivar that has a pleasing outline.

Transplant container-grown plants in spring. Forsythia looks best when pruned annually just after it finishes blooming. Trim wayward stems and suckers. Forsythia has no major pests.

Names to watch for
There are many forsythia cultivars. **'Gold Cluster'** has flower-packed stems in spring.

YOU SHOULD KNOW
Plants like forsythia and flowering quince are susceptible to late-season frosts that will turn the petals of just-opened flowers brown. Hard freezes often damage swollen buds set to open in a few days. Late spring frosts and freezes rarely harm plants. They simply temper the bloom show for the year.

Fothergilla
(*Fothergilla* species)

One of the best native shrubs for fall color, fothergilla has a tidy round shape and sweetly fragrant flowers in spring. This multiseason plant is perfect for foundation plantings and mixed borders and is also a good addition to containers.

Best site
Fothergilla grows best in full sun or partial shade. It flowers more prolifically and develops better fall color in full sun. For best results it requires moist, well-drained soil that has plenty of organic matter. Zones 5–8.

Growing
A small to medium shrub, fothergilla grows 2 to 8 feet tall and wide. Its leathery dark green leaves turn hot shades of yellow, orange, and scarlet in fall. Before the leaves emerge in spring, the plant debuts bottlebrush-like white flowers. The fragrant flowers perfume the garden.

Transplant container-grown plants in spring. Water plants regularly for at least eight weeks after transplanting to ensure they develop a strong root system. Fothergilla rarely requires pruning. If necessary, prune in late spring after blooms fade. Plants are generally pest-free.

Names to watch for
'Mt. Airy' has blue-green summer foliage and consistent yellow-orange and red fall color.

Gardenia
(*Gardenia jasminoides*)

Gardenias make their presence known with an intoxicating fragrance that will waft to the neighbor's home. Waxy evergreen foliage is a perfect backdrop to the shrub's spectacular white flowers, which remain open for weeks in summer.

Best site
Gardenias grow best in full sun or partial shade and moist, well-drained soil that is high in organic matter. The best location is near a patio or entryway where their beauty and fragrance will be appreciated. Zones 8–10.

Growing
A medium shrub, gardenia grows 4 to 6 feet tall and wide. It has a dense upright habit. Transplant container-grown plants in spring. Water plants regularly for at least eight weeks after planting to encourage the development of a strong fibrous root system.

Prune plants as needed in late winter. Several pests may trouble gardenias, but none cause serious damage.

Names to watch for
'August Beauty' produces hundreds of flowers from May through October. **'Chuck Hayes'** is an especially hardy cultivar (to Zone 7) with semidouble flowers. It blooms in early summer and again in September.

Glossy abelia
(Abelia × grandiflora)

Evergreen to semievergreen, glossy abelia is decorated with fragrant bell-shape flowers from late spring to fall. Some varieties have striking variegated foliage. Glossy abelia beckons butterflies and is a lovely plant for a hedge or mixed border.

Best site
Glossy abelia grows best in full sun or partial shade. It thrives in well-drained, moist soil. It is grown as an herbaceous perennial in Zone 5; winter temperatures kill all stems above ground, but the plant quickly regrows from its roots. It is reliably hardy in Zones 6–9.

Growing
A medium shrub, glossy abelia grows 3 to 6 feet tall and wide. It has a dense rounded habit with many arching branches.

Transplant container-grown or balled-and-burlapped plants in early spring. Prune glossy abelia in late winter or early spring. In Zones 5 and 6, remove copious amounts of deadwood in spring. Glossy abelia is generally pest-free.

Names to watch for
'Little Richard' is a compact variety that grows 3 feet tall and wide. Its green foliage takes on orange-pink hues in fall. **'Mardi Gras'** has pink-white-and-green-variegated foliage. It is a great shrub for containers as well as the landscape.

Heavenly bamboo
(Nandina domestica)

A rare combination of durability and elegance makes heavenly bamboo an all-star shrub. This medium-height evergreen has flower clusters in spring and showy bright red berries in fall. It's a great plant for mixed borders and foundation plantings.

Best site
Heavenly bamboo grows well in a variety of light conditions—from full sun to dense shade. When grown in full sun, its evergreen foliage takes on reddish hues in winter. It grows best in moist, fertile soil. Zones 6–10.

Growing
Heavenly bamboo grows 6 to 8 feet tall and slowly spreads by suckering to form a colony 10 feet wide. It has a distinctly upright growth habit and requires annual pruning to maintain its dense growth.

Transplant container-grown plants in spring. Prune heavenly bamboo annually in spring. Begin by removing one-third of the plant's oldest canes. Prune remaining canes back by one-third to one-half their length to promote dense new growth. Heavenly bamboo is relatively pest-free.

Names to watch for
'Firepower' has leaves that glow red in winter. 2 feet tall and wide. **'Gulf Stream'** has good winter color. 3 feet tall and wide.

Holly (*Ilex* species)

Bright red fall berries and spiny evergreen foliage are hallmarks of holly, but this large group of plants is diverse and includes deciduous shrubs as well as those that bear purple-black fruit. All hollies are tough, reliable plants and make excellent hedge and mixed border plants. Grow several varieties and enjoy their unique habits, berries, and foliage. Male and female plants are necessary for fruit production.

YOU SHOULD KNOW

Hollies require a male plant and a female plant for fruit production. If a plant has fruit it is a female. Fruitless plants are males. The best holly pairs are species or varieties that bloom at the same time. Plant tags on female plants often indicate good choices to use as pollinators.

Best site

Holly is very adaptable. It grows well in sun or part shade. Moist, well-drained soil encourages vigorous growth and fruiting, but plants stand up to heat and drought with ease. Zones 3–9, depending on species.

Growing

Hollies range from 3 to 15 feet tall and 3 to 10 feet wide. Some holly shrubs can be sculpted into small trees. Evergreen shrubby hollies include Chinese and Japanese holly, and inkberry. Their shiny dark green leaves are an asset year-round, adding color and texture to the landscape. Winterberry is a deciduous holly.

Holly plants bear female flowers or male flowers only. When at the nursery, check a cultivar's plant tag to learn if it is a male or female. Male pollinator cultivars are often suggested on the plant tag of female holly plants. One male pollinator plant will pollinate six or more female plants. Recently, growers have begun planting male and female cultivars in the same container, eliminating the need to purchase two separate holly plants.

Transplant container-grown plants in spring. Water plants regularly for at least eight weeks after planting to encourage them to develop a strong root system. Holly tolerates pruning but often is most pleasing when it is pruned minimally and develops a natural form. Prune plants as needed in late winter.

Spider mites and scale are occasionally problematic. Most hollies are relatively pest-free.

Names to watch for

CHINESE HOLLY (*I. cornuta*) is referred to as a bulletproof holly. It is evergreen and extremely adaptable to tough growing conditions. It shows great resistance to heat and drought. It has brilliant red berries. Zones 7–9. There are more than a hundred cultivars of Chinese holly. A few notable ones include: **'Dwarf Burford'**, with its good berry production and dense growth habit; **'Needlepoint'**, prized for its good fruit production and upright form, is good for hedges and screens.

JAPANESE HOLLY (*I. crenata*) has a dense, refined habit without pruning. It has lustrous dark green foliage and black fruit. Its small rounded leaves provide a great textural contrast in the landscape. Zones 6–8. Great cultivars include: **'Chesapeake'**, with its dense, upright pyramidal form; **'Helleri'**, a popular hedge holly growing 4 feet tall and 5 feet wide.

INKBERRY (*I. glabra*) is a North American native holly that tolerates shade and wet soil with ease. It has purple-black fruit and shiny dark green leaves. It is evergreen. Inkberry's slightly open form gives it a softer texture than other hollies. Zones 5–9.

WINTERBERRY (*I. verticillata*) is a deciduous holly with bright red berries that often persist into winter in cold regions. Because this holly loses it leaves in winter, the fruits are especially prominent. Zones 3–9. There are many excellent winterberry cultivars. Select plants that mature to a size that complements your landscape.

holly species and varieties:

1 **'CARISSA'** (*I. cornuta*) is a low-growing cultivar that is perfect for creating a hedge. 3 to 4 feet tall and wide. Zones 7–9.

2 **'BURFORDII'** (*I. cornuta*) will produce large red berries without a pollenizer and when planted with a pollenizer it will produce a prolific number of berries. It has an upright habit and grows fast. 15 feet tall and 10 feet wide. Zones 7–9.

3 **NORDIC** (*I. glabra*) is a fruitless plant with deep green foliage and a rounded shape. It is a male selection and is a good pollenizer for other inkberry hollies. 3 to 4 feet tall and wide. Zones 3–9.

4 **'AFTERGLOW'** (*I. verticillata*) is a deciduous holly with large clusters of bright red berries. It has glossy large dark green leaves. **'Jim Dandy'** holly is a good pollenizer for 'Afterglow.' 6 to 8 feet tall and wide. Zones 3–9.

5 **'CHINA GIRL'** (*I. × meserveae*) is a mounding evergreen holly that produces bright red berries. Pair this evergreen holly with **'China Boy'** for good fruit set. 8 to 10 feet tall and 6 to 8 feet wide. Zones 4–9.

6 **'WINTER GOLD'** (*I. verticillata*) is a deciduous holly with unique golden yellow berries. **'Southern Gentleman'** is a good pollenizer for 'Winter Gold'. 8 feet tall and 10 feet wide. Zones 4–9.

Hydrangea (*Hydrangea* species)

With a bloom season that stretches from early summer to fall, hydrangeas are some of the most prolific flowering shrubs. Hydrangeas planted in moist, fertile soil and sun or part shade will yield hundreds of big, showy blooms over the course of a growing season. Use dwarf cultivars in small-space gardens and perennial plantings. Reserve large plants for mixed shrub borders or group several together to create a long-blooming hedge.

Best site

There are several types of hydrangeas, and each type thrives in specific growing conditions. Learn more about a specific hydrangea's optimal growing conditions in the summaries on the following pages. In general, hydrangeas thrive in moist, well-drained soil that is rich in organic matter.

Most hydrangeas thrive in partial shade. Some shade is essential in warm regions where hydrangeas suffer in intense heat. Full sun is acceptable in cool regions, provided the soil is moist. Zones 3–9, depending on hydrangea type.

Growing

Hydrangeas grow 3 to 10 feet tall and wide. Smooth and panicle hydrangeas spread slowly by suckers to form a large colony. Bigleaf and oakleaf hydrangeas are more apt to maintain a constant width over time.

Choosing the right hydrangea for your landscape begins with choosing a plant hardy in your area. Gardeners in cold-winter areas can grow smooth, panicle, oakleaf, and a few bigleaf hydrangeas. Gardeners in warm-winter areas have most success with bigleaf and oakleaf hydrangeas. Panicle hydrangeas are the most adaptable hydrangeas and are best suited for harsh climates or growing conditions.

Transplant container-grown hydrangeas in spring. Incorporate a 2-inch-thick layer of compost into the soil before planting. Spread a 2-inch-thick layer of compost or organic mulch over the root zone to keep roots cool, limit soil moisture loss, and improve soil fertility. Water hydrangeas deeply in drought. Plants wilt quickly when the root zone dries.

Hydrangeas are generally pest-free, and consistently moist, well-drained soil is key to healthy, vigorous plants.

Names to watch for

BIGLEAF HYDRANGEA (*H. macrophylla*) is the showy, colorful hydrangea that has flowers in shades of pink or blue. Thick, waxy, dark green foliage is a pretty backdrop to the often massive flowers. Recent plant introductions have made this group of hydrangeas more adaptable. Once relegated to cool, moderate climates like the Pacific Northwest and mild areas of the Eastern Seaboard, new reblooming cultivars make it possible to grow bigleaf hydrangea in climates with temperature extremes.

Most bigleaf hydrangeas bloom on old wood. Winter damage results in no flowers on these cultivars. New cultivars, such as **Endless Summer**, bloom on both new and old wood, making it possible to have flowers in harsh-winter areas such as the Midwest.

The color of bigleaf hydrangea blossoms is determined by the acidity of the soil. Acidic soils, those with a pH measure of 5.0 to 5.5, create deep blue flowers. Soils with a pH above 6.5 will develop pink flowers. In between, purple flowers result. Adjust soil pH and hydrangea flower colors with wettable sulfur or dolomitic lime. Both products are available at garden centers. For blue flowers, broadcast ½ cup of wettable sulfur over 10 square feet of soil and water it in well. For pink flowers, broadcast 1 cup of dolomitic lime over 10 square feet of soil and water it in. It may take several months for the soil pH to change and influence the hydrangea's flower color.

Mophead bigleaf hydrangea varieties:

1 ENDLESS SUMMER is an easy-to-grow bigleaf hydrangea for cold regions. It blooms on new and old wood, ensuring flowers even when the winters are particularly cold. 3 to 5 feet tall and wide. Zones 4–9. **Blushing Bride** is a white cultivar that blooms on new wood and **Twist-n-Shout** has pink-and-purple flowers on its new wood.

2 'BERLIN' is part of the **Cityline** series and has sturdy upright stems and a compact habit that highlights its color-rich flowers. 1 to 3 feet tall and wide. Zones 5–9. There are several members of the **Cityline** series and all are known for their strong upright habit.

3 'ALL SUMMER BEAUTY' has large pink-and-blue ball-shape flower clusters in neutral soil and rich blue flowers in acidic soil. It is a great cultivar for cutting flowers. 3 to 5 feet tall and wide. Zones 5–9.

4 'LEMON DADDY' is a bold-color shrub for brightening up a dark corner. Grown more for its chartreuse foliage than its flowers, it has bright green foliage from early spring through fall. 3 to 5 feet tall and wide. Zones 6–9.

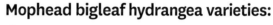

YOU SHOULD KNOW

Hydrangeas are great for container gardening. Panicle and bigleaf types thrive in containers. Complement an upright hydrangea with trailing plants such as bacopa or calibrachoa.

LACECAP BIGLEAF HYDRANGEA

(*H. macrophylla*) Flat-top flower clusters are characteristic of lacecap hydrangeas. The fertile flowers in the center of the cluster are surrounded by showy infertile flowers. As with mophead hydrangeas, the flower color of lacecaps is dependent on soil pH.

lacecap bigleaf hydrangea varieties:

- **⑤ 'LANARTH WHITE'** is an elegant cultivar with white flowers and a broad, spreading habit. 3 to 4 feet tall and wide.
- **⑥ ENDLESS SUMMER TWIST-N-SHOUT** is a reblooming lacecap hydrangea that sports pink-and-blue flowers. 5 feet tall and wide.
- **⑦ MIDNIGHT DUCHESS** has dark green foliage, purple-black stems, and clusters of pink flowers that mature to green. 4 to 6 feet tall and wide.

OAKLEAF HYDRANGEA (*H. quercifolia*) is grown as much for its beautiful foliage as it is for its large flower clusters. Oakleaf hydrangea's leaves are shaped like those of red oak, as its name implies. The large leaves turn shades of red, orange, and yellow. No other hydrangeas boast such a colorful fall show.

Oakleaf hydrangea is hardy to Zone 5, but because it blooms on old wood, occasionally the tender buds are damaged during harsh winters and the plant does not bloom the following year. The spectacular foliage nearly makes up for the lack of bloom. In Zone 5, plant oakleaf hydrangea in a protected location.

This medium shrub grows 5 to 10 feet tall and wide. It has an upright, irregular habit and is best integrated into a mixed shrub border or planted in large groups and used as a hedge. It has white flowers that turn tawny brown in fall.

Prune oakleaf hydrangea in August after the blooms fade. Zones 5–9.

oakleaf hydrangea varieties:

- **⑧ 'ALICE'** has 10- to 14-inch-long flower clusters and burgundy-red autumn color.
- **⑨ 'SNOWFLAKE'** is known for its dense flower spikes and strong stems.

PANICLE HYDRANGEA (*H. paniculata*) is the most cold-hardy hydrangea—it grows well in Zone 3. Blooming on new wood, panicle hydrangea is not bothered by extreme winter temperatures. Cut it back to 6 inches above ground level in late fall or early spring, and it will send up new stems and bloom with gusto in summer. Pruned plants grow 3 to 5 feet tall and wide.

Panicle hydrangea has pyramidal flower clusters that are white when they open and slowly fade to maroon or pink as they age. The flowers are often showy for eight weeks or more in summer as they slowly change colors. This long bloom show makes panicle hydrangea a welcome member of a mixed shrub border, perennial garden, or entryway garden where easy-care color is always appreciated.

Panicle hydrangea is the most adaptable hydrangea. It tolerates soil ranging from moist to sandy. It grows best in moist, well-drained soil and partial shade. Unlike most hydrangeas, it tolerates full sun well in Zones 3–5. Grow in part shade or shade in Zones 6–8. Zones 3–8.

panicle hydrangea varieties:

10 TARDIVA is a late summer blooming cultivar with many cone-shape white flower clusters.

11 LIMELIGHT produces chartreuse blooms in midsummer. The flowers change to pink in fall.

12 PINKY WINKY has unique two-tone flowers that open white and then turn dark pink from the bottom of the flower cluster up.

13 VANILLA STRAWBERRY has 10-inch blooms that debut white and then turn light pink before darkening to magenta.

YOU SHOULD KNOW

Hydrangea flowers are easy to preserve; the dried flowers are lovely year-round. Harvest flowers after the blooms are fully opened. Cut stems 10 to 12 inches below the flowers. Remove any leaves and gather the stems in bundles of six to eight. Tie the bundles together with a piece of twine and hang them in a dry, dark place. The hydrangeas will be thoroughly dry in about six weeks.

SMOOTH HYDRANGEA. (*H. arborescens*) is a hardy hydrangea with large white flowers. A vigorous grower, it grows 3 to 5 feet tall and wide and spreads to form large colonies in rich, moist soil.

Smooth hydrangea develops the best habit when it is pruned back to 6 inches above the ground in fall or early spring. Plants bloom on new wood. The long-lasting flowers add color for four weeks or more in the South and eight weeks or more in the North. Zones 4–9.

smooth hydrangea varieties:

14 INCREDIBALL has massive white flowers on sturdy stems that resist flopping. The flowers open green, mature to white, and fade to green.

15 'ANNABELLE' has 12-inch-wide white blooms. Stake plants to prevent the stems from bending to the ground.

16 BELLA ANNA has unique magenta-pink flowers on strong stems.

Japanese barberry
(*Berberis thunbergii*)

An easy-to-grow shrub with colorful foliage, Japanese barberry is a popular shrub for foundation plantings and shrub borders. It spreads invasively in some areas. Use it with caution, and don't grow it where cultivation of it is restricted.

Best site
Barberry tolerates a wide range of growing conditions—from blazing sun and dry soil to partially shaded sites with slow-draining soil. It thrives in urban environments where many other shrubs fail. Zones 4–10.

Growing
A small to medium shrub, Japanese barberry grows 2 to 6 feet tall and 2 to 7 feet wide. Green-, burgundy-, and yellow-leaf cultivars are available. Expect barberry to put on a good fall color show. Its showy red berries create a decorative effect into winter.

Transplant container-grown plants in spring or summer. Prune Japanese barberry in spring or summer. This tough shrub is usually pest-free.

Names to watch for
'Crimson Pygmy' is the most popular barberry in the market place. It is petite—growing just 2 feet tall and wide. It has deep crimson foliage throughout the growing season. **Golden Ruby** has yellow-and-burgundy-variegated leaves.

YOU SHOULD KNOW Japanese barberry is so tolerant of adverse growing conditions that it has become invasive in some locations. New Hampshire and Massachusetts have banned the sale of barberry. Plant breeders are focusing on developing sterile cultivars that have a well-behaved garden presence. Stay tuned!

Japanese pieris
(*Pieris japonica*)

A graceful plant for foundations or borders, Japanese pieris has clusters of fragrant white flowers in spring. An evergreen, it thrives in part shade and is a good complement to perennials and small shrubs that also thrive in shade.

Best site
Japanese pieris grows in moist, organic soil and partial shade. It is a great companion plant for azaleas and rhododendrons. Zones 6–8.

Growing
Count on Japanese pieris to have an upright, arching habit and grow 4 to 6 feet tall and wide. Its glossy evergreen foliage has apple green, bronze, or rich red tones when it debuts. The new foliage turns medium green with age.

Plant container-grown plants in spring. Water transplanted plants regularly for eight weeks after planting to encourage them to develop a strong root system. Prune Japanese pieris in spring after flowers fade. Lace bugs are problematic. They suck sap from leaves, which turn shades of cream, yellow, and green.

Names to watch for
'Mountain Fire' has fiery red new growth that matures to deep green. **'White Cascade'** is beloved for its five-week-long flower show. **'Valley Valentine'** has maroon flowers.

Juniper
(*Juniperus* species)

A tough-as-nails evergreen shrub, juniper is prized for its ability to stand strong in hot, dry soils. Ranging from ground-hugging varieties that suppress weeds to medium shrubs and even large trees, junipers are valuable throughout the landscape.

Best site

Junipers grow best in full sun and well-drained soil. They grow well in part shade, where their form will be more open and their growth will be slower than if planted in full sun. Generally junipers prosper in any planting location except wet soil. Zones 3–9.

Growing

Groundcover junipers grow 1 to 2 feet tall and 8 to 10 feet wide. Shrub forms range from 2 to 10 feet tall and 2 to 8 feet wide. Many cultivars of these evergreen plants have prickly needles or scaly foliage, which makes them a good barrier hedge. Cultivars with medium to dark green foliage as well as ones with blue-green and silvery foliage forms are available. In cold regions juniper foliage takes on a purplish-blue cast in winter.

Transplant container-grown plants in spring or summer. Water plants regularly for about eight weeks after transplanting to encourage development of a strong root system.

Prune junipers in spring or summer. These easy-to-grow shrubs can be sculpted into tidy compact forms. Their most pleasing appearance, though, is usually their natural form. Cedar apple rust, bagworms, and mites are problematic on junipers. Plants growing in wet soil are most often plagued by pests. When grown in quick-draining soil and sun or part shade, junipers are usually problem-free.

Names to watch for

GROUNDCOVER TYPES Also called creeping or spreading junipers, groundcover types hug the ground and suppress weeds. They are particularly useful in mixed shrub borders. **'Golden Carpet', Gold Strike',** and **'Maiden Gold',** have yellow-green foliage.
SHRUB FORMS Spreading, horizontal branches give shrub-form junipers a graceful habit. There are hundreds of cultivars.

varieties:

1. **BLUE CHIP** is a groundcover type. It is a blue-needled form that grows 8 to 12 inches tall and 10 to 12 feet wide.
2. **'WILTONII'** is also called 'Blue Rug'. It has a carpetlike form with rich blue foliage that turns slightly mauve in winter. 6 inches tall and 6 to 8 feet wide.
3. **'GOLD FEVER'** is a groundcover type that has striking yellow-green foliage. 1 foot tall and 5 to 6 feet wide.
4. **'GOLD LACE'** is a shrub type with golden foliage in all seasons. It grows 3 to 4 feet tall and 5 to 6 feet wide.

Lilac (*Syringa* species)

Possessing the sweet fragrance of spring, lilacs are must-have shrubs for many northern gardens. Flower-packed bloom clusters in shades of white, lavender, purple, or pink decorate these easy-to-grow plants for two weeks or more in mid- to late spring. Plant tall vintage varieties together to form a fragrant hedge. Use the new smaller cultivars in mixed borders and foundation plantings.

 YOU SHOULD KNOW Lilacs have notable drought tolerance. Established plants will survive extended dry spells and bloom with gusto the following spring. Severe, long-lasting droughty conditions call for supplemental watering. Water plants deeply every week or two during extreme drought.

Best site
Full sun is essential for lilacs. Plants growing in part shade will not flower nearly as prolifically as those planted in full sun. These deciduous shrubs tolerate a variety of soils but grow best in moist, well-drained soil. Zones 3–9, depending on species.

Growing
Old-fashioned lilacs grow 12 to 15 feet tall and 8 to 12 feet wide. They develop a lanky habit with age and their foliage is concentrated on the top half of the plant. Littleleaf, Manchurian, cutleaf, and Meyer lilacs all mature to compact shrubs that are well-suited to residential landscapes. These smaller lilacs grow 4 to 10 feet tall and 3 to 7 feet wide.

Lilacs are easy to establish in the landscape. Transplant container-grown plants in spring. Water plants regularly for eight weeks after transplanting to encourage them to develop a strong root system.

Pruning is essential for dense growth and bushels of flower clusters. As soon as blooms fade in spring, remove easy-to-reach spent flowers on common lilacs to prevent plants from using valuable energy to produce seeds. Don't bother removing flowers on littleleaf, Manchurian, cutleaf, and Meyer lilacs. These small lilacs expend little energy producing seeds.

In late spring or early summer, remove one-third of a lilac shrub's oldest stems. When pruning overgrown plants, remove as many as one-third of the total stems, leaving the young, vigorous stems.

Powdery mildew is the greatest lilac pest problem. Common or old-fashioned lilacs are most susceptible. Prevent powdery mildew by pruning regularly and encouraging good air circulation around plants.

Names to watch for
COMMON LILAC (*S. vulgaris*) is the heirloom species that is found growing around abandoned farmhouses. Its 6- to 10-inch-tall bloom clusters have intense fragrance and make wonderful spring bouquets. Zones 3–7. There are more than 2,000 common lilac cultivars. A few of the most fragrant include **'Charles Joly'**, **'Henri Robert'**, **'Jeanne D'Arc'**, **'President Roosevelt'**, and **'Sensation.'**

CUTLEAF LILAC (*S. × laciniata*) is the most heat-tolerant lilac. It has a rounded outline and fragrant, pale purple flowers. It grows 6 to 8 feet tall and wide. Zones 4–9.

LITTLELEAF LILAC (*S. pubescens microphylla*) is a small shrub with 2- to 3-inch-tall rosy pink flower clusters and small leaves. It grows 6 feet tall and 9 to 12 feet wide. Zones 3–7.

MANCHURIAN LILAC (*S. patula*) has leathery, dark green leaves and a rounded habit. Its flowers open in May and June, after common lilac flowers. 8 to 10 feet tall and 6 to 8 feet wide. Zones 3–7.

MEYER LILAC (*S. meyeri*) is covered with flower clusters from ground level to the top of its rounded outline. A dense, easy-to-grow plant, it is a great choice for mixed borders or as a hedge. It grows 4 to 8 feet tall and 6 to 12 feet wide. Zones 3–7. **'Palibin'** is a compact form with red-purple buds and pink flowers. 4 to 5 feet tall and 6 to 8 feet wide.

PERSIAN LILAC (*S. × persica*) is common in the East and Midwest. Small dark green leaves and pale lavender flowers are hallmarks of this rounded shrub. It grows 8 feet tall and wide. Zones 3–7.

lilac species and varieties:

1. **'SENSATION'** (*S. vulgaris*) is a common lilac that is grown for its large trusses of purple flowers that are edged in white. It has a mild fragrance and grows 10 feet tall and 6 feet wide.

2. **CUTLEAF LILAC** (*S. × laciniata*) is grown just as much for its lacy, deeply cut foliage as it is for its loose panicles of fragrant pale lavender flowers. Cutleaf lilac has good heat tolerance. 6 to 8 feet tall and wide.

3. **'SUPERBA'** (*S. pubescens microphylla*) is a spreading littleleaf lilac that makes an excellent hedge. It has pink-purple flowers in late spring and early summer. 6 feet tall and 9 to 12 feet wide.

4. **'MISS KIM'** (*S. patula*) is a petite Manchurian lilac with thousands of tiny fragrant flowers in spring. It blooms about a week after common lilac. Prune this easy-to-grow lilac to maintain its small stature. 6 to 8 feet tall and wide.

5. **'BLOOMERANG'** (*S. meyeri*) is a new Meyer lilac that blooms abundantly in spring and then continues blooming sporadically through summer. It has fragrant, small flowers. 4 to 5 feet tall and wide.

6. **PERSIAN LILAC** (*S. × persica*) is grown for its exceptionally fragrant flowers. Smaller than common lilac, Persian lilac grows 8 feet tall and wide. Its small flowers are pale lavender.

Mexican orange
(*Choisya ternata*)

Shiny evergreen foliage, fragrant white flowers in spring, and a tidy rounded habit make Mexican orange an ideal foundation or border shrub for gardens in warm climates. It has good deer resistance.

YOU SHOULD KNOW
Mexican orange gets its name from the aroma of its foliage. When crushed, a Mexican orange leaf emits a strong citrus scent that is most similar to that of an orange.

Best site
Mexican orange thrives in part to full shade and moist, well-drained soil. It is a great plant for the north or east side of a house. Grow it in the shadow of trees to create ground level interest. Zones 7–10.

Growing
A broad, rounded shrub, Mexican orange grows 6 to 8 feet tall and wide. Its evergreen nature makes it useful as a low hedge. Mexican orange flowers prolifically in spring and then sporadically through summer and into fall.

Transplant container-grown plants in spring. Water regularly for eight weeks after planting to promote a strong root system.

Prune plants in summer after their blooms fade. Plants can be sheared for a formal appearance. Mexican orange is nearly pest-free.

Names to watch for
'Sundance' has golden yellow leaves year-round. It adds great color and contrast to mixed shrub borders.

Mockorange
(*Philadelphus coronarius*)

Mockorange blossoms waft their sweet scent through the landscape for a couple of weeks in late spring. Pair this large shrub with small shrubs and perennials that shine in summer and fall.

Best site
Mockorange grows in full sun or partial shade and soil ranging from dry to wet. This tough shrub adapts to a variety of growing conditions. Zones 4–8.

Growing
A medium, upright shrub, mockorange grows 6 to 8 feet tall and wide. It is a single-season plant in that its only notable landscape characteristic is its fragrant white flowers in spring. In other seasons it recedes into the background.

Transplant container-grown plants in spring. Pruning is essential to keep mockorange in good form. Remove one-third of the oldest stems in spring after the blooms fade. Mockorange can also be rejuvenated by pruning it back to 6 to 8 inches tall in early spring.

Names to watch for
'Dwarf Snowflake' grows just 3 to 4 feet tall and has arching branches. **'Belle Etoile'** is an old-fashioned variety that grows 5 to 6 feet tall.

Mountain laurel
(Kalmia latifolia)

A North American native, mountain laurel has magnificent flowers and leathery evergreen foliage. It's a great plant for partial shade and mixed shrub borders. Or use it at the back of a perennial border.

Best site
Plant mountain laurel in full sun or part shade and moist, acidic, well-drained soil. Zones 4–9.

Growing
Mountain laurel grows 3 to 15 feet tall and wide. It is a slow-growing plant and will take many years to reach its mature size. Several dwarf cultivars are available, making it possible to grow this shrub with multiseason interest in small-space gardens or large containers.

Transplant container-grown plants in spring. Mountain laurel thrives in cool, moist soil. Spread a 2-inch-thick layer of organic mulch over the plant's root zone to keep roots cool and prevent soil moisture loss.

Prune plants in summer after the flowers fade. Leaf spot, blight, and a few other pests attack mountain laurel, but vigorous plants usually fend them off without excessive damage.

Names to watch for
'Elf' is a small mountain laurel with pink flowers. It grows 3 to 4 feet tall and wide.

Mugo pine
(Pinus mugo mugo)

A slow-growing needled evergreen, mugo pine is an excellent shrub for adding unique texture to mixed borders and foundation plantings. Because it grows slowly, it is nearly maintenance-free.

Best site
Plant mugo in full sun or partial shade and moist, well-drained soil. It will tolerate dry situations but grows best in slightly moist soil. Zones 3–7.

Growing
Shrub-form pines range from 1 to 10 foot tall and wide. There are many cultivars of mugo pine. Choose a cultivar that matures to the optimal size for your landscape.

Transplant container-grown or balled-and-burlapped plants in spring. Water plants regularly for at least six weeks after planting to encourage them to develop a strong root system. Rusts, borers, and scale often trouble mugo pine. Plants growing in moist, well-drained soil are rarely attacked by pests.

Names to watch for
When buying a mugo pine, be sure to read the plant tag carefully; there is tremendous variation in size. **'Mops'** is a dwarf round form that grows 3 feet tall and wide.

Myrtle
(*Myrtus communis*)

An easy-care evergreen hedge plant, myrtle is heat-, drought-, and salt-tolerant. It takes pruning well and can be sculpted into formal shapes with ease. Plant myrtle in containers for a lovely dark green backdrop.

Best site

Myrtle grows best in full sun or light shade and well-drained soil. Plants succumb in high humidity and wet soil. Zones 8–11.

Growing

Myrtle grows 8 to 10 feet tall and wide, but the plants are easily, and commonly, sheared to smaller forms. Plants are slow growing and require many years to reach their mature size.

Transplant container-grown plants in winter or spring. Once established, plants need supplemental watering only during periods of extreme drought.

Prune myrtle in spring or summer. Mites and scale occasionally trouble myrtle, but vigorous, thriving plants are rarely damaged.

Names to watch for

'Variegata' has creamy-white leaf edges and small blue-back berries. It is a great cultivar for brightening up dark areas. 8 to 10 feet tall and wide. **'Compacta'** is a dwarf myrtle that is commonly used in knot gardens and foundation beds. 2 to 3 feet tall and wide.

Ninebark
(*Physocarpus opulifolius*)

A tough, easy-to-grow shrub, ninebark has color-rich foliage and summer flowers. Use it as a hedge plant or in a mixed shrub border where its chartreuse or burgundy foliage will add interest.

Best site

Ninebark grows best in full sun and moist, well-drained soil. It tolerates dry soil and partial shade with ease. Ninebark is similar to the popular landscape shrub spirea in that it will grow almost anywhere. Zones 2–7.

Growing

A medium shrub with a coarse texture year-round, ninebark grows 5 to 10 feet tall and wide. Plants can be maintained at a smaller size with regular pruning.

Plant container-grown plants in spring. Water plants regularly for at least six weeks after transplanting to encourage them to develop a strong root system. Ninebark will develop a sprawling, irregular habit if not pruned annually. Prune plants in early spring before growth begins. Remove one-third of the oldest canes and cut existing canes back as necessary to keep the plant's size in check.

Ninebark is rarely troubled by pests.

Names to watch for

Summer Wine has delicately cut small leaves and pretty pink summer flowers. **Diablo** is a dense shrub with burgundy foliage.

Oleander
(Nerium oleander)

A spring to fall flower show and evergreen leaves make oleander a favorite plant for warm regions. Often grown as a container shrub in cooler zones, oleander tolerates a wide range of growing conditions.

Best site
This easy-to-grow shrub thrives in sun or partial shade and well-drained soil. It tolerates salt well, making it an excellent seaside plant. It also has excellent drought tolerance and withstands soggy soil. Zones 8–11.

Growing
Oleander usually grows 6 to 12 feet tall and wide, but in the Deep South where freezing temperatures are rare, it regularly reaches 20 feet tall. Its medium green evergreen foliage makes it a great hedge plant.

Transplant container-grown plants in spring. Water plants regularly for at least six weeks after transplanting to encourage them to develop a strong root system. Prune plants anytime during the growing season. Rejuvenate oleander by cutting stems back to 6 inches above ground level. Oleander is rarely troubled by pests.

Names to watch for
'Big Pink' has large hot pink flowers. **'Snow Frost'** is exceptionally hardy and has cream-color flowers.

Oregon grapeholly
(Mahonia aquifolium)

An evergreen shrub with glossy dark green leaves, Oregon grapeholly spreads rather slowly to form low-maintenance colonies. Use it in a mixed border or as a foundation plant in shaded areas.

Best site
Shade is a must for Oregon grapeholly. The leaves will scorch and turn brown when the plant is grown in full sun. Moist, well-drained soil is also essential. It does not grow well in dry soil. Zones 5–8.

Growing
Oregon grapeholly grows 3 to 6 feet tall and spreads 3 to 5 feet wide. A slow-growing evergreen shrub, it will take several years to reach its mature size. Plants bloom in spring with showy bright-yellow flowers. The glossy leaves have spiny margins.

Transplant container-grown plants in spring. Water plants regularly for at least six weeks after transplanting to encourage them to develop a strong root system. Prune plants in spring after blooms fade.

Names to watch for
'Compact' has bronze-red new growth and purple-red winter color. It grows 2 to 3 feet tall and 3 to 4 feet wide. **'Orange Flame'** has bronze-orange new leaves. It makes a good barrier plant.

YOU SHOULD KNOW
All parts of oleander are poisonous. Avoid planting this shrub where children or animals might ingest its leaves, flowers, or stems.

Pittosporum
(Pittosporum tobira)

A compact, slow-spreading evergreen shrub, pittosporum is popular in the South. Sometimes overused, it is a good plant for creating a low-maintenance hedge or barrier. Flowers are very fragrant.

Best site
Pittosporum grows well in full sun or heavy shade. It grows in sandy soil or clay soil as long as the soil drains quickly. A long-lived plant, it thrives in hot, dry sites and tolerates salt spray. Zones 8–10.

Growing
Pittosporum grows 10 to 12 feet tall and up to 24 feet wide. It takes pruning well and can easily be kept smaller. Wonderfully fragrant white-yellow flowers bloom in mid-spring. The flowers have an orange blossom scent.

Transplant container-grown plants in spring or early summer. Pittosporum is rarely attacked by pests.

Names to watch for
Cream De Mint is a dwarf variety with creamy-white leaf edges. It grows 24 to 30 inches tall and wide. **KOHUHU** (*P. tenuifolium*) is another member of the pittosporum genus and offers an upright habit. **Oliver Twist kohuhu** has silvery-green leaves on black stems. It grows 8 to 10 feet tall and 5 to 7 feet wide.

Potentilla
(Potentilla fruticosa)

A plant that falls squarely in the tough-as-nails category, potentilla is a small shrub that resists deer, blooms for weeks through drought, and attracts butterflies. Use it in mixed border plantings.

Best site
Potentilla grows best in full sun and well-drained soil. Fertile, moist soil is optimal, but it grows well in dry, infertile soil too. Potentilla has excellent drought and cold tolerance. Zones 2–8.

Growing
A small to medium shrub, potentilla grows 1 to 4 feet tall and 2 to 4 feet wide. It is a slow-growing plant and tolerates pruning well. This twiggy shrub begins blooming in early summer and unfurls white, pink, yellow, or red flowers until frost.

Transplant container-grown plants in spring. Regular pruning is essential for maintaining good form. Each spring remove one-third of the canes or cut back the plant to 6 inches above ground level in late winter. Without pruning, it becomes loose and ragged. Potentilla can develop spider mites in dry, sunny sites.

Names to watch for
'Abbotswood' has bluish-green foliage and large white flowers. **'Gold Star'** has deep golden yellow flowers that are 2 inches in diameter. **'Pink Beauty'** has large soft pink flowers.

Privet
(*Ligustrum* species)

A stalwart of landscapes in the South and West, privet is an evergreen shrub that is commonly employed as a living screen or short hedge. It is invasive in some areas and planting is prohibited there.

Best site
Privet is adaptable to full sun or heavy shade and grows well in all soils except those that are permanently wet. Zones 7–10.

Growing
Privet grows 6 to 12 feet tall and wide. It is commonly pruned into shapes ranging from geometric hedges to curvaceous topiaries. Remove privet's lowest limbs and it will become a sculptural tree. Privet has showy, cream-color, fragrant flowers in late spring. The flowers are followed by black fruit that is sometimes eaten by birds.

Transplant container-grown plants in spring. Water plants regularly for at least six weeks after transplanting to encourage them to develop a strong root system. Prune privet in spring after plants bloom. Privet has no serious pests.

Names to watch for
'Jack Frost' has shiny, leathery green leaves with creamy-white edges. **'Variegatum'** is similar to 'Jack Frost' in that it is variegated, but it has blotches on the center of its leaves as well as cream-color leaf margins.

Redtip photinia
(*Photinia* × *fraseri*)

A widely used evergreen shrub, redtip photinia is a common hedge plant in warm regions. In recent years a fungal disease has damaged many established plantings. Plant it with caution.

Best site
A bulletproof shrub until a devastating fungal disease came along, redtip photinia grows well in full sun or heavy shade and soils ranging from sand to clay. Zones 7–10.

Growing
Redtip photinia grows 10 to 15 feet tall and 5 to 10 feet wide. Its ruby-red new growth is most prolific in spring. The shiny evergreen leaves turn green in a few weeks. Often plants produce a second flush of growth in early summer.

When using redtip photinia as a hedge, space plants at least 6 to 8 feet apart to promote good air circulation. Fungal leaf spot is a problem on plants that are planted too close together.

Transplant container-grown plants in spring. Prune plants in winter when they are dormant to avoid spreading fungal disease. Prevent rampant spread of fungal disease by raking and discarding fallen leaves in winter.

Names to watch for
Cracklin' Red, **Dynamo Bronze**, and **Fireball** have shown good disease resistance.

Rhododendron and azalea
(*Rhododendron* species)

Spring beauties grown from Florida to Minnesota, rhododendrons and azaleas are some of the most popular flowering shrubs. Their white, pink, red, yellow, or purple flower clusters decorate the evergreen or deciduous plants for weeks in spring. Lovely plants for partial shade, rhododendrons and azaleas add color to sun-dappled beds and borders.

YOU SHOULD KNOW
All azaleas and rhododendrons are botanically classified as *Rhododendron*. The common name azalea refers to native deciduous species and some evergreen Asian types. Rhododendron refers to species that have large, leathery evergreen leaves. No sharp division can be made, and it is always accurate to call any plant in this genus a rhododendron.

Best site

There are many species and varieties of rhododendron, including some that are native to North America. They thrive in moist, well-drained, acidic soil that is rich in organic matter. Planting sites near pine trees are particularly suitable because the soil tends to be acidic.

Sun requirements range from partial shade to full shade, depending on the variety. Most plants do well when planted where they will receive morning sun and afternoon shade. Plant rhododendrons and azaleas on the north or east side of a house for a pleasing mix of sun and shade. Zones 4–9, depending on variety.

Growing

Rhododendrons and azaleas range from small plants that are 2 feet tall and wide to large shrubs growing 15 to 20 feet tall and 10 to 15 feet wide. They have a round and irregular outline. Rhododendrons bloom in mid- to late spring. Some new varieties bloom again in early fall.

Plant container-grown rhododendrons and azaleas in spring. The plants have fibrous root systems, making them easy to transplant. Their threadlike roots also dry out quickly, so be sure to water plants regularly for at least eight weeks after transplanting. Blanket the soil over the root zone with a 2-inch-thick layer of organic mulch. Pine straw is best because it will provide valuable nutrients as it breaks down and contributes to the acidic nature of the soil around plants.

Some growers suggest fertilizing plants with a product designed especially for rhododendrons, but it is not necessary for a healthy plant.

Rhododendrons and azaleas are slow growing and rarely require extensive pruning. Prune plants after the blooms fade in late spring.

Several insects and diseases affect rhododendrons and azaleas. Lacebugs are particularly troublesome. Healthy, vigorous plants usually shrug off pests.

deciduous varieties:

① 'HINO CRIMSON' has a profusion of rich crimson blooms. This shrub makes a delightful hedge. Zones 6–9.

② EXBURY HYBRIDS are a large group of hardy azaleas that are available in shades of orange, yellow, pink, and cream. Zones 5–7.

③ WHITE LIGHTS is one of the **Northern Lights hybrids,** which were developed in Minnesota and are known for their winter hardiness. Plants are compact and can grow to 6 feet tall and wide. Zones 4–8. Look for variety names including **Orchid Lights**, **Rosy Lights**, **Spicy Lights**, and **Golden Lights**.

④ KOREAN AZALEA (*R. yedoense poukanense*) is deciduous in cold climates but evergreen in warm climates. Its foliage turns orange red in autumn. Zones 4–9.

evergreen varieties:

⑤ **'ENGLISH ROSEUM'** has large clusters of lavender-pink flowers. 5 to 10 feet tall and wide. Zones 4–8.

⑥ **KURUME HYBRIDS** is a popular group of evergreen rhododendrons. Plants include a rainbow of flower colors. 3 to 5 feet tall and wide. Zones 6–9.

⑦ **BLOOM-A-THON RED** is a reblooming evergreen azalea that blooms in spring and then begins blooming again in July and continues into fall. 3 feet tall and wide. Zones 6–9.

⑧ **AUTUMN TWIST** blooms in spring, summer, and fall. Its purple-and-white-striped flowers are 4 inches across. 4 to 6 feet tall. Zones 7–9.

⑨ **AUTUMN EMBERS** is part of the **Encore** series, which flower in spring and then resume flowering in late summer and fall. 3 feet tall and 4 feet wide. Zones 6–9.

⑩ **'HAAGA'** has massive clusters of pink flowers. It grows best in cool regions. 3 feet tall and wide. Zones 4–8.

Rock rose
(*Cistus* species)

A drought-tolerant evergreen shrub with long-blooming pink or white flowers, rock rose is a good choice for low-water landscapes. Use it in mixed borders or on banks for erosion control—anywhere you need an easy-care plant.

YOU SHOULD KNOW Waterwise plants like rock rose—those that have excellent drought tolerance—can be enjoyed in almost any landscape. If your region generally receives adequate rainfall, waterwise plants likely have a place in dry areas such as those found under eaves, near the base of established trees, or in sun-baked parking strips.

Best site

Rock rose thrives in dry, infertile soil and full sun. It will grow with gusto in moist, well-drained soil, but it will have limited blooms. It is deer-resistant, salt-tolerant, and exceptionally drought-tolerant. Zones 8–11.

Growing

Rock rose grows 2 to 4 feet tall and 4 to 8 feet wide. It spreads slowly, making it a good choice for planting in an undeveloped area where it will blanket the open space with foliage. Rock rose blooms for many weeks beginning in spring.

Transplant container-grown plants in spring. Pruning is rarely needed. When necessary, control the size of your plant by pruning in late summer after blossoms fade. Rock roses are generally pest-free.

Names to watch for

'**Brilliancy**' has magenta flowers and grows 2 to 3 feet tall and 6 to 8 feet wide. Its extensive spreading ability makes it a good choice for erosion control on slopes.

Rose of Sharon
(*Hibiscus syriacus*)

A spectacular container shrub or garden plant, rose of Sharon has bold, showy flowers all summer. Use it in mixed borders for a burst of energetic color, or mass plants to create a blooming hedge. Plants thrive in moist or dry soil.

Best site

Rose of Sharon grows best in full sun or partial shade and moist, well-drained soil. It will grow nearly anywhere except in soil that is permanently wet or extremely dry. Rose of Sharon thrives in heat and may not begin actively growing until early summer in cool climates. Zones 4–9.

Growing

Rose of Sharon ranges from 3 to 8 feet tall and 2 to 6 feet wide. Many small cultivars are available for use in container gardens. Rose of Sharon flowers in many colors, including some bicolors.

Transplant container-grown plants in spring. Keep plants neat and tidy by pruning them back to 6 to 12 inches above ground level in early spring. Japanese beetles attack rose of Sharon.

Names to watch for

There are many varieties of rose of Sharon. They differ in mature size and flower color. Choose the best for your landscaping situation.

Russian arborvitae
(*Microbiota decussata*)

A soft evergreen groundcover, Russian arborvitae grows well in part shade and moist, well-drained soil. Use it in mixed borders where it will ramble around other shrubs, or employ it on a bank to hold soil in place.

Best site

Russian arborvitae, also called Russian cypress, thrives in moist, well-drained soil and partial shade. It is adaptable to poor or dry soil and in cool regions will grow well in full sun. Zones 3–7.

Growing

A groundcover shrub, Russian arborvitae grows 1 foot tall and about 6 feet wide. It is a slow-growing shrub and requires several years to reach its mature size.

Transplant container-grown plants in spring. Water plants regularly for at least six weeks after transplanting to encourage them to develop a strong root system.

Prune Russian arborvitae as needed in early spring. This easy-care shrub is generally pest-free, making it an ideal plant for a low-maintenance landscape.

Names to watch for

There are no notable cultivars.

Sea buckthorn
(*Hippophae rhamnoides*)

An exceptional shrub for sandy, infertile soil, sea buckthorn is useful for stabilizing banks and creating hedges. Its narrow leaves and bright orange fruit add interesting color and texture to the landscape. It grows best in infertile soil.

Best site

Sea buckthorn, also called seaberry, grows best in full sun and well-drained, sandy soil. It often succumbs in rich, loamy soil but does well in infertile soil. It withstands salt spray and is drought-tolerant. Zones 4–7.

Growing

A medium to large shrub, sea buckthorn grows 10 to 20 feet tall and 10 to 40 feet wide: it spreads slowly to form large colonies. Female plants produce bright orange berries in September. Male and female plants are needed for fruit set, but it is currently impossible to determine whether young plants are male or female. Best advice—plant several to increase your chances of planting male and female plants.

Transplant container-grown plants in spring. Prune plants as necessary in early spring. Sea buckthorn has no notable pests.

Names to watch for

Golden Sweet has sweet large fruit. **Orange Delight** has reddish fruits.

Seven-son flower
(*Heptacodium miconioides*)

Add structure to the back of the border and screen views with seven-son flower. Blooming in late summer and fall and attracting butterflies, it is a unique plant with pleasingly fragrant flowers.

Best site

Seven-son flower grows best in moist, well-drained soil that is rich in organic matter. It suffers in drought and infertile soil. Site it carefully for best growth and bloom. Zones 5–8.

Growing

A medium to large shrub with an upright, loose habit, seven-son flower usually grows about 20 feet tall and 10 to 15 feet wide. Fragrant white flowers open in August. They turn pink and decorate the plant until frost. The flowers are a valuable late-season nectar source for butterflies. Grow it with forsythia, hydrangea, and viburnum for a season-long color show.

Transplant container-grown plants in spring. Spread a 2-inch-thick layer of mulch over the root zone to help with water retention. Prune seven-son flower as needed in early spring. It has no notable pests.

Names to watch for

There are no named cultivars of seven-son flower available in the nursery trade.

Shrub rose
(*Rosa* species)

Shrub roses are all about easy-care color. These tough beauties are not plagued by pests that affect many hybrid roses. Add shrub roses to mixed borders and wherever you need a spot of color.

Best site

Shrub roses grow best in full sun and moist, well-drained soil. Many shrub roses will tolerate short periods of drought with ease. Zones 4–10, depending on variety.

Growing

Shrub roses grow 2 to 4 feet tall and wide. They bloom in many shades of red, pink, white, and yellow. The plants grow quickly and usually begin blooming in early summer. Expect new flowers to open periodically until frost. Shrub roses continue blooming even without deadheading.

Plant container-grown plants in spring. Water plants regularly for best flowering. Prune shrub roses in early spring before growth begins. Prune as needed to create a plant with the desired shape and size. Diseases rarely affect shrub roses. Japanese beetles can attack the flowers.

Names to watch for

Knock Out series roses are the most popular shrub roses on the market. They are nearly disease-free and their bloom show is outstanding. Zones 5–10.

Siberian peashrub
(*Caragana arborescens*)

Ideal for frigid climates and heavy, dry soil, Siberian peashrub is useful as a hedge, screen, or windbreak. It has yellow flowers in late spring and light green foliage that turns medium green in summer.

Best site
Peashrub grows best in full sun and well-drained soil. It is exceptionally cold-tolerant, making it a great flowering shrub for Zones 2 and 3, where flowering shrub choices are limited. Peashrub is drought-tolerant. Zones 2–6.

Growing
A medium to large shrub in most areas, Siberian peashrub grows 6 to 15 feet tall and wide. It has an oval outline and often sparse branches. Its overall appearance is a bit untidy, but in extreme regions where cold hardiness limits the plant palette, it is a good choice.

Transplant container-grown plants in spring. Prune peashrub as needed to maintain the desired size and shape. If necessary, rejuvenate it by cutting it back to 6 inches above ground level in spring. The plant is rarely troubled by pests.

Names to watch for
'**Nana**' is a dwarf form with contorted branches. '**Pendula**' is a stiffly weeping form that has branches cascading toward the ground.

Smoke tree
(*Cotinus coggygria*)

Airy flower clusters give smoke tree its common name. An intriguing shrub for mixed borders and foundation plantings, it is easy to grow and usually looks best when planted in a mass or cluster.

Best site
Smoke tree grows best in full sun or part shade and well-drained soil. It is adaptable to a wide range of soils, including dry, rocky soil, as well as soil with a high clay content. Zones 5–9.

Growing
Smoke tree grows 10 to 15 feet tall and wide. It has an upright habit and a spreading, irregular outline. Long-lasting flowers debut in June and are effective through September. Smoke tree usually has excellent fall color, ranging from red to burgundy to fiery orange.

Transplant container-grown plants in spring. Prune smoke tree in spring. Purple-leaf cultivars are often cut to the ground in spring to encourage new, vigorous shoots that have an intense leaf color. Easy-to-grow smoke tree has no serious pests.

Names to watch for
'**Flame**' has brilliant orange-red fall coloration. '**Royal Purple**' has rich maroon-red foliage that darkens to almost purple-red or black in summer.

YOU SHOULD KNOW The best time to remove broken, dead, or diseased branches is as soon as you see them. Prevent diseases from spreading and pests from entering the damaged plant by removing the troubled branches as soon as possible.

Spirea (*Spiraea* species)

Clusters of dainty flowers—fragrant in some spireas and not in others—decorate spirea for several weeks in late spring and early summer. Old-fashioned Vanhoutte spirea and new cultivars of Japanese spirea create a diverse group of long-lived, easy-care plants. Spireas fare best in sun and well-drained soil, but they will tolerate some shade and grow and flower well in adverse soil conditions. Use these small to medium shrubs in beds and borders or as an informal hedge.

YOU SHOULD KNOW
Vanhoutte spirea is one of the most fragrant spireas. Its canes are cloaked with fragrant flowers in late spring. One shrub will perfume an entire residential landscape. Plant it near a window where you can enjoy the fragrance from inside the house too.

Best site

Spireas grow best in full sun and moist, well-drained soil. They tolerate drought well and will grow in heavy clay as long as it drains. Most spireas are cold-hardy and adaptable to a wide range of growing conditions. Zones 3–8, depending on variety.

Growing

Spireas range from petite plants 1 foot tall and wide to shrubs that grow 10 feet tall and wide. Plants tolerate pruning well and can be sheared annually to keep their size in check. Flower colors range from white to pale pink to dark pink. Foliage may also exhibit valuable color. Blue-green foliage is common on several members of the group. Japanese spireas are known for their yellow leaf color.

Transplant container-grown plants in spring and water plants well after planting. Prune in early summer after the blooms fade. Avoid late-winter pruning; it will eliminate flower buds and spring bloom. Pests rarely trouble spirea.

Names to watch for

BIRCHLEAF SPIREA (*S. betulifolia aemiliana*) has rounded leaves with toothed margins and white flowers. 24 to 30 inches tall. Zones 4–6.
BRIDAL WREATH SPIREA (*S. prunifolia*) is a well-known spirea, but many other species are superior. Bridal wreath has an open habit and limited foliage. 4 to 9 feet tall and 6 to 8 feet wide. Zones 4–8.

JAPANESE SPIREA (*S. japonica*) is the most popular spirea at garden centers. Used throughout the landscape, but particularly popular in foundation plantings and areas where easy-care plants are needed, Japanese spirea is prized for its long-lasting flowers and clean foliage. It flowers in shades of white, pink, and red-pink. Yellow-leaf selections expand the color power of this versatile shrub. 2 to 5 feet tall and wide. Zones 4–8. There are hundreds of Japanese spirea cultivars.

white-blooming spirea species:

❶ VANHOUTTE SPIREA (*S. × vanhouttei*) has long arching branches that are covered with dainty, fragrant white flowers for two weeks in late spring. It is a superior plant to bridal wreath spirea. 6 to 8 feet tall and 10 to 12 feet wide. Zones 3–8.

❷ BRIDAL WREATH SPIREA (*S. prunifolia*) has white flowers and arching canes, but it tends to have an open, floppy habit with age and limited foliage on the bottom half of its stems. 4 to 9 feet tall and 6 to 8 feet wide. Zones 4–8.

❸ SNOWMOUND SPIREA (*S. nipponica* 'Snowmound) is smaller than Vanhoutte spirea, but it has many of the same admirable characteristics. 3 to 5 feet tall and wide. Zones 4–8.

pink-blooming spirea varieties:

④ **DOUBLE PLAY GOLD** (*S. japonica*) has green-gold foliage that contrasts well with pink flowers in spring. It has a neat, compact habit. 16 to 24 inches tall and wide. Zones 4–9.

⑤ **MAGIC CARPET** (*S. japonica*) has bright burgundy new foliage that matures to chartreuse. In fall the foliage turns russet. It has small clusters of pink flowers. 16 to 24 inches tall and wide. Zones 4–9.

⑥ **FROEBEL** (*S. japonica*) has pink flowers in spring and long-lasting green foliage. 3 to 4 feet tall and wide. Zones 3–8.

⑦ **PINK PARASOLS** (*S. fritschiana*) has large pink flower clusters. It is a larger plant than many other pink-blooming varieties. 2 to 3 feet tall and 4 to 5 feet wide. Zones 4–8.

⑧ **'NEON FLASH'** (*S. japonica*) has bright pink flowers for weeks in spring. Its rich green foliage turns dark burgundy in fall. 3 feet tall and wide. Zones 4–9.

⑨ **'GOLDMOUND'** (*S. japonica*) has bright yellow leaves in spring. The foliage turns yellow-green in summer and yellow-orange in fall. 2 to 3 feet tall and 4 feet wide. Zones 4–8.

Spruce
(*Picea* species)

Dwarf spruces are perfect for adding year-round interest to any landscape. They are especially useful near entrances and walkways where they contribute color and texture when deciduous plants are leafless.

Best site

Spruces grow well in full sun and moist, well-drained soil. They tolerate partial shade well and will grow in sandy soil provided they receive ample moisture. Zones 3–8.

Growing

Dwarf and shrub-type spruces range from petite plants growing just 1 foot tall and wide to plants that grow 5 to 10 feet tall and wide. There are hundreds of cultivars available. In general, shrubby spruces are slow growing. Expect them to expand just a few inches each year.

Transplant container-grown or balled-and-burlapped plants in spring. Prune plants in late winter. Mites, aphids, and bagworms are the most prevalent pests of spruce. Vigorously growing plants are rarely troubled. Water during times of drought to promote healthy plants.

Names to watch for

DWARF ALBERTA SPRUCE (*P. glauca* 'Conica'), a popular small spruce, has a pyramidal shape and matures to a height of 10 to 12 feet in 25 years. **'Fat Albert'** is similar.

St. Johnswort
(*Hypericum* species)

Sulfur-yellow flowers light up this easy-to-grow small shrub for weeks in summer. Add it to mixed borders, perennial beds, or foundation plantings for a hefty dose of easy-care color.

Best site

St. Johnswort grows best in full sun and well-drained soil. It does extremely well in dry, rocky soils and also tolerates heavy, dry soils with ease. It is very adaptable and will be at home in almost any sunny landscape. Zones 4–8.

Growing

St. Johnswort grows 2 to 4 feet tall and wide. It tolerates pruning well and can be maintained at 2 feet tall and wide with ease. Its buttercup yellow flowers debut in June and continue to open throughout the summer. The flowers are followed by seed heads in showy capsules.

Transplant container-grown plants in spring. Prune St. Johnswort as needed in early spring. It naturally develops a pleasing round outline. Prune to control its size, if desired.

St. Johnswort is rarely troubled by pests.

Names to watch for

'Ames' is a semievergreen cultivar that grows 2 to 3 feet tall and wide. It has golden yellow flowers. **'Hidcote'** has 3-inch-wide bright yellow flowers and dark green foliage.

Staghorn sumac
(Rhus typhina)

An open, spreading shrub with branches resembling antlers of a deer, staghorn sumac is a good plant for stabilizing banks and for naturalized areas. It offers spectacular fall color and winter food for wildlife.

Best site

Staghorn sumac grows best in well-drained soil and full sun. It thrives in infertile, dry soil but is not a good choice for wet, heavy soil. It spreads by suckers, forming a large colony in areas where it flourishes. Zones 4–8.

Growing

Staghorn sumac usually grows 15 to 25 feet tall, although some new cultivars top out at 6 feet tall. Bright green leaves turn glowing shades of yellow, orange, and scarlet in fall. Because staghorn sumac spreads readily by suckers, it can be hard to keep contained or to eradicate.

Transplant container-grown plants in spring or summer. Prune staghorn sumac in late winter. Rejuvenate it by cutting it back to 6 inches above the ground. Staghorn sumac has no serious pests.

Names to watch for

Tiger Eyes has finely cut yellow leaves that contrast nicely with the plant's rosy-pink stems. **FRAGRANT SUMAC** (*R. aromatica*) is a 3-foot-tall mounded shrub. It spreads readily and makes a good groundcover.

Summersweet clethra
(Clethra alnifolia)

Excellent for shady sites and wet soil, summersweet clethra is a North American native with showy spires of delightfully fragrant summer flowers. Add it to mixed borders or plant it en masse.

Best site

Summersweet clethra grows best in moist soil that is rich in organic matter. In nature it is found growing near streams and creeks. It grows well in sun or shade, and it tolerates salty conditions near the seashore. Zones 4–9.

Growing

Summersweet clethra grows 4 to 8 feet tall and 4 to 6 feet wide. It has a dense, rounded habit and often spreads by suckers to form broad colonies. Its white or pink flower spikes are a favorite nectar source for bees and butterflies.

Transplant container-grown plants in spring. Prior to planting, enrich the planting area by incorporating a generous amount of compost.

Pruning is rarely needed because plants usually develop a tidy shape on their own. Prune in late winter if necessary. Summersweet clethra is usually pest-free.

Names to watch for

'Hummingbird' has long white flower spikes and a compact habit. 3 to 4 feet tall and wide.

YOU SHOULD KNOW Staghorn sumac and fragrant sumac are North American natives. In natural landscapes they can be found on banks and rocky areas where other plants would struggle to survive. Use them in similar areas in a residential landscape and you'll enjoy success.

Sweet acacia
(*Acacia farnesiana*)

A drought-tolerant native shrub, sweet acacia is semievergreen and has sharp thorns. This shrub makes a good barrier hedge and nesting site for songbirds. Its long-lasting fruit is popular with birds and other wildlife.

Best site
Sweet acacia grows best in full sun. It tolerates a wide range of soils—from clay to sand and well-drained to occasionally wet. It has good drought and salt tolerance. Zones 9–11.

Growing
A medium to large shrub or small tree, sweet acacia grows 15 to 25 feet tall and wide. Its slow growth is a great benefit in small landscapes. In late winter the plant is decorated with yellow puffball-like flowers that are very fragrant. The plant blooms sporadically throughout the rest of the year.

Transplant container-grown plants in spring. Water plants regularly for at least six weeks after transplanting to encourage them to develop a strong root system. Prune sweet acacia in late summer or fall as needed. The plant has no major pests.

Names to watch for
There are no notable sweet acacia cultivars.

Sweet olive
(*Osmanthus fragrans*)

A delightful apricot-like fragrance perfumes the landscape around fragrant olive. This large evergreen shrub is an old-fashioned favorite and a good plant for the back of a border or in a foundation planting in warm regions.

Best site
Sweet olive grows best in full sun and moist, well-drained soil. In hot areas, provide afternoon shade. Shrubs are moderately drought-tolerant after they establish a strong root system. Sweet olive grows well in containers. Zones 8–11.

Growing
Sweet olive grows 10 feet tall and 6 to 8 feet wide. It is a slow growing evergreen. Plants produce white blooms over a long period beginning in fall and extending into winter.

Transplant container-grown plants in spring. Sweet olive rarely needs pruning since it usually forms a pleasing shape on its own. If needed, prune plants in spring before growth begins. Sweet olive blooms on new growth, and pruning in early spring will not disturb flowering. Sweet olive is generally pest-free.

Names to watch for
'Conger Yellow' has butter-yellow flowers. **'Fudingzhu'** has an exceptionally long flowering period and creamy-white flowers.

Sweetshrub
(*Calycanthus floridus*)

Sweetshrub's maroon flowers exude an intensely fruity fragrance for weeks beginning in mid-spring. In fall the dark green leaves take on brilliant hues. It is an adaptable plant and good for mixed borders. Keep it watered well.

Best site
Sweetshrub grows best in moist, rich soil and full sun or part shade. Unlike many shrubs, it grows equally well in shade, although it will grow taller there than a plant growing in full sun. Zones 4–9.

Growing
A medium to large shrub, sweetshrub grows 6 to 9 feet tall and 6 to 12 feet wide. The plant's flowers vary greatly in fragrance. Aim to shop for sweetshrub at the garden center in April and May when the plants are in bloom. Many varieties produce intense golden yellow fall color.

Transplant container-grown plants in spring. Spread a 2-inch-thick layer of mulch around plants to prevent soil moisture loss.

Sweetshrub blooms on new and old wood. Early summer, after flowers fade, is the best time to prune. The plant is rarely troubled by pests.

Names to watch for
'Edith Wilder' and **'Michael Lindsey'** are known for their warm yellow fall color. **Chinese wax flower,** *Sinocalycanthus chinensis,* is a closely related species with camellia-like blooms.

Trailing indigo bush
(*Dalea greggii*)

A desert native and spreading groundcover shrub, trailing indigo bush is an excellent plant for low-water-use landscapes. It rambles around drought-tolerant shrubs, creating a weed barrier.

Best site
Trailing indigo bush grows best in full sun and well-drained soil. It thrives when watered at least every two weeks but tolerates long stretches between watering. Zones 7–10.

Growing
A creeping groundcover, trailing indigo bush grows 1 to 2 feet tall and 9 feet or more wide. It has fuzzy silvery-green foliage and small lavender flowers that color the plant beginning in February and extending through summer.

Transplant container-grown plants in spring. Water plants regularly for about six weeks after transplanting to encourage them to develop a strong root system.

Trailing indigo bush looks best when it is allowed to grow without pruning. Cut plants back as needed to remove excessive woody growth and encourage new blooms. Plants are generally pest-free.

Names to watch for
There are no cultivars of trailing indigo bush.

Viburnum (*Viburnum* species)

North American natives with outstanding flowers, intense fragrance, and fruit that delights wildlife, viburnums are an essential part of many landscapes. Use them as focal points in mixed borders or plant them en masse to create an informal hedge that will beckon birds. Viburnums range from 2 feet tall to nearly 30 feet tall—there are types of these native plants for nearly every garden.

Best site

Viburnums thrive in moist, well-drained soil and full sun or partial shade. They are an adaptable group of shrubs, growing in a variety of landscape situations. Once established, they tolerate drought well. They also grow well in heavy soil provided standing water is not present. Zones 2–9, depending on species.

Growing

Some viburnums are far too large for today's landscapes. But many new small cultivars are available in the marketplace, making it possible to enjoy a greater number of these easy-to-grow plants. Viburnums range from 4 feet tall and wide to 20 feet tall and wide. Some sport fragrant flowers; others have flowers with virtually no scent. White is the most common flower color, although some species have pink-tinged blooms. Most viburnums produce fruit that is devoured by wildlife, and fall leaf color is often notable.

Transplant container-grown or balled-and-burlapped plants in spring or early summer. Water plants regularly for at least six weeks after transplanting to encourage them to develop a strong root system.

Prune viburnums as needed to maintain a desired size. Plants generally develop a pleasing shape without pruning. If pruning is necessary, do so in late spring or early summer after flowers fade. For a natural appearance, selectively remove one-third of the oldest stems and trim back remaining stems as needed.

Viburnums are generally pest-free. Adequate moisture promotes strong, healthy growth that thwarts most pest attacks. Water viburnums deeply if a drought extends for more than two weeks during the growing season.

Names to watch for

AMERICAN CRANBERRYBUSH (*V. trilobum*) has excellent fall color and bright red berries in early fall. American cranberrybush does not tolerate long periods of drought or standing water. 8 to 12 feet tall and wide. Zones 2–7.

ARROWWOOD VIBURNUM (*V. dentatum*) is a tough and durable viburnum that is good for hedges, masses, and filler in a shrub border. It flowers in late spring and its blue-black fruit ripens in September and October. Arrowwood is one of the most adaptable viburnums. 6 to 8 feet tall and wide. Zones 3–8.

BURKWOOD VIBURNUM (*V. × burkwoodii*) is an excellent choice for a mixed shrub border, or employ several plants to create a hedge. It is exceptionally fragrant. 8 to 10 feet tall and 5 to 7 feet wide. Zones 5–8.

DOUBLEFILE VIBURNUM (*V. plicatum tomentosum*) has horizontal branching and consistent red-purple fall color, making it one of the most elegant viburnums. Its nonfragrant flowers are snow-white and very showy. It is intolerant of heavy clay soil. 8 to 10 feet tall and wide. Zones 5–7.

EUROPEAN CRANBERRYBUSH VIBURNUM (*V. opulus*) has flat-topped flowers in late spring and long-lasting bright fruit ripening in September and October. Leaves turn shades of yellow-red and reddish purple in fall. 8 to 12 feet tall and wide. Zones 3–8.

KOREANSPICE VIBURNUM (*V. carlesii*) is known for its fragrance, as its name suggests. Its clove-scented flowers are a wonderful addition to the landscape. Its pink flower buds open to form roundish white flower clusters. 4 to 6 feet tall and wide. Zones 5–7.

viburnum species and varieties:

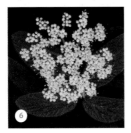

1 **'MOHAWK'** (*V. × burkwoodii*) has spicy-scented white flowers in mid-spring that are followed by red fruit that changes to black at maturity. It has brilliant red flower buds and striking orange-red fall color. 8 to 10 feet tall and 5 to 7 feet wide. Zones 5–8.

2 **AMERICAN CRANBERRYBUSH** (*V. trilobum*) has shiny dark green leaves that turn yellow or red-purple in fall. Its large, white flat-top flowers are followed by bright red fruit that remains on the plant through much of the winter. 8 to 12 feet tall and wide. Zones 2–7. **'Compactum'** is a good choice for small landscapes—it grows 6 feet tall and wide.

3 **DOUBLEFILE VIBURNUM** (*V. plicatum tomentosum*) has red-purple fall color and showy white flowers. 8 to 10 feet tall and wide. Zones 5–7. **'Shasta'** has abundant 6-inch-wide white flower clusters.

4 **'BLUE MUFFIN'** (*V. dentatum*) has large white flower clusters and copious quantities of blue berries in fall. The fruit is relished by wildlife. As an arrowwood viburnum, it is one of the most adaptable viburnums, growing in urban and difficult conditions. 6 to 8 feet tall and wide. Zones 3–8.

5 **'CAYUGA'** (*V. carlesii*) has good disease resistance and large flowers. A Koreanspice viburnum, it is known for its fragrant pinkish-white flower clusters. 4 to 6 feet tall and wide. Zones 5–7.

6 **LEATHERLEAF VIBURNUM** (*V. rhytidophyllum*) will retain most of its dark green leaves in cold climates and is evergreen in the South. It has large flat-top yellow-white flowers. It is a useful shrub for hedges and screens. 10 to 15 feet tall and wide. Zones 5–9.

Weigela
(*Weigela florida*)

Weigela rings in summer with a flush of colorful flowers. This tough, easy-to-grow shrub is adaptable to a wide range of soil conditions. It makes a lovely mass planting, informal hedge, or grouping in a shrub border.

Best site
Weigela grows best in full sun and moist, well-drained soil. It will grow in rocky, dry soil as well as heavy clay. In hot climates weigela benefits from afternoon shade. Zones 5–8.

Growing
A small to medium shrub, weigela grows 2 to 10 feet tall and wide. Many new cultivars mature at 2 to 4 feet tall and wide. Flower colors range from pink to cherry red. Foliage is medium green, chartreuse, creamy white-variegated, or burgundy, with no notable fall color.

Transplant container-grown plants in spring. Weigela has the best form when it is pruned annually. Prune plants in early summer after their main flush of flowers fade. Cut plants back by several inches or selectively remove one-third of the oldest canes. Weigela is generally pest-free.

Names to watch for
My Monet is a dwarf variegated form with pink flowers. It grows 18 to 24 inches tall and wide.

Wintercreeper euonymus
(*Euonymus fortunei*)

Growing in full sun or heavy shade, evergreen wintercreeper euonymus is a woody groundcover. It rambles around small trees and shrubs. Cultivars with variegated foliage add interest at ground level.

Best site
Wintercreeper euonymus grows well in most soils, except swampy, extremely wet locations. It thrives in full sun or full shade. This tough, easy-to-grow plant is a good choice for areas with difficult growing conditions. Zones 5–8.

Growing
Hugging the ground, wintercreeper euonymus grows 4 to 12 inches tall with an indefinite spread. Also a clinging vine, it will scramble 40 to 70 feet up a structure if allowed.

Transplant container-grown plants in spring. Water plants regularly for at least six weeks after transplanting to encourage them to develop a strong root systems. Prune wintercreeper as needed to keep it in bounds. It sometimes is attacked by scale insects.

Names to watch for
'Emerald 'N Gold' has bright yellow leaf margins. It has a mounding habit and can grow 2 to 3 feet tall. **'Moonshadow'** has deep green leaves with a bright yellow blotch in the center.

Witch hazel
(*Hamamelis* × *intermedia*)

Blooming in late winter, witch hazel's color-rich red or yellow flowers add beauty and fragrance at a time when the landscape is still cloaked in drab winter tones. Many cultivars have good fall color. Use witch hazel in a mixed shrub border.

Best site

Witch hazel grows best in moist, well-drained soil that is rich in organic matter. It thrives in full sun or partial shade. Zones 5–8.

Growing

A large shrub with an open, irregular outline, witch hazel often grows 10 to 20 feet tall and wide. The branches have a wide, spreading habit, giving the plant an informal appearance. Witch hazel blooms for several weeks between January through mid-March. Its medium green leaves reliably turn warm shades of yellow, red, and orange in fall.

Transplant container-grown plants in spring. Prune witch hazel as needed in late spring after flowers fade. Plants are rarely troubled by pests.

Names to watch for

'Arnold Promise' boasts a copious display of clear yellow flowers in spring. It rivals forsythia in flower power and is very fragrant. **'Diane'** has coppery-red flowers and intense orange-red foliage in fall.

Yew
(*Taxus* species)

Among the best evergreen shrubs for landscapes, yews are slow growing and disease-resistant. They have excellent dark green color and are available in many shapes and sizes. For a fresh, modern look, pair them with perennials.

Best site

Yews grow equally well in sun or shade. These shrubs demand soil with excellent drainage. Anything less than well-drained soil will result in root rot and plant death. A loose, rich soil is best. Zones 2–7.

Growing

There is wide variation in plant size and shape. Nearly all cultivars are compact and retain their dense character with age without extensive pruning. Yews can be maintained at 2 feet tall and wide or allowed to surpass 20 feet tall and wide, depending on cultivar.

Transplant container-grown or balled-and-burlapped plants in spring. Prune as needed in early spring to maintain the desired size and shape. Deer browse yews.

Names to watch for

There are a multitude of yew cultivars. **'Brownii'** has a rounded form and can be maintained at any height. **'Capitata'** is a pyramidal form that grows 25 to 30 feet tall.

 YOU SHOULD KNOW
Yews are among the most toxic plants, yet they are rarely problematic in a residential landscape. The foliage, bark, and seeds are all poisonous. Yew's red berries contain seeds, which are toxic, but the fleshy red seed covering is not toxic. The seeds are not digested by the human body and pass through harmlessly.

USDA Plant Hardiness Zone Map

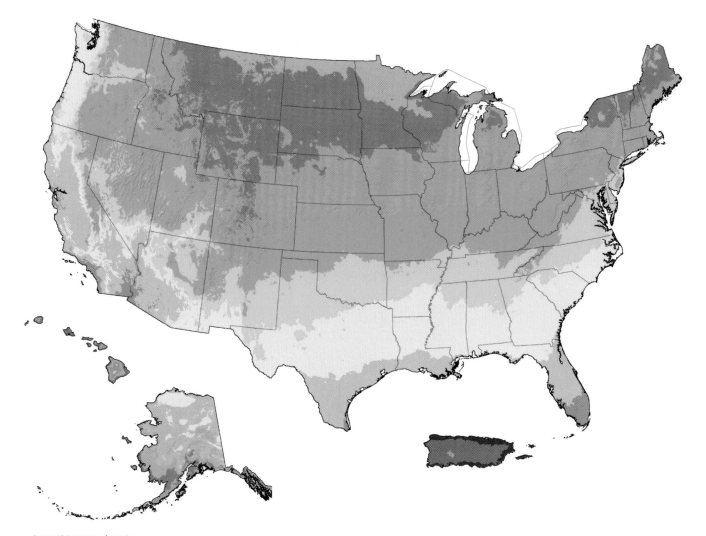

Source: U.S. Department of Agriculture

Average Annual Extreme Minimum Temperature for Each Zone

3 Zone 3: -40 to -30°F (-40 to -35°C)

4 Zone 4: -30 to -20°F (-34 to -29°C)

5 Zone 5: -20 to -10°F (-29 to -23°C)

6 Zone 6: -10 to 0°F (-23 to -18°C)

7 Zone 7: 0 to 10°F (-18 to -12°C)

8 Zone 8: 10 to 20°F (-12 to -7°C)

9 Zone 9: 20 to 30°F (-7 to -1°C)

10 Zone 10: 30 to 40°F (-1 to 4°C)

11 Zone 11: 40 to 50°F (4.5°C to 10°C)

Plants

CAMELLIA FOREST NURSERY
9701 Carrie Road
Chapel Hill, NC 27516
919/968-0504
www.camforest.com

FORESTFARM
990 Tetherow Road
Williams, OR 97544
541/846-7269
www.forestfarm.com

HIGH COUNTRY GARDENS
2902 Rufina Street
Santa Fe, NM 87507
800/925-9387
www.highcountrygardens.com

HYDRANGEAS PLUS
P.O. Box 389
Aurora, OR 97002
866/433-7896
hydrangeasplus.com

KLEHM'S SONG SPARROW
13101 E. Rye Road
Avalon, WI 53505
800/553-3715
www.songsparrow.com

MENDOCINO MAPLES NURSERY
41569 Little Lake Road
Mendocino, CA 95460
707/973-1189
www.mendocinomaples.com

MONROVIA NURSERY
Sells wholesale only;
for retail sources in your area,
www.monrovia.com

WAYSIDE GARDENS
1 Garden Lane
Hodges, SC 29695
800/846-1124
www.waysidegardens.com

WHITE FLOWER FARM
P.O. Box, 50, Rte. 63
Litchfield, CT 06759
800/503-9624
www.whiteflowerfarm.com

Specialty Supplies

CORONA
22440 Temescal Canyon Road
Corona, CA 92883
800/847-7863
www.coronatoolsusa.com

GARDENER'S SUPPLY CO.
128 Intervale Road
Burlington, VT 05401
888/833-1412
www.gardeners.com

KINSMAN CO.
P.O. Box 428
Pipersville, PA 18947
800/733-4146
www.kinsmangarden.com

LEE VALLEY TOOLS
P.O. Box 1780
Ogdensburg, NY 13669-6780
800/267-8735
www.leevalley.com

index

Looking for more
gardening inspiration?

See what the experts at
Better Homes and Gardens have to offer.

Available where all great books are sold.

WILEY